e-Learning Standards

A Guide to Purchasing, Developing, and Deploying Standards-Conformant e-Learning

e-Learning Standards

Carol Fallon and Sharon Brown

A Guide to Purchasing, Developing, and Deploying Standards-Conformant e-Learning

St L

ST. LUCIE PRESS

A CRC Press Company
Boca Raton London New York Washington, D.C.

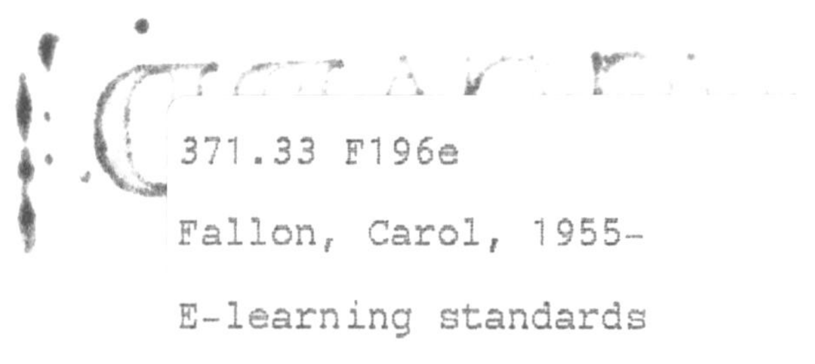

Sun, Sun Microsystems, the Sun Logo, and JavaScript are trademarks or registered trademarks of Sun Microsystems, Inc. in the United States and other countries.

Library of Congress Cataloging-in-Publication Data

Fallon, Carol, 1955-
E-learning standards : a guide to purchasing, developing, and deploying standards-conformant e-learning / Carol Fallon, Sharon Brown.
p. cm.
Includes bibliographical references and index.
ISBN 1-57444-345-3
1. Educational technology--Standards. I. Brown, Sharon, 1949- II. Title.
LB1028.3 .F35 2003
371.33--dc21 2002035739

Direct all inquiries to CRC Press LLC, 2000 N.W. Corporate Blvd., Boca Raton, Florida 33431.

Visit the CRC Press Web site at www.crcpress.com

St. Lucie Press is an imprint of CRC Press LLC

No claim to original U.S. Government works
International Standard Book Number 1-57444-345-3
Library of Congress Card Number 2002035739
Printed in the United States of America 1 2 3 4 5 6 7 8 9 0
Printed on acid-free paper

Foreword

The phenomenon of training material delivered via a computer is not new. In fact, it is well over 30 years old. And, yet, although this neat little technology trick is an old one, many more people than ever before are experiencing it for the first time. Using a computer to train people is still a new discovery for many, and it is an old discovery made new for others.

During my 14-year tenure in this fascinating field, I have seen computer-based training rediscovered twice, once with the advent of the multimedia (Windows-based) PC, and later with the discovery that the Internet could be used for training. Rediscovery of this kind is a sign of maturity in the industry. Another sign of maturity in this (or any other) industry is standardization. Standardization has the same implications and benefits for the learning technology industry as it does for other industries: reduction in costs through economies of scale and overall expansion of the market.

We are only just now beginning to see the benefits of learning-technology standards. Specifications that allow for interchangeability of learning content and learning management systems not only exist but also are actually implemented in many major learning systems and products. When I first became involved in the development of such standards in 1992, I had no idea that they would gain the level of acceptance that they enjoy today. Early progress in this arena was slow until it was stimulated by the rapid spread of the Internet in the late 1990s. Now we enjoy a level of content interoperability never seen before, and amazingly, it is still only the early days for these standards.

Anyone who is planning to develop learning content, management, or tools can no longer ignore these standards. Even though these standards are very young, customers have "discovered" them and are demanding their implementation in learning technology products. Although this seems great to consumers, it is a royal pain for some developers. Unfortunately, these first-generation learning-technology standards, although extremely useful, are technically dense and difficult to follow for some. I can certainly attest to the difficulty that developers have with some of these standards based on the large volume of questions that I receive on the hot topic of how to implement them.

Trying to approach and understand the technical specifications for these learning-technology standards can be bewildering for a newcomer to this arena. However, if you are reading this book, you are most fortunate! You have found the best (and quite probably only) *real* roadmap for understanding what these standards really mean to you.

Supporting learning technology standards is a community service that I perform for my industry. Many people do not understand that learning-technology standards are developed largely by volunteers. These volunteers have day jobs but still make time to help promote these standards. I think that I and all others who participate in this process are most fortunate also. We can now refer people to this book as well!

I leave you in the capable hands of Carol Fallon and Sharon Brown.

William A. McDonald
AICC (Aviation Industry Computer-Based Training Committee)
Independent Test Lab Chair

Learning Technology Architect —
FlightSafetyBoeing

Preface

The last few years have seen an explosion of interest in e-learning. Many organizations have leaped on the possibilities offered by the deployment of educational training material over the World Wide Web. Universal access, continuous availability, and the potential for large cost savings have excited managers and training specialists alike. In the early days, e-learning was viewed by many as a natural progression from computer-based training (CBT), which is delivered via CD-ROM or via an organization's local area network (LAN). Organizations familiar with using or developing CBT had at least a subset of the skills and knowledge required to set up an e-learning infrastructure. However, contrary to expectations, many organizations that never used CBT have become interested in e-learning. This has resulted in steep learning curves for personnel tasked with setting up an e-learning infrastructure. These are the people whom this book sets out to help.

As e-learning consultants, we deal daily with questions on many facets of e-learning. Standards are certainly one of the areas that cause the greatest concern. We decided to write this book because we realized that many people whom we will never have the opportunity to meet are struggling with standards-related issues, and we believed that we were qualified to help.

So why did we feel so qualified? We are not standards experts. We do not sit on any standards committees or working groups. We applaud those who do. They do great work in a difficult and challenging area, and without them e-learning would not be where it is today. However, we are learning management system (LMS) vendors and courseware developers who have "been there, done that, bought the T-shirt." We are part of the team that developed the world's first LMS to be certified for Web-based interoperability by the Airline Industry CBT Committee. Over the last 5 years, we have developed dozens of lessons for standards-conformant e-learning courses. We have helped our clients build e-learning environments for their organizations and taught them how to develop their own standards-conformant courses. We felt that this book was an opportunity to share the fruits of our experience to benefit others like us.

These days there is an abundance of information about e-learning standards — probably an overabundance. During our research, several trees were sacrificed just to print the information available on the World Wide Web. However, once we sifted through it, we found that very little of this information provides hard-core practical advice about the how-to of implementing e-learning standards. The standards specification documents generally do their job very well. But they are standards specifications and not intended to be developer's guides.

We also hear many horror stories about e-learning products that have not fulfilled their purchasers' expectations. So we also set out to help buyers make well-informed decisions about their e-learning purchases.

Our goal for this book, then, was to provide just enough information to help two different groups of people: those who have to make e-learning purchase decisions and those who have to work with the standards. In many organizations these are the same people; in others they are quite separate. So we have created this book in two parts. The first part is intended for all readers. It provides an overview of e-learning and its components and gives practical advice for those who make or have input into purchasing decisions. It also provides high-level descriptions of the most prominent specifications. The second part is intended for courseware developers or those who are just curious to learn more technical detail about the standards. It serves as an entry ramp to the specifications themselves and provides practical advice for applying the specifications to different courseware development situations.

One problem that has plagued us throughout the writing of this book is that e-learning standards are evolving and changing constantly. In addition, it was not practical to include such items as samples of code for specific authoring tools. To address these issues, we have created a Web site, http://www.elearning-standards.com, where we have posted further information, such as downloadable code samples and the latest news on the standards. Please use the Web site in conjunction with this book.

Now we will finish with a disclaimer. As we explain in Chapter 1, e-learning standards are still in a relatively early stage of their evolutionary cycle. There are many parts of the standards that are only just being put to the test of working in real-world situations. The standards specifications themselves also contain certain ambiguities and gray areas. We have based our advice on our own experience and made our best efforts to accurately interpret the specifications documents and other information about areas in which we have more limited practical experience. If we have been unable to obtain a firm ruling on any point, we have said so. We have given you the most accurate information that we can, but we cannot accept responsibility for any errors or omissions in this text.

We hope that you find our book useful. Please use the contact link on the Web site to let us know how well we have met our goal and how we can make any improvements.

Carol Fallon
President, Integrity eLearning

Sharon Brown
Integrity eLearning

About the Authors

Carol Fallon is the founder of Integrity eLearning, based in Anaheim Hills, California. She is a 27-year computer industry veteran who has worked as an analyst and programmer, designer, project manager, and training and development manager. She first became involved in computer-based training in 1992, when she moved to the United States from England to work for a courseware vendor specializing in technology training. Carol cofounded Integrity eLearning with her husband, Dave Fallon, in 1996. They started out by developing Web-based training (WBT) for messaging middleware applications. Since then, Integrity has developed numerous custom online learning courses for clients in a wide variety of industries.

In 1999, Integrity launched WBT Manager, a learning management system (LMS). WBT Manager was the first LMS ever to be certified as conformant with the Aviation Industry Computer-Based Training Committee specification for Web-based LMSs. It was this certification process that sparked Carol's interest in e-learning standards and specifications.

While promoting WBT Manager, Carol discovered the confusion surrounding the subject of standards for e-learning. As a consultant, she has helped many organizations develop, purchase, or implement standards-compliant e-learning environments. She is a regular speaker on the subject of standards for e-learning at trade shows and conferences in the United States and Europe.

In 2000, Carol coauthored a book for Macromedia, *Getting Started in Online Learning.*

Sharon Brown has been an instructional designer for over 20 years and has been involved in online training development since 1998. She holds a master's degree in English from the University of California at Los Angeles. She was a founding member of the Orange County, California chapter of the International Society for Performance Improvement (formerly the National Society for Performance and Instruction) and served as their newsletter editor for several years.

Upon entering the online-learning arena, Sharon was immediately plunged into the emerging world of standards; her initial assignment was to write the documentation for Integrity eLearning's WBT

Manager, the first Web-based learning management system to receive Aviation Industry Computer-Based Training Committee (AICC) certification. Since that time, she has increased her knowledge of standards both by maintaining and improving the WBT Manager documentation through several upgrades and by hands-on experience with developing standards-based courseware using a wide variety of authoring tools. In addition to developing standards-based courseware for a number of clients, Sharon also developed AICC-compliant sample lessons with accompanying documentation for several well-known authoring tools and courseware generation systems.

Acknowledgments

Many people have contributed directly and indirectly to our being able to create this book.

In particular we would like to thank the following: Mark Schupp, without whom this book would never have been written, for it was he who first introduced us to the standards; Candy Ludewig for her endless enthusiasm and willingness to tackle anything from typing up illegible scrawl to researching trademarks; and the rest of the team at Integrity, who have tolerated our preoccupation and long absences. We also thank Dick Davies for his help on learning content management systems; Rick Zanotti, David Mauldin, and Rita Moore for their help with case studies; Leopold Kause for his input and offers of help; and Joe Ganci for his inspiration and support.

Finally, we thank all those who participate in the development of standards for e-learning. Without your efforts we would not have today's vibrant and exciting e-learning industry.

Dedication

To Dave, for all the meals, laundry, school runs, and countless other thoughtful things he's done to give me more "book time." Also to Abi, Jenny, and Sophie for all their love, patience, and support.

— Carol

To my husband, Wes, who has oft suffered the slings and arrows of an outrageously grumpy wife and been forced to sacrifice much-needed help with troubleshooting his computer, recreational opportunities, and the occasional meal on the altar of "that blankety-blank book." Also, to my mother, who upon calling and asking if I was busy, has all too often been told, "yes."

— Sharon

Contents

Part 1 — A Guide for Decision Makers

1 The Vital Role of Standards in E-Learning Environments

2 The Evolution of Standards for E-Learning

6 Standards for Importing and Exporting Entire Courses

7 Standards for Tests and Test Questions

Part 2 — A Guide for Designers and Developers

8 Working with Standards: How to Author Standards-Based Content

9 Creating Interoperable Learning Objects

10 A Guide to Creating Meta-Data Files

Part 1

A Guide for Decision Makers

1

The Vital Role of Standards in E-Learning Environments

Pssst. Hey, I hear you've got some stuff you want to teach people. A lot of people, all over the place. I've got just what you need: e-learning. You know, on the Internet, like e-mail and e-commerce. It's WBT, like CBT only better. If it's not on the 'Net these days, it's nowhere. Now, I can get you started with a great LMS. And I'll throw in a bunch of LOs and SCOs and AUs to help you out. Later on, maybe you can even move up to an LCMS. That's even cooler. Now, our LMS can launch your LOs like lightning, and it'll track everything about your learners. I mean everything! It'll give you their scores and how long it takes them to do their work, and every click they make on their computers. I tell ya, you can find out what color socks they're wearing. And it's got all the accessories, chat rooms, videoconferencing....

Oh, uh, standards? Um... sure, it supports all the latest standards — AICC, SCORM, HACP, API, QTI, IMS, IEEE/LTSC, ISO, ABC, XYZ.... everything that's out there. We're compliant, conformant, even certified. We're always on top of the latest thing....

What's that? Will it work with someone else's courses? Of course it will. Standards, remember? And yeah, you can write your own stuff, too. Just use the standards and it will be as easy as pie.

How's it work? Well...uh...I'm a sales guy, you see, not a programmer. A demo? I'll have to get back to you on that. But you know you can trust it to work. It's all done according to the standards.

Introduction

If you're confused about e-learning and e-learning standards, you're not alone. To the uninitiated, it seems like a confusing alphabet soup of arcane acronyms, pie-in-the-sky promises, and very little practical information. This book is designed to offer clarity and hype-free useful information to help you make intelligent decisions regarding e-learning in your organization.

Although e-learning has become a hot topic in training and education organizations around the globe, there is considerable variance in opinion about just what it is. In this chapter we set the scene for the rest of the book by defining e-learning and its components. Then we take a look at the reasons that the successful growth of e-learning depends on the widespread adoption of standards. Finally, to understand how today's e-learning standards have evolved, we will take a look at the standards lifecycle that begins with a problem, produces a solution to that problem, and standardizes the solution until ultimately it becomes an accredited standard.

What Is This Thing Called E-Learning?

E-learning is a relatively new term in the world of computer-delivered training and education. Every time you pick up any book or magazine on the subject, you will almost certainly find a different definition. One commonly held view is that e-learning encompasses any type of learning content that is delivered electronically. Under this definition, information sent in the body of an e-mail or contained in a Microsoft Word document could be construed to be e-learning. Although we do not wish to take issue with this definition, it is too broad for the purposes of this book. We have limited the scope of this book to include only those standards that concern the purchasers and developers of Internet-based learning technologies and content. We define e-learning as follows: "any learning, training or education that is facilitated by the use of well-known and proven computer technologies, specifically networks based on Internet technology."

Use of Internet technologies means that learning content is stored on a Web server and that learners access the content by using well-known and widely used network technologies such as Web browsers and the TCP–IP network protocol.

Types of E-Learning

E-learning can be classified based on the degree to which it differs from traditional learning strategies. Often it is only one component in a comprehensive learning system that may include such other methods as instructor-led training, self-study, books, videos, and so on. Sometimes this situation occurs when an organization is in transition from traditional learning to e-learning. But more recently, people have begun to recognize that in many instances, such an approach is the perfect solution to a given learning need. This approach is often called *blended learning*.

Pure e-learning can be classified into two broad categories, synchronous and asynchronous. Although the standards covered in this book apply primarily to asynchronous e-learning, we will define both categories here.

Synchronous e-learning uses a learning model that emulates a classroom course, lecture, or meeting using Internet technologies. It is specified as "synchronous" because it requires all participants to be present at the same time. There are several special software packages designed specifically for this purpose, offering presentation delivery, interactive online chat, electronic whiteboards, and so on. These types of software packages are commonly known as *collaboration tools.* Interestingly, some packages allow interactive sessions or presentations to be recorded for later viewing — then they become asynchronous. The standards that are discussed in this book may be relevant to such saved sessions.

Asynchronous e-learning is the Web-based version of computer-based training (CBT), which is typically offered on a CD-ROM or across an organization's local area network. In the case of e-learning, the learning content or *courseware* is served from a Web server and delivered on demand to the learner's workstation. Learners can thus take courses at their own pace. Courseware is normally available to learners 24 hours per day, 7 days per week (24/7) and, subject to the setting of the appropriate permissions, can be accessed from any workstation connected to the Internet or to an organization's intranet. The courseware may be comprised of any combination of text, still images, animations, sound, or movies. The courseware, or at any rate good courseware, is interactive and is often combined with some type of assessment. Typically such courseware is managed and monitored by a learning management system (LMS). Such systems provide learners with access to their assigned courses via a personalized menu, and track and record learner progress in those courses. Most of the work done on e-learning standards to date is concerned with asynchronous e-learning.

The Components of E-Learning

To make sense of e-learning and the standards it employs, we must distinguish between two categories of components. One category contains those components that can be called *physical.* These components have a physical (or at least electronic) existence. They include such things as learning content files, management software, and databases. The other category contains components that are *conceptual,* such as courses and lessons. A clear understanding of these conceptual components is critical to any discussion of e-learning, so we will address this category first.

Conceptual E-Learning Components

Learning Objects — The Conceptual Building Blocks of E-Learning

A learning object (LO) is the smallest chunk of content that can stand by itself as a meaningful unit of learning. The exact size of an LO can vary, but it is considered best practice for a single LO to map onto a single learning objective or concept. Each LO should be self-contained but independent of context; that is, it should not depend upon any other piece of learning content to be complete. This means that each LO can be shared by and reused in multiple lessons or courses.

Although this sounds as though LOs must be quite small and focused, their actual size and scope is left to their authors and often reflects practical rather than ideal considerations. It important to note, however, that whatever its size, an LO is the smallest unit of learning that can be automatically managed and tracked.

LOs can be considered the building blocks of e-learning content. They can be used to construct any desired type of learning experience. LOs are often compared with LEGO® blocks. Provided that they all conform to the same or compatible standards, you can use them in any combination, and they will fit together seamlessly. Therefore, LOs can be assembled to form larger chunks of learning content such as topics, lessons, or complete courses. Without standardization, however, there is no guarantee of a usable combination. (See Figure 1.1.)

Reusability Is the Key

Perhaps the most important characteristic of LOs is that they are designed to be reused in different contexts. Imagine, for example, that you purchase a course on using Microsoft Excel® 2000. After reviewing the course, you decide that the section on charting is poorly done and that you need an additional LO specific to your own organization's use of spreadsheets. You find a better charting LO that you can purchase individually and assign your in-house training department to create the organization-specific LO. If all the LOs conform to the same standard, you can build a custom course from the components you have gathered. (See Figure 1.2.)

Smaller, more focused LOs offer even more opportunities for reusability. You can use a given LO in as many composite learning components as you wish. Consider, for example, the wide range of learning contexts in which you might include an LO devoted to selecting text in a Microsoft Windows® application.

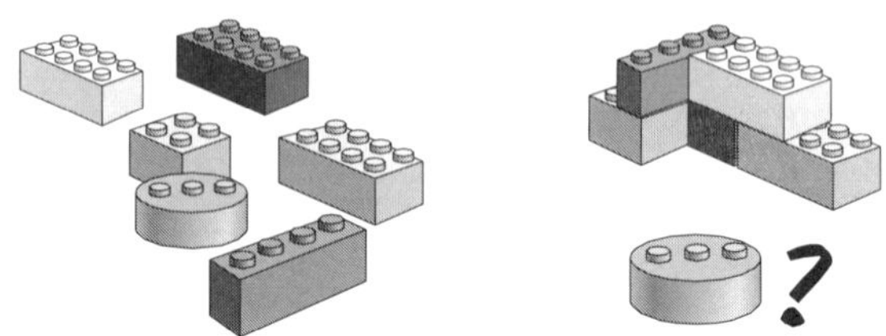

FIGURE 1.1
Sharable Content Object Reference Model. Adapted from Dodds, P. V. W., *Demystifying SCORM*, paper presented at the e-Learning Conference, Washington, D.C., April 2002, slide 6. Available at: http://www.adlnet.org. With permission.

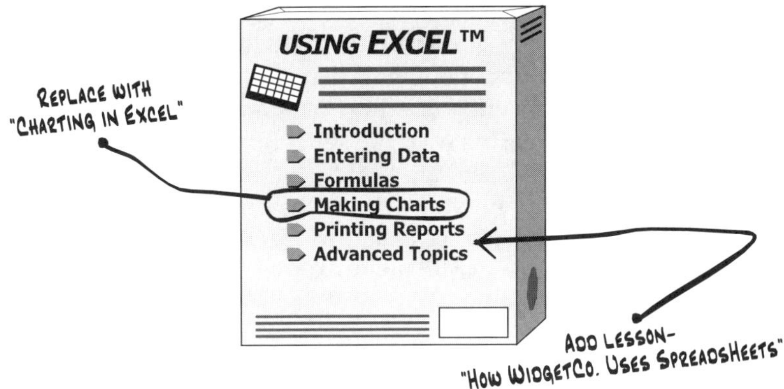

FIGURE 1.2
Reusable learning objects.

How Is Reusability Enabled?

To enable sharing and reusability, each LO needs a descriptive "wrapper." This wrapper provides information such as a description of the content of the LO, its identifier, the learning objectives it meets, who built it, the target audience, and so on. It may help to think of an LO as a candy bar. The learning content is the candy. It is enclosed in a wrapper on which is printed its name, ingredients, nutritional information, manufacturer, and so on. This information enables you to choose a candy bar that is to your taste without removing the wrapper and taking a bite. (See Figure 1.3.)You can use the wrapper of an LO in the same way, but for this to be possible, the information must be provided in a standard and universally understood format. This problem is solved by the use of meta-data, which is by definition "data about data." To facilitate the ability to find and share LOs, various standards groups have worked together to define a consistent set of meta-data to be provided

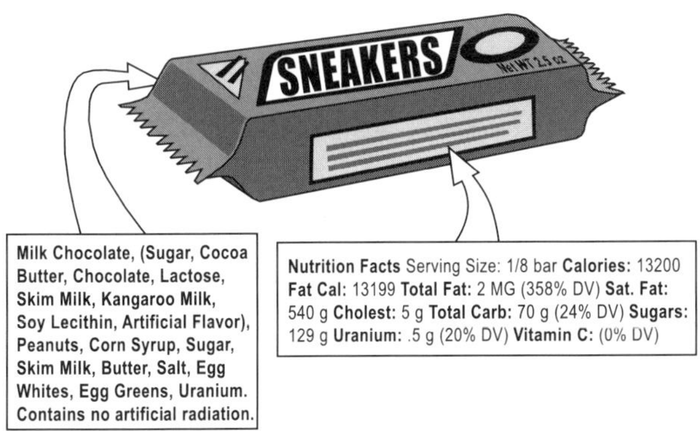

FIGURE 1.3
Meta-data wrapper.

for each LO. The meta-data is not part of the LO itself. Rather, it is held in a separate document designed to travel along with the LO, and that document can be accessed without opening or displaying the actual LO. LOs can be stored in large databases known as LO or content repositories, which can easily be searched by comparing each LO's meta-data with specified criteria. For example, suppose you wanted to build a course about car maintenance. You could build your course by searching the content repository for LOs whose description includes phrases such as *checking tire pressure, changing windshield wipers,* and *cleaning spark plugs.*

Content Structures

As we have seen, LOs can be considered the building blocks of e-learning content. Building blocks, however, are not particularly useful unless they are used in larger structures. In this section we will see how content structures based on LOs are represented within the major standards.

Most learning content, regardless of how it is delivered, uses some sort of hierarchical structure. A course may be divided into lessons, for example, and a lesson into topics. There are many possible ways to construct courses. A major requirement for e-learning specifications is to provide a simple but flexible method for representing a wide variety of content structures.

Curricular Taxonomies

A *curricular taxonomy* is a fancy term for a defined set of named hierarchical learning levels. A curricular taxonomy may have only one or two levels, such as *Course > Lesson,* or it may consist of many levels, such as those shown in Table 1.1.

Formally defined curricular taxonomy models such as these are probably the exception rather than the rule. In a more typical scenario, the taxonomy would evolve during development to fit the requirements of each course.

TABLE 1.1

Examples of Curricular Taxonomy Models

Army	Air Force	Marine Corps	Canadian
Course	Course	Course	Course
Module	Block	Phase	Performance objective
Lesson	Module	SubCourse (annex)	Enabling objective
Learning objective	Lesson	Lesson	Teaching point
Learning step	Learning objective	Task	
		Learning objective	
		Learning step	

Source: From Advanced Distributed Learning Initiative, Sharable Content Object Reference Model (SCORM) version 1.2, *The SCORM Content Aggregation Model,* October 2001, Table 2.3.2.2a. With permission.

The higher levels of the taxonomy might be named, whereas lower levels are only implied in the structure of the content.

Confronted with the wide range of possible curricular taxonomies, the standards groups have developed simple, expandable content hierarchy models. These models are neutral in terms of content complexity, number of taxonomic levels, and instructional approach.

Standards exist for two different models that describe the way in which courses are constructed from LOs. One model forms part of the Sharable Content Object Reference Model (SCORM) developed by the Advanced Distributed Learning Initiative (ADL). The other model was developed by the Aviation Industry CBT Committee (AICC). We will have much more to say about these organizations and their specifications in the course of this book. However, for now we will simply introduce the two content structure models.

The SCORM Content Hierarchy

The SCORM content hierarchy includes three types of components:

- Content aggregation — A group of learning resources that can stand by itself. Course-level content always constitutes a content aggregation. Lower-level blocks of content may be treated as content aggregations if they are sufficiently independent to be used outside the context in which they were developed.
- Sharable content object (SCO) — The SCORM's LO. This is the level at which the learner interacts directly with the learning content and at which the LMS tracks the results.
- Asset — A small, single-purpose learning resource that could be used in multiple contexts. Assets are not tracked by the LMS. They are normally "called" by SCOs, although it is allowable for them to be launched directly by an LMS. Assets typically consist of media such as graphics, sounds, and movies, although there is no restriction on what they can contain.

You may have noticed that these three components don't cover all the territory necessary to fully represent most content structures. There is no provision for blocks of content that are not designed to stand alone. This obvious gap is handled in the *manifest* document that must be packaged with all content aggregations. This document describes the aggregation's components, structure, and special behaviors. It may also reference the meta-data associated with the individual components of the aggregation. SCORM content structure and manifest documents are discussed more fully in Chapter 6.

The AICC Content Hierarchy

The AICC content hierarchy also has three components, as described below:

- Course — The top level of the hierarchy. This is the level at which content is assigned to learners.
- Instructional block — An optional intermediate grouping of smaller learning units. Instructional blocks can be nested inside one another to provide any number of levels. These levels can be mapped to a given curricular taxonomy.
- Assignable unit (AU) — The AICC's LO.

The AICC content hierarchy was developed before the LO concept reached today's level of refinement. The specification often refers to AUs as *lessons,* which implies a relatively large chunk of content. However, by nesting AUs inside a number of instructional-block levels, the granularity of a typical LO can be reproduced.

Physical E-Learning Components

The components of an organization's e-learning infrastructure may originate from a variety of providers or vendors. However, these components must be integrated to provide a seamless interface to learners and administrators. Later we will learn how standards play a major role in enabling this integration.

Courseware

Easily the most recognizable and understandable component of e-learning is the learning content or courseware itself. Courseware may be presented in a format as simple as that of a downloadable text file or hypertext markup language (HTML) page, or one as complex as interactive, rich multimedia that includes sound, animation, or movie files. More complex content will have almost certainly been authored using an authoring tool such as Macromedia Authorware®, Dreamweaver®, Flash®, or Click2Learn ToolBook Instructor.

Courseware originates from two main sources:

- *Off-the-shelf content* is sourced from one of the growing number of content development companies that produce generic content for the mass market or niche markets. New titles appear almost daily on subjects as diverse as sexual harassment training, statutory safety training, sales training, law, accounting, medicine, technical training, computer networks, software development, and many more.

- *Custom content* is required when there is no suitable off-the-shelf content available. Typical examples of custom content are instruction in business procedures and processes unique to your organization such as product sales training, new-hire orientation, or turnkey computer software. Custom content is either developed in house by a special e-learning team or by a third-party content developer to exactly meet your organization's needs.

A traditional e-learning course is modeled on the classic educational paradigm. It is literally a course of study designed as a set of sequential lessons, to be taken one after another. Each lesson may have its own built-in assessment, and successful completion of a lesson may be required before the learner is allowed to move on to the next lesson. The learner may also be required to take and pass a final assessment to graduate from the course.

Learning Management Systems

What Is an LMS?

Although it is easy enough to provide access to a piece of e-learning content directly from a Web page, many organizations want to control access to the courseware and track data such as who is using the content, the level of usage of the content, and the outcome of the usage. An LMS is a Web server–based software application that provides the administrative and data-tracking functions necessary to do this. The specific features and functions of LMSs vary considerably from one system to another, but generally they offer the following:

- *Administrative functions* such as course setup, learner registration, course assignment, and reporting of learners' progress by tracking data such as the scores from any tests or quizzes, the time spent in courses, and the completion status of each course. Figure 1.4 shows the basic interactions between an administrator and the LMS.
- *Learner interface* by which learners log in to the LMS using a personal identifier with or without a password and receive access to e-learning content via a personalized menu of their assigned courses. Usually they can also monitor their own progress by viewing test scores, completion status for LOs and courses, and so on. Figure 1.5 shows the basic interfaces between a learner and the LMS.

LMSs are also responsible for sequencing learner access to LOs within courses, such as allowing learners to access the LOs on their personal menus in any order they wish or forcing them to access the LOs in a linear sequence. More complex schemes, which are not available in all LMSs, include setting

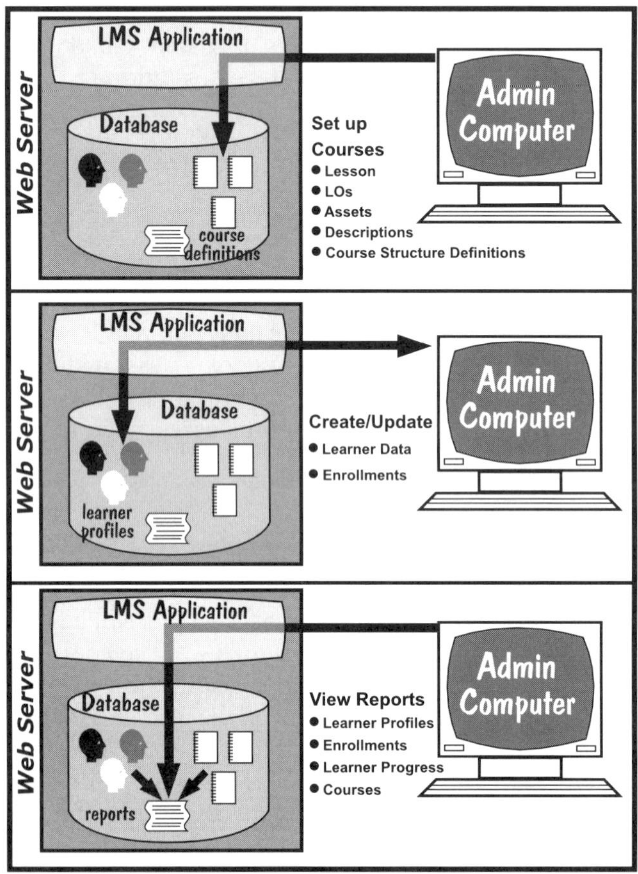

FIGURE 1.4
LMS functions — administrator view.

prerequisites or applying completion criteria such as allowing the learners to skip an LO by passing a pretest. However, it is important to note that LOs manage their own internal sequencing.

Do I Need an LMS?

If your organization's e-learning content is a mandatory part of job training or training required to comply with statutory requirements, it is obvious that you will need to monitor learner progress and results. Unless your organization is very small, you will probably need an LMS to handle this monitoring. You will also need an LMS if you want to control access to the e-learning content and the sequence in which LOs are presented. If your e-learning content is optional educational material provided for self-improvement purposes only, you may feel that an LMS is an unnecessary

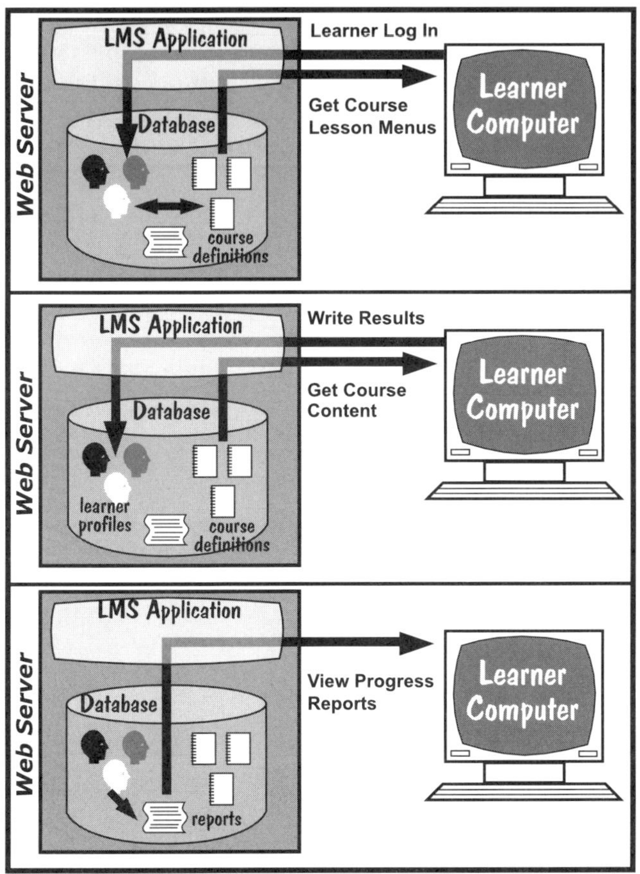

FIGURE 1.5
LMS functions — learner view.

frill in your e-learning infrastructure. However, you should consider some of the other benefits of an LMS. Setting up e-learning for your organization will not be inexpensive, so you or your management will want to know whether it is beneficial. You may have such questions as the following:

- Is anyone actually using the courses?
- Do most people who try the courses complete them?
- Do people come back for more after completing one course?
- How many learners pass the assessments?
- Are the assessments too difficult or too easy?

An LMS will enable you to collect data about the level of usage and effectiveness of your e-learning courses. Usage data includes the number of learners taking a course, the average amount of time spent on a course, and the number of learners completing a course. Having this data enables you to take any necessary measures to increase usage, for example by heightening awareness of the availability of the e-learning or finding out why learners don't stick with the courses. Data for measuring effectiveness may include the overall results for each course, such as the average score, as well as very detailed data about the result of every individual assessment question. Analysis of such data can point to ineffective areas of the content or poorly worded assessment questions. For example, if a high percentage of learners have consistently answered a particular question incorrectly, it probably indicates either that the question is badly designed or that the concept it is testing is not well explained in the content. Having this information gives you the opportunity to fix such problems and improve the effectiveness of your courses.

Learning Content Management Systems

The recent appearance of another genre of administrative systems known as learning content management systems (LCMS) on the e-learning scene has added a further layer of confusion for purchasers of e-learning components. These systems have been produced in anticipation of the wide-scale availability of standards-conformant LOs. A natural result of the adoption of LO technology is that there will be a much larger number of content pieces to deal with. Table 1.2 contrasts a traditional course structure against that of a course built from multiple LOs.

LCMSs were born of the realization that more advanced content management, organization, and search capabilities would be required to handle LOs than exist in a typical LMS. LCMSs are designed to meet the following requirements:

- Generate unique descriptions for each LO
- Discover (search for and locate) the required LO
- Provide multiple hierarchies for storing and organizing LOs
- Facilitate the assembly of complex course structures

TABLE 1.2

Traditional Course Structure Compared with Learning Objects (LOs)

Traditional Computer-Based Training	LOs
Few content pieces (typically fewer than 20 lessons)	Many content pieces (possibly thousands)
Few levels (perhaps 1–3) of hierarchy in course structure	Many layers of hierarchy in course structure
Each lesson can be easily located by its title	LOs need to be carefully described
Simple course structure	Complex course structure

A typical LCMS includes the following components:

- Authoring tools for producing content objects
- Content tagging and assembly functions for creating LOs from lower-level content objects and for grouping LOs to form larger learning content structures such as topics, lessons and courses
- A content repository for storing assets, LOs, content aggregations, and other content structures
- A delivery interface including functions for searching and organizing LOs to provide individualized learning experiences

Figure 1.6 shows the architecture of a typical LCMS.

Do I Need an LCMS?

Your requirement for an LCMS depends on how you plan to purchase and develop your e-learning content and how much content you will have to deal with. If you are taking an object-oriented approach by purchasing or

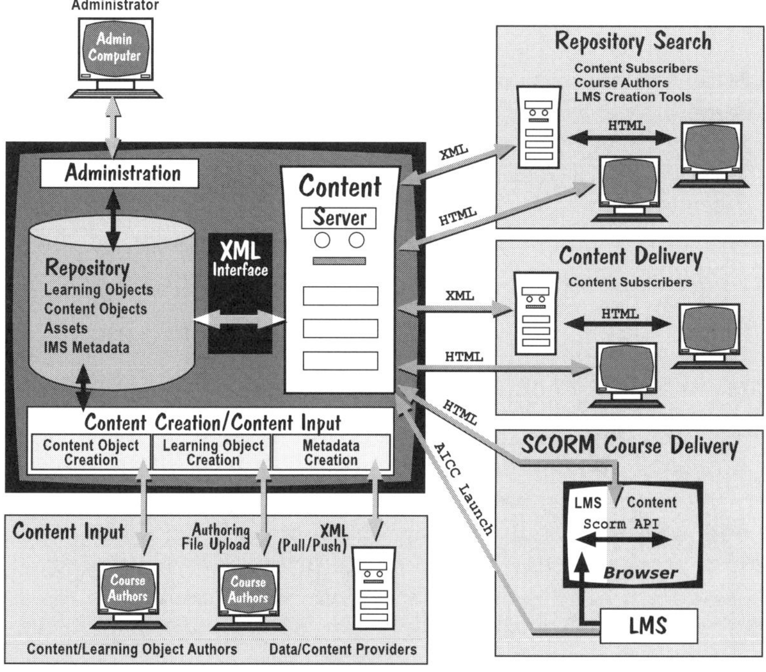

FIGURE 1.6
Sample LCMS architecture. (Adapted from Davies, D., Constructing Custom Courseware Factories, The Online Courseware Factory, unpublished marketing presentation, March 2002, slide 11.)

developing many small LOs, then you will likely need an LCMS. However, at the time of writing, the availability of off-the-shelf LOs is limited, and the design and production of context-independent reusable LOs offers a daunting challenge for a fledgling e-learning department. Over time the availability of premade LOs and the expertise in producing them will increase. Also, more design and development tools to aid the novice developer will appear on the market. Perhaps the question is better phrased, "how soon will we need an LCMS?"

In the short term, if you are planning to implement more traditional e-learning courses, use relatively few LOs, or be mainly concerned with learner administration and tracking, you will not need an LCMS. An LMS will adequately meet your needs.

Assessment Systems

Assessment systems are dedicated software systems used to present assessments to learners and to grade the learner's responses. Generically, such software is called an *assessment engine*. An assessment engine has two main components, one for displaying the assessment items (questions) and the other for processing the learner's responses (answers) to them.

Testing of all types can be easily included in conventional LOs, of course. In fact, it is not unusual for a course to include one or more test-only AUs or SCOs. So why might you need a separate system?

Assessment systems provide comprehensive sets of easy-to-use templates for question generation. They can also be used to store and transport entire libraries of individual test questions, structured groups of questions, and complete tests.

Generally speaking, assessment systems are useful for organizations that need to generate large banks of assessment questions on a regular basis.

Development and Authoring Tools

Those planning to produce their own courseware in house need to consider purchasing one or more of the specialized development tools for authoring e-learning content. Generally, the sophistication and cost of such tools will increase in direct proportion to the complexity of the e-learning content that they are capable of producing. Incidentally, so will the learning curve for achieving proficiency in using the tools. Very simple content with low interactivity can be produced using a Web site development tool such as Microsoft FrontPage®. More specialized tools such as Macromedia Authorware or Click2Learn Toolbook Instructor make it easier to produce content with a high level of interactivity once the developer is proficient with the tool. Chapter 9 offers a list of some of the best standards-friendly authoring tools.

Collaboration Tools

Collaboration tools is a term used to describe a group of components that enable contact among groups of learners, between learners and faculty, or both. Some of these tools are used to create the synchronous e-learning environments described earlier. Collaboration tools use Internet technologies for communication in environments such as chat rooms and video conferences. A common paradigm is the Webcast, or online presentation in which a speaker presents to a distributed audience who view a series of slides or an electronic whiteboard displayed on their own computers, with a voice-over via an Internet connection. Learners are able to ask questions by typing a text message to the presenter or to chat among themselves in a separate window. Some collaboration tools are asynchronous, including e-mail and discussion forums in which messages are sent or posted and a reply is not expected until later. Some LMSs offer built-in collaboration tools. Although at the time of writing there is work being done on standards for collaboration tools, there is not sufficient public information available to include them in this book.

Why Do E-Learning Standards Matter?

Standard vs. Proprietary

Why should you care about standards for e-learning? There are several reasons. First, imagine that you are setting up your organization's new e-learning portal. You like the pricing and scalability of an LMS from vendor A. For courseware, you really like vendor B's industrial safety courses but much prefer vendor C's software application courses. Provided that all of these components use a common standard for their data-passing methods and protocols, you can be confident that they will interoperate correctly.

Until the emergence of standards in the e-learning industry, organizations were often constrained to buying all their e-learning products from a single vendor. Courses came complete with their LMS software already integrated, and although data flowed freely between the LMS and the courseware, there was no way that the courses or LMS could interoperate with another vendor's system. Decision-makers had to choose between having multiple learning systems within their organizations or limiting their choice of courseware to a single content provider and sticking with that provider's offerings — good, bad, and indifferent. That situation was rather like trying to build a library for which all of the books have to be supplied by the same publisher. Today, as more vendors adopt the emerging standards, it is possible to achieve the mix-and-match scenario described above. And because organizations now have the freedom to pick and choose courseware, increased competition for courseware dollars inevitably will drive the quality of the available courseware up and its costs down.

In addition to mixing content from different vendors, perhaps you plan to develop some custom courseware for a particular process within your own organization, such as a special in-house sales training class or instruction on using a turnkey computer application. You may be developing this courseware in house or having an external specialist do it for you. In either case, this custom courseware can be added easily to your existing e-learning infrastructure, provided that it is developed to the correct standards.

Earlier in this chapter we discussed how an LO-based approach to developing courseware enables reusability of content in multiple contexts. Such reuse of LOs depends on each one being built to the same standards. Similarly, the *discovery* (search and location) of LOs relies on the use of a standard method for describing each one.

In summary, the benefits offered by standards-conformant e-learning over proprietary e-learning are as follows:

- Freedom of choice
- Cost savings
- Portable courses
- Courses from mixed sources
- Reusable and discoverable content

Case Studies

The following four case studies illustrate how e-learning standards are significant in e-learning implementations.

Accountants Inc.

Accountants Inc. is a national specialty-staffing service with more than 30 offices in markets across the United States. Its business is to provide accounting and finance staffing solutions for clients, and career opportunities in accounting and finance for candidates. Founded in 1986, Accountants Inc. is headquartered in Burlingame, California and is a member of the Select Appointments (Holdings) Limited Group of Companies, a division of Vedior, NV, the third largest global staffing company in the world.

Multiple needs dictated Accountants Inc.'s e-learning initiatives, including the following:

- The geographic distribution of its branch offices
- A significant increase in new employee hiring in the field offices

- A desire to take advantage of the opportunity for "any time" learning and training
- The need to provide training content that can be easily changed and updated without necessitating redistribution of paper documents
- The need to provide a method to efficiently and effectively respond to the training needs of new hires, who typically come aboard one at a time in the branch offices

The goal and objectives of the e-learning initiative were as follows:

- Provide basic sales training and a foundation of knowledge for new employees
- Integrate existing first-generation e-learning and other training products into the soon-to-be-launched corporate intranet
- Develop a foundation for future content and course offerings
- Create content that could be updated easily and without costly production and distribution requirements
- Provide a method for measuring and tracking training completion

The chosen e-learning solution included an LMS certified to the AICC CMI specification (WBT Manager from Integrity eLearning) and custom courses designed by Accountants Inc.'s training department and developed by a third-party e-learning vendor using Macromedia Authorware. Accountants Inc.'s course designer applied instructional design and communication standards to do the following:

- Chunk information
- Limit the amount of information on a page
- Limit scrolling
- Create or add interactivity every few screens (typically three to five screens)
- Provide continuity of screen design, layout, and navigation

Each topic of the courseware was designed to do the following:

- Present the foundation information
- Provide an example
- Apply or test the knowledge via a practice exercise

All the courseware was developed to the AICC CMI specification using functions already built into the Authorware function set. The data tracked include the following:

- Learner's score on each individual assessment
- Learner's final score
- Time spent in each LO
- A bookmark to enable the learner to resume partway through an LO
- Completion status (not started, incomplete, or complete) of each LO

This information is used to monitor learner progress and to measure course effectiveness and usage.

Accountants Inc. selected an AICC-certified LMS so that they could mix custom-developed and off-the-shelf content using the same LMS. Conversely, by developing their existing custom courseware to the AICC CMI specification, they also left the door open for migration of their courseware to another LMS should their current LMS be unable to meet their future requirements.

Accountants Inc. achieved its objectives. Future plans for its e-learning infrastructure include adding more custom course content and deploying off-the-shelf content via the existing LMS.

Western and Southern Life Insurance Company

The Western and Southern Life Insurance Company consists of more than 200 offices operating in 22 states and the District of Columbia. These offices are staffed by more than 3,000 licensed, experienced field personnel. The Western Southern Financial group consists of more than 12 wholly owned subsidiaries and approximately 5,000 associates, and it is recognized as a leader in consumer and business financial services providing life insurance, annuities, mutual funds, and investment management for millions of people throughout the United States.

In an industry with traditionally low sales force retention rates, Western-Southern Life recognized the need to provide a world-class training environment for their field associates. The ability to provide up-to-date training in a quickly changing, geographically dispersed environment was critical. Western-Southern Life also recognized that to improve the quality of training, they must be able to see its results. They felt that an e-learning infrastructure would enable them to meet their objectives.

Western-Southern Life's goal was to be able to deliver a clearly communicated educational program to their field sales force. They wanted the ability to blend their learning between self-paced 24/7 asynchronous e-learning, live synchronous online learning, and management-led practical application instruction. They wanted to ensure that the learner, management, and home office would have the appropriate reporting tools to see that everyone stays on pace and accomplishes their educational goals.

Finally, they wanted to expand their course offerings to include industry designations and state-required training, making their online university the only place that their associates would need to go for *all* of their corporate-sponsored training.

Western-Southern Life selected three primary tools to comprise their e-learning infrastructure:

- A learning management system
- Courseware
- A collaboration tool

They chose WBT Manager from Integrity eLearning as their learning management system, Macromedia Authorware as their content design and development tool, and HorizonLive as their collaboration tool.

When selecting e-learning partners, standards played a significant role in the decision-making process. Western-Southern Life wanted a solution that offered open architecture to enable them to customize the look, feel, and even some features of the systems. They needed the ability to make all three pieces work together. Without standards it would simply not have been possible to meet these requirements. At the time of review of their consultant report in the year 2000, there were only two LMS vendors that were actually AICC certified (at the time of this writing there are more than 20). Both of these made the company's "top 3" list of LMS choices. WBT Manager came out on top because it was not only AICC certified but used open-source active server pages (ASPs) that allowed them to customize how the application worked. Because their information systems department already supported the use of ASP code, it was a natural fit into their existing infrastructure.

Western-Southern Life has completed its delivery and tracking system and is now focusing on improving its learning content. Initially, its instructional designers built content without using standards. The designers' philosophy was that if the content owners were not concerned about standard tracking abilities, they did not need to be concerned either. However, as they moved forward, they learned how critical standards are. The organization now sees the power of standards-conformant courses and expects all training to meet those standards. As a result they now need to convert some of their original content to meet this new requirement. Online University Project Manager Dave Mauldin said, "It is a wonderful problem to have when you create a higher standard and expectation for an enterprise. Now we are leveraging the e-learning standards to meet these unforeseen expectations."

Western-Southern Life managed to meet all of their phase 1 deliverables on time and under budget. They held more than 200 live online classes in the first 6 months and have transitioned huge amounts of legacy data from their old mainframe systems. They now have well over 150 self-paced e-learning courses and more than 30 courses that offer continuing education (CE) credits in most states. They now even offer e-learning courses that are part of the LUTC industry designation.

Western-Southern Life's key driver is the New Agent Introduction (NAI) program. It is a 4-year program with a 26-week fast-start component. Successfully completing the fast start within the 26 weeks, as well as hitting several other key checkpoints in the program, is contractually required training. Because of this and the need for state licensing–required CE credits, Western-Southern drives over 100 new learners per month and 2000 learners annually through the learning management system.

Western-Southern Life feels that in an industry that is compliance driven, the ability to record and validate that competencies have been properly delivered is a must. The ability to see a global view of training results allows them to track the effectiveness of the content and see where areas of improvement are needed, and they have realized cost savings by using standards-conformant e-learning.

Southern California Edison

Southern California Edison (SCE) is the largest and most advanced utility in the United States. As with all utilities, it must comply with many governmental and labor requirements. For SCE, training its workforce is a necessary and crucial step toward improving productivity, ensuring safety, and meeting regulatory requirements.

In 1997, SCE selected an AICC-certified LMS, which was later acquired by IBM-Lotus and became part of that corporation's LearningSpace® application.

The LMS had to be integrated into SCE's existing data-processing infrastructure, which included the following:

- Oracle® database
- PeopleSoft® HRMS human resources management system
- A data warehouse

SCE's needs were as diverse as their power offerings, and e-learning was tracked for the following departments:

- Customer Service Business Unit — Responsible for all customer service functions as well as for meter readers and assorted field personnel and for safety
- Transmission and Distribution — Responsible for all aspects of power management and distribution over the electricity grid
- Human Resources — Responsible for human resources compliance training, Family Medical Leave Act compliance, payroll processing, and so on

- San Onofre Nuclear Group — Responsible for the training and maintenance associated with the largest nuclear reactor on the West Coast
- Environmental Safety
- Procurement
- Other groups

The requirements for tracking vary by department and were based on regulatory needs, productivity requirements, compliance issues, and company indemnification. Once information is stored in the LMS, it is merged with human resources (HR) data and moved to the SCE corporate data warehouse, where departments can run reports or query the tracking data by employee, department, division, and so on.

The courseware was acquired from multiple sources, including in-house and third-party developers and off-the-shelf vendors. By developing and acquiring AICC-conformant courseware, it was possible to integrate all the courseware, whatever its source, into the AICC-certified LMS.

Implementing the e-learning infrastructure companywide took SCE approximately 2 years because of the large amounts of data that needed to be integrated. The larger the enterprise, the more complex the requirements and the greater the effort needed for data integration, custom modifications, departmental needs analysis, consensus gathering, and planning. Most e-learning implementations do not take as long as SCE's did.

Initially, a single group spearheaded the implementation. However, as news spread throughout the organization that e-elearning was now available, a committee was formed comprised of management from all critical divisions and from their information technology department. The committee steered the direction of the implementation and made sure that the whole enterprise was taken care of adequately.

Five years after implementing e-learning, some of the measurable benefits include the following:

- Increased productivity among substation operators and decreased power downtime
- A reduction in accidents by more than 30%
- Improved management–labor relationships
- Decreased maintenance downtime for the nuclear plants
- Improved understanding of HR compliance issues

As with most e-learning implementations, SCE did not know up front what the eventual results of implementing the software would be. But now that the software is running as part of a normal production schedule, SCE is not sure how they managed without it.

Standards played a major role in the success of SCE's e-learning implementation by enabling the integration of courseware from multiple sources, used in diverse parts of the organization, into a single enterprise-wide LMS.

Mitchell International

Mitchell International, in San Diego, California, is a leading provider of software and actuarial services for the insurance industry. The company specializes in estimating, decision support, claims management, collision shop management, medical casualty claims, and total loss, as well as training and education services.

As a major provider of software to small companies in the automotive, truck, and medical industries, training clients was a major endeavor. But small-company budgets did not allow for big-company training. Mitchell needed a way to increase customer knowledge to decrease the costs of supporting their software. An initiative was launched to create the online Mitchell University.

Mitchell knew that offering training via the Web would improve customer satisfaction and reduce customer service costs. Time would prove that they were correct.

The first step was to purchase an LMS. The system had to be AICC conformant so that it would be able to track custom learner information as needed. Mitchell recognized the importance of being able to launch and track content from mixed sources. After reviewing five major providers, they selected Pathlore® Learning Management System, an AICC-certified LMS.

They developed most of the content in house. A small amount of development was outsourced to a third party.

The implementation was a great success, and Mitchell was able to quantify the following:

- Cost of sales dropped as more marketing materials were placed online, and the Mitchell University became a value-added component of their product suite.
- Customer service calls dropped by nearly 75% because customers were required to obtain an online certification on the specific product's usage. This alone was an enormous savings and increased customer satisfaction dramatically.
- The training department could roll out new courses on a more timely basis that corresponded with product delivery.
- Staff training costs were greatly reduced.

The e-learning implementation has also helped Mitchell's sales and marketing groups because they can run reports on customer training. This helps them identify weaknesses in the training and areas that need improvement. Mitchell

University has been a great success and cost saver for Mitchell, proving that a well-thought-out implementation of standards-conformant e-learning can result in quantifiable business improvements. By adopting the AICC CMI specification, they also ensured interoperability with content that they might obtain from other sources in the future.

So Does My Organization Really Need Standards?

If you are still unsure about the need to follow e-learning standards in your organization, consider the following:

- Do you need to control learner access to courseware, track learner progress, or monitor the effectiveness of your e-learning content?
- Do you want to be able to control the learner's path through the content in some way?
- Do you plan to develop content in house and also purchase content from one or more third-party content vendors?
- Do you plan to use the content for multiple new audiences in the future?
- Do you plan to reuse parts of the content in future courses?
- Are you planning to redistribute or sell the content to another organization?

If your answer to one or more of the above questions is "yes," then it would be very prudent for you to purchase or develop standards-conformant e-learning components.

So What Is a Standard?

Understanding the Term *Standards*

Standards are an integral part of everyday life that we take for granted most of the time. Electrical plugs that only fit one way into their sockets, clocks (both analog and digital), stop lights, and 35mm film are all examples of widely known and accepted standards. However, although it is fairly difficult to insert an electrical plug into its socket the wrong way round, many standards, such as those concerned with computer software, are much more complex and need extensive documentation.

According to the International Organization for Standardization (ISO), standards are "documented agreements containing technical specifications or other precise criteria to be used consistently as rules, guidelines, or definitions of characteristics, to ensure that materials, products, processes and services are fit for their purpose."[1]

The term *standard* as it is commonly used actually refers to *accredited* standards, which have been processed and approved by an accredited standards body such as ISO or the Institute of Electrical and Electronics Engineers (IEEE) Standards Association. The e-learning standards to which we refer throughout this book are not standards according to this definition. They are in fact a mixture of requirements, specifications, and implementation models that are in the process of evolving toward becoming accredited standards. It is important that buyers and vendors alike are clear about this distinction when discussing conformance with existing e-learning standards. So let's take a brief look at the steps that lead to the publication of an accredited standard.

The Life Cycle of a Standard

The standardization process usually starts as a result of a problem. In the case of e-learning, several problems were encountered by early adopters of the technology. One of these was the inability to mix and match courseware from different sources and vendors under the control of a single LMS or to move completed courses between LMSs. The efforts to resolve such a problem typically pass through a number of stages that ultimately lead to the publishing of an accredited standard. A simplified view of a standards life cycle is given in Figure 1.7.

Specifications

The next stage is for the interested parties to develop a specification that solves the problem. In the case of the interoperability problem mentioned above, this was the AICC CMI specification. More information on the AICC CMI specification will be found in succeeding chapters.

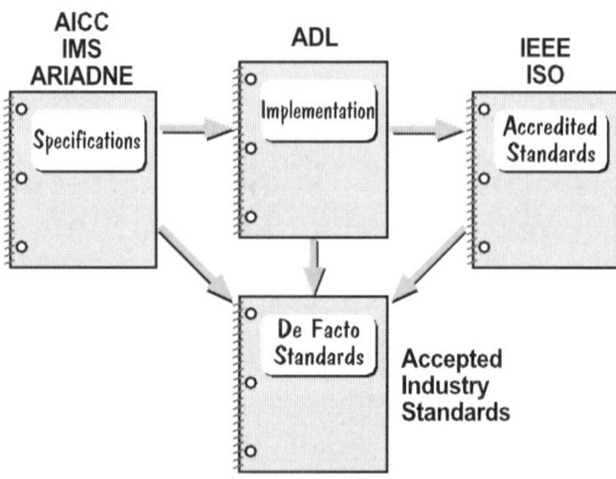

FIGURE 1.7
E-learning standards evolution.

Implementations

During the implementation phase, the specification is tested in real-world situations. If it is successful, it may become widely accepted and implemented. When such widespread adoption occurs, the specification becomes an *industry* or *de facto* standard. The ADL SCORM is an example of such an implementation. It is comprised of several specifications from various standards bodies. We will discuss the ADL SCORM further later in thebook.

Accredited Standards

Accredited standards are the result of a formal standardization process carried out by an accredited standards body. During this standardization process, the specification is reviewed to ensure that it is broadly or globally applicable and does not contain any specifics of given industries or originators. For example, the standards body checks that it does not favor any particular vendor and that it is applicable to all relevant types of organizations.

There are three major bodies in the world that are responsible for technology standards accreditation, the IEEE-SA (IEEE Standards Association), ISO, and CEN/ISSS (European Committee for Standardization/Information Society Standardization System), which is responsible for accredited standards for the European Union.

Once a standard becomes an accredited or *de jure* standard, it generally enjoys widespread acceptance, implementation, and use. This increased experience typically leads to the discovery of new problems and requirements, which can then be fed back into the standardization process. The process then cycles around again to produce new or revised specifications and standards.

The Downside of Standards

The life cycle of standards, as described above, leads to certain difficulties. The standardization process typically takes about 10 years, and most technological industries simply cannot wait that long. Although this situation often leads to rapid adoption and validation of specifications as industry standards, the specifications are often inadequate for such widespread use. For example, the AICC CMI specification is generally accepted as the interoperability *de facto* standard for courseware and LMSs. However, although conformance of products to the specification is a very good start, it is not an absolute guarantee that two such products will work together. This may be due to vague or missing areas in the specification, leading to inconsistencies in the way that it is interpreted by different vendors. An important part of the standardization process is to resolve such inadequacies in specifications. The rule of thumb when buying products that claim to be conformant with a specification that is not yet an accredited standard is to ask the vendor to demonstrate the product's conformance.

So Are Standards Really Worth the Trouble?

The reaction of some people to the pitfalls in the standards life cycle is to ignore standards altogether until they become accredited. They feel that the specifications that exist today are not stable and mature enough to be regarded as standards. Although it is certainly true that standards will develop further and change over time, they are the best that we have right now. The adoption of AICC certification, AICC conformance, and SCORM conformance by many major e-learning vendors is a good indication of how important the vendors feel standards to be. Although there are e-learning providers who claim to be a one-stop shop for all e-learning needs, most are realistic enough to realize that they cannot survive without the ability to interoperate with products from other vendors and their clients' own systems. By sticking to vendors that have committed to conforming with the emerging standards, one can have some degree of certainty that those vendors will keep their products in line with those standards as they develop, become established, and are eventually accredited.

Bear in mind that standards bodies want organizations to continue to adhere to their specifications. This gives them the incentive to make transitioning between old and new versions of specifications as easy as possible. For example, as the ADL makes updates to the SCORM data model, it will provide mapping between data elements in the old and new models to simplify updates whenever possible.

Also consider the following. Suppose that you follow one of today's standards for e-learning components that you purchase or develop and that by the time the standard becomes accredited, 30% of it has changed. Under this scenario, your e-learning component will still be 70% conformant with the appropriate accredited standards. However, if you ignore today's standards, your components may be as little as 0% conformant when the standards become accredited. Clearly, in this case you will have a lot further to go to achieve full standards conformance.

Conclusion

In this chapter we have discussed the conceptual and physical components of e-learning and how they are named and defined in the AICC and SCORM specifications. We have also seen the role of standards in enabling successful e-learning implementations. In the chapters that follow we will take a look at what is included in these specifications and how they are actually used. We will start in Chapter 2 by discussing the history of e-learning standards, where they are today, and what is planned for the future.

Reference

1. International Organization for Standardization (ISO). *About ISO, Introduction.* Available at: http://www.iso.org/iso/en/aboutiso/introduction/index.html.

2

The Evolution of Standards for E-Learning

Introduction

This chapter offers a brief history of e-learning standards, describing how they came into being and are progressing along the path to accreditation. The standards that we have today are the result of the work of a number of standards bodies. We will meet the key players and explore the relationship between the various standards bodies. Finally we will take a look at likely future directions for the standards and discuss what you can do to keep up-to-date with further developments.

The Rise of Standards for E-Learning

In the early 1980s, the aviation industry was one of the first industries to adopt computer-based training (CBT) on a large scale. As aviation technology advanced and aircraft became more sophisticated, it became very difficult to keep airline staff adequately trained to maintain and operate a variety of aircraft. Obviously, for safety reasons in the aviation business, it is vital that personnel are kept up-to-date with the most current information available. The aircraft manufacturers found that CBT was the ideal delivery medium to meet that training need for several reasons:

- Media-rich interactive CBT is a far more effective training tool than printed manuals.
- The addition of assessment and data tracking means that management can be assured that their personnel meet the required standards.
- CBT is available to personnel 24 hours per day, 7 days per week (24/7).

- Personnel can access the training material on a just-in-time basis, so that they can carry out a particular task immediately after reviewing the latest information.

As a result of this success, the aviation industry invested millions of dollars in producing CBTs. However, as the adoption of CBT spread through the aviation business, one problem quickly emerged. In the 1980s CBTs were not only developed using proprietary software but also ran on proprietary hardware. So CBTs supplied by Boeing, Airbus, McDonnell-Douglas, and other manufacturers all needed their own unique set of hardware. Consequently airlines had to buy a discrete set of computers for each type of airplane they owned. Needless to say they were extremely unhappy about the resulting high costs and the inconvenience of having sets of records for each learner on multiple computers.

The Aviation Industry CBT Committee (AICC) was founded in 1988 to address these problems. The AICC is an international group of aircraft manufacturers, aviation trainers (military, commercial, and civilian), government and regulatory agencies, e-learning tools vendors, and e-learning courseware developers. The AICC first turned its attention to standardizing the hardware for CBT delivery by developing platform guidelines. They continued with a DOS-based digital audio guideline that was released before the advent of Windows-based multimedia standards. The guideline enabled end users to use one standard audio card for multiple vendors' CBT courseware. Because of the huge amount of CBT legacy courseware in the aviation industry, this guideline is still in use.

In 1993 the AICC produced its best-known CBT guideline, which specified a standard mechanism for computer-managed instruction (CMI) interoperability. CMI is the predecessor of today's learning management systems (LMS). These days, CMI is generally regarded as a subset of LMS. However, for the purposes of any discussion about interoperability, the terms *CMI* and *LMS* are essentially synonymous. The interoperability guideline resulted in the ability of LMSs to share data with local area network (LAN)–based CBT courseware from multiple sources or vendors.

In January 1998, the AICC's CMI specification was updated to include Web-based CBT, now better known as Web-based training, or WBT. The Web-based guideline was the first published specification for interoperability on the Web.

As we have already discussed, the AICC was born of a need to standardize the delivery platforms for CBT and e-learning content and consequently reduce the cost of these learning strategies. The AICC recognized that this cost reduction could only be achieved by promoting interoperability standards that vendors can use across multiple types of organizations, thereby enabling them to sell their products to a broader market. So the AICC recommendations, particularly those for CMI interoperability, were designed to be applicable to most types of e-learning. Many other organizations soon recognized the applicability of these specifications to CBT and WBT in general. As a result, the AICC's CMI specification became the first widely adopted industry standard for e-learning.[1]

Another key development in e-learning standards arose in part as a result of the Gulf War in 1991. After that war, the U.S. Congress carried out studies to assess the readiness of the reserve forces when those forces were called to Operation Desert Storm. These studies concluded that the reserve forces needed improved access to education and training to achieve better readiness for future action. As a result, Congress gave funds to the National Guard to prototype e-learning classrooms and networks as a delivery mechanism for the required education and training resources. In 1997, the U.S. Department of Defense (DoD) decided to expand this work and founded the Advanced Distributed Learning Initiative, which is commonly referred to as "the ADL." The primary mission of the ADL was to modernize the delivery of training to the U.S. armed forces. However, its work is considered to be applicable in many other public and private sectors. The ADL Initiative published the first version of its e-learning specification, the *Sharable Content Object Reference Model* (SCORM), in 1999.[2]

Two other significant bodies became involved in e-learning standards in 1997. These were the IMS Project and the Institute of Electrical and Electronics Engineers (IEEE) Learning Technology Standards Committee (LTSC).

The IMS Project was founded as part of the National Learning Infrastructure Initiative of EDUCAUSE (then Educom) as a fee-based consortium of learning-technology vendors, publishers and users. Its members included many U.S. universities, and its original focus was on higher education. The IMS project produced specifications covering multiple areas of e-learning — meta-data, content, administrative systems, and learner information, each developed by its own working group. IMS later relaunched as a nonprofit organization with a more international outlook, the IMS Global Learning Consortium.[3]

The IEEE is a nonprofit, technical professional association that has more than 377,000 individual members representing 150 nations. Through its members, the IEEE is a leading authority in a broad range of technical areas, including computer engineering, biomedical technology, telecommunications, electric power, aerospace, and consumer electronics.[4] Groups affiliated with or sponsored by the IEEE include the IEEE Standards Association (IEEE-SA)[5] and the IEEE Computer Society.[6] In 1997, the IEEE Computer Society Standards Activity Board chartered the LTSC to develop standards for information technology as used in learning, education, and training.[7] The chartering of the LTSC opened the way to accreditation for e-learning standards.

An Overview of the Standards Bodies

In this section we discuss the individual bodies that are involved in the development of e-learning standards and describe the work that they are doing today.

The ADL Initiative

The ADL's common technical framework, the SCORM, comprises the following:

- Interrelated technical specifications from a variety of different standards bodies
- A content model
- A standardized e-learning run-time environment

Although it was conceived by the DoD, the SCORM is being developed through active collaboration between private industry, education, and the U.S. federal government with the goal of producing guidelines that meet the common needs of all sectors. To facilitate this collaboration, the ADL established the ADL Co-Laboratory Network, which provides an open collaborative environment for sharing and testing learning technology research, development, and assessments.[8] The ADL Co-Laboratory hosts regular public events called Plugfests, at which e-learning vendors and content developers can bring their products and test their conformance to the SCORM and their interoperability with other e-learning products and content. Plugfests provide a valuable opportunity for all interested parties to cooperate in identifying the strengths and weaknesses of the SCORM and to exchange ideas and information. For example, content developers can test the interoperability of their courses with LMSs from various vendors, and vice versa.[9]

The SCORM document, which is available on the ADL's Web site (http://www.adlnet.org), includes specifications based on the work of other standards bodies, namely the AICC, IMS, IEEE/LTSC, and Alliance of Remote Instructional Authoring & Distribution Networks for Europe (ARIADNE). The work being done by these organizations is discussed later in this chapter.

Rather than reinventing the wheel, the SCORM leverages the work of the standards bodies by bringing together their disparate specifications and adapting them to form an integrated and cohesive implementation model. Figure 2.1, which is adapted from the SCORM version 1.2 Overview document, groups these specifications into three books:

- *The SCORM Overview* provides a general overview of the purpose and structure of the SCORM.
- *The SCORM Content Aggregation Model* contains specifications for identifying, finding, and moving e-learning content. The content of this book is based on input from the following specifications:
  - IEEE/LTSC Learning Object Meta-data (LOM) Standard
  - IMS XML Meta-data Binding Specification (from the IMS Learning Resource Meta-data Specification, version 1.2)
  - IMS Content Packaging Specification

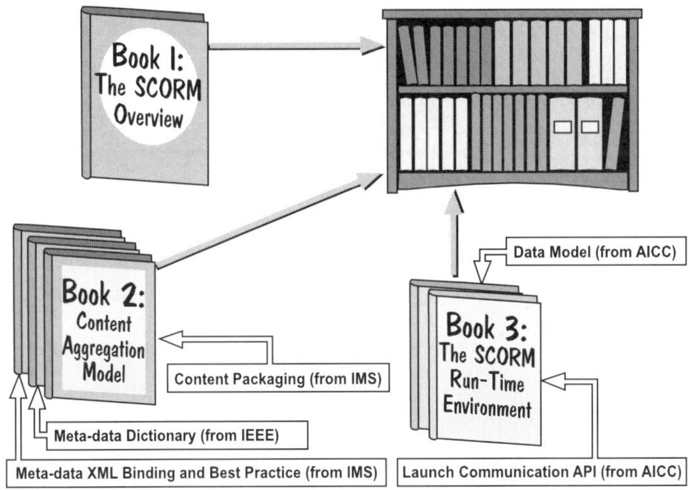

FIGURE 2.1
The SCORM "books." (Adapted from ADL, *Sharable Content Object Reference Model (SCORM) Version 1.2, The SCORM Overview,* 2001, Table 1.1.3a. Available at http://www.adlet.org)

- *The SCORM Run-Time Environment* includes specifications that define how LMSs should launch content and track learner progress with that content within a Web-based environment. It is based on a combination of content derived from the AICC CMI specification and further collaborative effort between ADL and AICC, which extended the AICC's specification to include a standardized Application Programming Interface (API) for LMS and content communication.

The SCORM document is constantly evolving as further specifications are refined and added to the model.

At the time of this writing, the ADL provides a SCORM Conformance Test Suite designed to help organizations test their conformance to the SCORM. ADL is planning to make certification testing available through third-party organizations. For the latest information, go to the ADL Web site, http://www.adlnet.org.

Aviation Industry CBT Committee

The AICC develops technical guidelines known as AICC Guidelines & Recommendations (AGRs). An AGR is a short document that usually references a detailed specification document. AGR 010 is the AICC's guideline for interoperability between Web-based courseware and LMSs. It references another document, CMI001 – "CMI Guidelines for Interoperability," which is commonly referred to in the e-learning industry as "the AICC CMI specification."

The AICC offers certification testing for the AGR 010 CMI interoperability guidelines, as well as for the AGR 006 guidelines, which apply to LAN-based management systems. Certification is available for the following types of e-learning products:

- Assignable unit (AU) — A unit of e-learning content (learning object) that can be launched and tracked by an AICC-conformant LMS
- Course — A group of AUs assembled using the AICC course interchange files
- LMS — A system that manages and launches AUs and tracks student progress
- Application service provider (ASP) — An LMS installed at a central data center provided by an organization; this organization, the ASP, offers LMS services to multiple customer organizations rather than licensing or selling LMS system software
- Courseware generation and assessment system — Content creation and delivery system that can either communicate with an LMS directly as an AU *or* generate AUs such that some (or all) AICC communication data is automatically set or inspected by the system (and not directly by the content designer); examples of such systems are test bank systems, simulation systems, courseware engines, and courseware generators
- Authoring system — E-learning content creation and delivery system that allows content developers to directly control the inspection and setting of all AICC communication data in the design of AUs

To achieve AICC certification, products are put through a testing process by an independent third-party testing organization. Vendors are also able to self-test their products using the AICC test suite. This enables them to claim AICC conformance for their products. Note however that this is a self-test, and there is no guarantee that a product does in fact conform to the AICC guidelines.

IMS Global Consortium

IMS produces open specifications for locating and using e-learning content, tracking learner progress, reporting learner performance, and exchanging student records between administrative systems such as LMSs. Two of these specifications have been adapted for use in the SCORM version 1.2:

- *The IMS Learning Resources Meta-Data Specification,* which defines a method for describing learning resources so that they can be located using meta-data–aware search software
- *The IMS Content & Packaging Specification,* which defines how to create reusable LOs that can be accessed by a variety of administration systems such as LMSs and LCMSs

Other IMS specifications that are expected to be wholly or partially incorporated into the SCORM in the foreseeable future are the following:

- *The IMS Question & Test Interoperability Specification,* which addresses the need to be able to share test items and other assessment data across different administrative and assessment systems
- *The IMS Learner Profiles Specification,* which defines ways to organize learner information so that learning-administration systems such as LMSs and LCMSs can be more responsive to the specific needs of each user
- *The IMS Simple Sequencing Specification,* which defines a method for specifying adaptive rules that govern the sequence in which reusable LOs are to be presented to the learner

Vendors developing e-learning components to IMS specifications can self-declare that they have adopted and implemented those specifications or specified individual components thereof. Certification testing against IMS specifications that are included with the SCORM is expected to be available as part of the ADL SCORM certification.

IEEE Learning Technology Standards Committee

The IEEE/LTSC consists of individual working groups that develop technical standards in approximately 20 different areas of information technology for learning, education, and training. These groups develop technical standards, recommended practices, and guides for e-learning–related software, tools, technologies, and design methods. Their focus is on the development, deployment, maintenance, and interoperation of e-learning components and systems.[10]

The IEEE/LTSC LOM Specification was derived from work done by the IMS and another group known as ARIADNE, which is described below. This specification, which forms the basis of the current IMS Learning Resource Meta-Data Information Model included in the SCORM, is the world's first accredited standard for e-learning.

Ultimately most of the standards developed by IEEE/LTSC will be advanced as international standards by the International Organization for Standardization (ISO), as discussed below.

Alliance of Remote Instructional Authoring & Distribution Networks for Europe

The ARIADNE European Projects (Phase I and Phase II) were formed to develop a set of e-learning tools and methodologies. The project, which was largely funded by the European Union and the Swiss government, ended in June 2000. Subsequently, the ARIADNE Foundation was formed to promote the widespread adoption of state-of-the-art and platform-independent education in Europe.[11]

International Organization for Standardization/International Electrotechnical Commission, *Joint Technical Committee 1, Sub-Committee 36*

The ISO is a worldwide federation of national standards bodies from some 140 countries.[12] It has created a Joint Technical Committee in cooperation with the International Electrotechnical Commission (IEC), which is the international standards and conformity assessment body for all fields of electrotechnology.[13] This technical committee, known as JTC1, includes a subcommittee known as SC36 (Sub-Committee 36), which is responsible for work on information technology for learning, education, and training.[14]

Other Standards Bodies

The standards bodies discussed in the preceding sections are those that have had a hand in developing the specifications discussed in this book. However, there are other bodies around the globe that are concerned with standards for e-learning. Readers are advised to check with industry-centric or geographically oriented bodies for any specifications or standards that may be applicable to their own industries or locations.

Relationships between the Standards Bodies

As we discussed earlier in this chapter, there is considerable overlap in the work of the standards bodies. For example, the IMS Learning Resources Meta-Data Information Model used in the SCORM was based on work done by both IMS and ARIADNE. Similarly, the SCORM Run-Time Environment includes the API developed jointly by ADL and the AICC. From time to time we have heard people express concern that the work of the AICC is not relevant to their type of organization or that the SCORM is for government only or is the "American standard." Although this concern is understandable and the standards bodies may vary to some degree in their focus, they are all working toward the common goal of attaining a set of international accredited standards for e-learning. The degree of synergy between these standards bodies is manifested by the fact that many of the individuals who participate in the various committees and working groups do so within two or more of the standards bodies simultaneously. So choosing the standards that you wish to follow is not a question of pitting IMS vs. AICC or ADL SCORM vs. IEEE. The choices are determined by the components that you choose for your e-learning infrastructure and by how you wish to integrate and interoperate those components with each other and possibly with other external e-learning infrastructures.

Future Directions for E-Learning Standards

Moving toward Accredited Standards

The existing specifications will continue to be developed as they roll toward standardization by one of the accredited standards bodies.

For example, the IEEE-LTSC LOM Specification (P1482) was approved as an accredited standard on June 13, 2002, just before this book went to press. This makes it the first accredited standard specifically for e-learning. Hereafter it will be put forward for acceptance as an ISO-accredited standard.

Working groups at IMS, IEEE, and ISO are developing several more specifications and accredited standards for various facets of e-learning, such as learner information and competency definitions. Some of these specifications will be added to the SCORM if considered appropriate. As noted earlier, at least three of the IMS specifications are already being considered for inclusion into the SCORM.

Keeping Up-To-Date

The best way to keep up-to-date as the e-learning standards continue to evolve and mature is to keep an eye on the news sections of the major standards organizations' Web sites. These Web sites are also useful resources for checking the certification and self-conformance tests available to vendors. For example, the AICC Web site has a list of all vendors who have been certified against its AGR 010 guidelines, including a report on each vendor's test results. At the very least, it would be prudent to check this list for the names of any vendors who claim that their product is AICC certified.

Several of the sites offer public discussion groups where you can post questions and comments about the relevant specifications or standards. For a list of Web sites, please see Appendix B.

Conclusion

After reading this chapter, you should have a good idea of the evolution of today's standards, the organizations that have been involved in their development, and the direction in which they are moving. In the next chapter we will focus on which standards are applicable to each type of e-learning product. We will also provide suggestions on how to deal with vendors when buying standards-conformant components.

References

1. Aviation Industry CBT Committee. *AICC FAQ (Frequently Asked Questions).* Accessed June 3, 2002. Available at: http://www.aicc.org/pages/aicc_faq.htm.
2. Advanced Distributed Learning Network (ADLNet). *Advanced Distributed Learning, SCORM Past.* Accessed June 3, 2002. Available at: http://www.adlnet.org/index.cfm?fuseaction=scormhist.
3. IMS Global Consortium, Inc. *IMS Background.* Accessed June 3, 2002. Available at: http://www.imsproject.com/background.html.
4. Institute of Electrical and Electronic Engineers, Inc. *About the IEEE.* Accessed June 3, 2002. Available at: http://www.ieee.org/home.
5. IEEE Standards Association. *IEEE Standards Association: Overview.* Accessed June 3, 2002. Available at: http://standards.ieee.org/sa/sa-view.html.
6. IEEE Computer Society. *About the Computer Society.* Accessed June 3, 2002. Available at: http://www.computer.org/csinfo/.
7. IEE/LTSC. *IEEE Learning Technology Standards Committee (LTSC), Mission.* Accessed June 3, 2002. Available at: http://grouper.ieee.org/groups/ltsc/index.html.
8. Advanced Distributed Learning Network (ADLNet). *ADL Co-Labs Overview.* Accessed June 3, 2002. Available at: http://www.adlnet.org/index.cfm?fuseaction=colabovr.
9. Advanced Distributed Learning Network (ADLNet). *Plugfest Overview.* Accessed June 3, 2002. Available at: http://www.adlnet.org/index.cfm?fuseaction=plugmulti.
10. Institute of Electrical and Electronic Engineers, Inc. *IEEE Learning Technology Standards Committee.* Accessed June 3, 2002. Available at: http://grouper.ieee.org/groups/ltsc/index.html.
11. The ARIADNE Foundation. *1.1_Foundation Presentation.* Accessed June 3, 2002. Available at: http://www.ariadne-eu.org/1_AF/1.1_Presentation/main.html#Top.
12. International Organization for Standards. *Introduction — What Is ISO?* Accessed June 3, 2002. Available at: http://www.iso.ch/iso/en/aboutiso/introduction/whatisISO.html.
13. International Electrotechnical Commission. *IEC / CEI — International Electrotechnical Commission — Home Page.* Accessed June 3, 2002. Available at: http://www.iec.ch/.

14. International Organization for Standardization/International Electrotechnical Commission JTC1 SC36. *ISO/IEC JTC1 SC36 Home Page*. Accessed June 3, 2002. Available at: http://jtc1sc36.org/.

3

Which Standards? Matching Standards to E-Learning Components

Introduction

The goal of this chapter is to equip you to make better decisions when purchasing or developing standards-conformant e-learning components. After deciding what components will be included in your e-learning infrastructure, you need to determine which standards apply to those components. We will look at how the standards map onto each of the major asynchronous e-learning components. Where more than one standard applies to a component, we will discuss the relative merits of each. Finally, we will offer some guidelines for talking about standards with e-learning vendors. For details on obtaining any specifications referenced in this chapter, please see Appendix B.

Standards for Courseware

The standards for courseware fall into two basic categories:

- The *interoperability* standards define how courseware communicates with administrative systems such as learning management systems (LMSs) and learning content management systems (LCMSs) to exchange data about learners and their progress. Data that can be exchanged include such items as the learner's identification, time spent in a learning object, and quiz scores.
- The *content-packaging* standards define how learning objects and groups of learning objects, including complete courses, should be packaged for import into administrative systems, transported between systems, and stored in content repositories so that they can be easily searched for, accessed, and reused.

Standards for Courseware Interoperability

The existing specifications that deal with courseware interoperability are the following:

- AICC AGR 010, which references the AICC CMI Specification (CMI001)
- SCORM Run-Time Environment

Probably one of the greatest areas of confusion around e-learning standards is the relationship between the SCORM and the AICC specifications. To help clear up this confusion, let's start by taking a look at the AICC CMI Specification. This specification includes two alternative methods for data exchange between content and administrative systems:

- HACP (pronounced *Hack-pea),* which stands for *HTTP-based AICC CMI Protocol*
- API, which stands for *Application Programming Interface*

The original Web-based AICC CMI specification included only HACP, which uses the most basic method of communicating information across the Internet (the HTTP protocol). This method is straightforward and reliable, but it requires learning objects to include some rather intensive programming. When the ADL began adapting and refining the AICC specification for inclusion in the SCORM, it felt that HACP was too challenging for the majority of content developers. The ADL also wanted to make the programming interface independent of the underlying communication software. The paired goals of providing an easy-to-use interface for developers and at the same time allowing LMS and LCMS vendors to use any desired communication protocol led the ADL to collaborate with the AICC in developing a new communication model. The resulting API communication interface, which provides content developers with a set of simple commands in the JavaScript® language, was added to the AICC specification as an alternative to HACP and was adopted as the only communication method specified in the SCORM. Please see Figure 3.1 for a comparison of HACP and the API.

If you want to develop or purchase content that is AICC conformant, you can choose between content that uses either of the two communication methods described above. However, if you want your courseware to be SCORM conformant or to conform to both standards, you must choose the API.

If you are developing or purchasing courseware for use with an in-house LMS only, you should choose whichever communication method works with your chosen LMS. If your LMS conforms to both the AICC and SCORM specifications, the API is usually a better choice. It is easier to use than HACP for in-house course development and is likely to be more widely supported in the future. However, there are some caveats regarding the use of the API

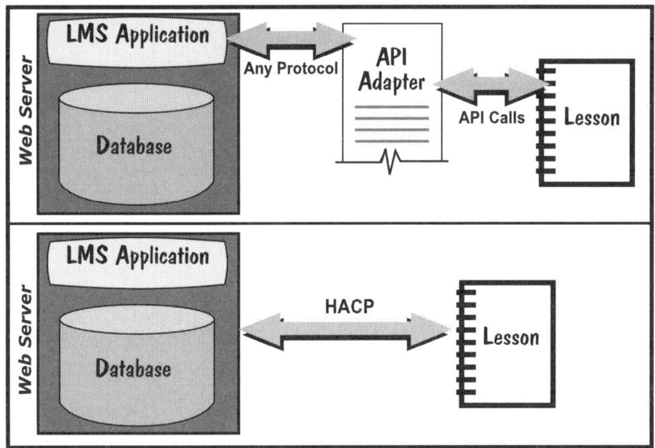

FIGURE 3.1
API and HACP communication methods.

that may affect your decision. See Chapter 4 for a more complete discussion of the pros, cons, and "gotchas" of the two communication methods.

Standards for Content Packaging

A content package for e-learning courseware is comparable to a package containing an item of self-assembly furniture such as a table. When you open the package you will find a number of items: the physical components of the table, such as pieces of wood and screws, a list of all the components included in the package, and a sheet of instructions for assembling those components into a completed table. Similarly, an e-learning content package contains the "physical" learning components, such as asset and learning object files, that make up a larger unit of instruction such as a course, chapter, or topic. The component list and "instruction sheet" consist of one or more files that describe how the individual components fit together to form the larger unit of instruction, as illustrated in Figure 3.2.

The existing specifications that deal with content packaging are the following:

- AICC AGR 010, which references the AICC CMI Specification
- SCORM Content Aggregation Model

Once again, there is some potential for confusion between these specifications. However, there is no actual overlap between the two content packaging methods.

The SCORM Content Aggregation Model includes two main components:

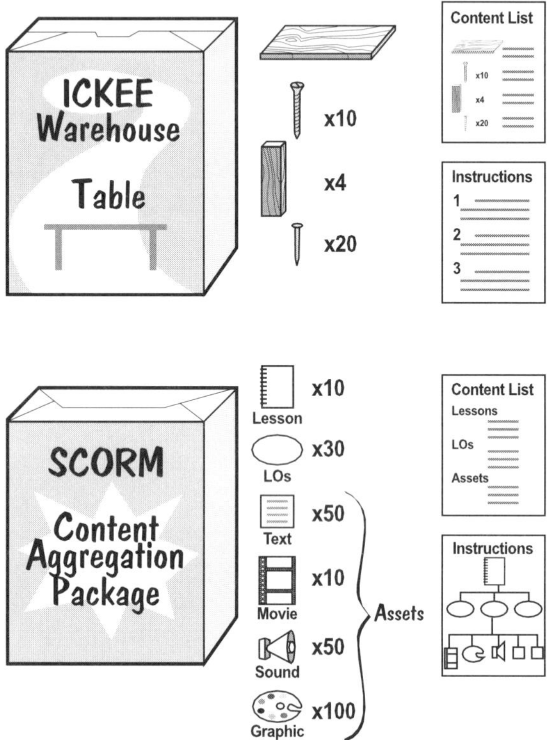

FIGURE 3.2
Content packages.

- A *content-packaging* specification, which specifies how to assemble a complete content package, ready for transfer between administrative systems
- A *meta-data* specification for describing individual content components

The AICC CMI specification includes an equivalent to the component list and instruction sheet portions of a content package, which it discusses in terms of *course interchange*. It does not, however, include any type of meta-data specification. The formats of the AICC and SCORM content packages are quite different, so you will need to produce two separate packages if you want your content to be conformant with both specifications.

Do I Need AICC or SCORM Content Packages?

The answer to this question largely depends on whether you want your courseware to be portable. You must produce one or both types of content packages if you need to prepare your courses to be imported into other standards-conformant administrative systems.

If you do not plan to reuse your content in another LMS or offer it for outside sale or distribution, you probably do not need to worry about content packaging. However, you should check with your LMS vendor. Although some LMSs have user-friendly interfaces for building courses internally, several of the best-known LMSs offer no such interface and require AICC or SCORM content packages for the initial setup of course content structures.

What About Meta-Data?

The AICC CMI specification does not include meta-data, and at the time of this writing the SCORM considers the use of meta-data to be optional. However, the SCORM does require that any meta-data used conform to its specification.

Chapter 5 has a more detailed discussion of meta-data and reasons that you might want to use it.

Certifications and Self-Tests for Courseware

The AICC offers certification testing for courseware. This certification is not as popular with courseware vendors as with LMS vendors, probably because the main criterion for courseware is that it will actually run in an AICC-conformant LMS, which is fairly easy to demonstrate. The AICC also offers a self-test that developers can use to pretest their courseware before testing with an LMS.

There are also self-tests for the SCORM, which developers can use to test that their courseware functions with the JavaScript API. Certification tests are expected soon.

Although there is little point in formal certification testing for content that you develop for use in house, the self-tests for AICC and SCORM can give you some degree of certainty that your courseware will function with a standards-conformant LMS. More detailed information on certification and self-testing can be found in Chapters 4 and 6.

A word about versions: the AICC and the ADL release new versions of their specifications on a regular basis. When testing courseware developed in house or when purchasing custom or off-the-shelf courseware, be sure that the courseware and the administrative system are tested against the same specification version.

Standards for Courseware Development Tools

Several courseware development tools are standards conformant in that they provide functions to assist with developing AICC or SCORM-conformant content. Once you have determined whether you will be using HACP or the API, you will be able to make a better assessment of which development tools are most suitable. Chapters 9 to 12, which address standards-based courseware authoring in some detail, include information on some of the more useful development tools. This book's Web site, http://www.elearning-standards.com, has additional up-to-date information about the standards capability of development tools.

It is important to be aware that none of the standards-conformant development tools has a magic button that automatically guarantees the output of standards-conformant content. Although the tools listed in this book and on the Web site have features that enable the production of standards-conformant courseware, none of them remove the need for developers to know and understand the standards specifications.

Standards for Assessment Tools

Chapters 7 and 12 of this book describe the Question & Test Interoperability (QTI) specification from IMS. This specification establishes a standard method of defining and exchanging test items and assessments, as well as storing and exchanging assessment results. It is expected that at least the results portion of this specification will eventually be incorporated into the SCORM. Those purchasing a test generation or assessment tool would be well advised to choose a QTI-conformant tool.

Standards for Administrative Systems

Standards that apply to administrative systems (LMSs and LCMSs) are basically the same as those for courseware: interoperability standards and content-packaging standards. This is not surprising because the main purpose of these standards is the integration of courseware and administrative systems. As might be expected, the same specifications that are relevant for courseware also apply to administrative systems:

- AICC AGR 010, which references the AICC CMI specification
- SCORM Run-Time Environment

AICC-Conformant LMSs

The Web-based version of the AICC CMI specification has enjoyed rapid adoption by LMS vendors since its introduction in 1998. Many vendors have also taken advantage of the AICC's independent certification testing program to prove their product's conformance. However, it is important to note that a good portion of the CMI specification is considered optional. The AICC certification test does not address these optional items and capabilities. Items that are not tested include the following:

- Lesson prerequisites
- Lesson completion requirements
- Objectives
- A large number of optional data elements

Also, at the time of this writing the certification test does not include the API method of communication with courseware. The ADL is currently developing certification tests for SCORM, and it is anticipated that the AICC will eventually adopt the API portion of those tests into its certification process. More details on what is included in the certification and self-tests can be found in Chapters 4 and 6.

Buyers should be cautious: if a vendor claims to be AICC certified (as opposed to AICC compliant or AICC conformant), buyers should verify that the vendor's product appears in the list of certified products on the AICC's Web site, http://www.aicc.org.

One should beware of vendors who claim that their product is AICC compliant or AICC conformant but who do not hold the official AICC certification. This includes those whose products carry the "Designed to AICC Guidelines" logo, which can be obtained with no independent testing. Ask these vendors to provide test data or, better still, insist that they demonstrate their products' AICC conformance.

SCORM-Conformant LMSs

Just as with the AICC CMI specification, many e-learning vendors are embracing the SCORM. True to its origins, SCORM conformance is becoming a mandated requirement for U.S. government and military applications. However, it is also becoming a recognized standard in commerce and education around the globe. Naturally, e-learning vendors are eager to meet the demands of this huge potential market. This means that the SCORM is a pretty safe bet as a choice of e-learning standards. The main drawback, as we mentioned in Chapter 1, is that the SCORM is still evolving with the addition of new specifications and publication of significantly revised versions on a regular basis.

Certification testing for SCORM is expected to be available soon. Currently, the ADL provides a self-test for SCORM conformance. As with AICC conformance, one should ask vendors to demonstrate their products' SCORM conformance or at least provide test data.

New Specification Versions and the Real World

There may be considerable lag time, sometimes a year or more, between the release of a new specification version and its adoption into administrative systems and courseware. This is particularly true of the SCORM because, as we have noted, it is still subject to fairly major changes. When shopping for an LMS, be sure to ask what versions of the specifications are supported and what kind of upgrade cycle to expect after updates to the specifications.

Some upgraded LMSs continue to provide support for earlier specification versions. This policy allows you to continue using older courseware. However, not all vendors provide this support, and some specification changes may not allow for backward compatibility. Before upgrading an LMS, check with its vendor on how the upgrade could impact existing courseware.

What about LCMSs?

LCMSs vary considerably in their breadth of functionality. Some are mainly concerned with the management and administration of content, limiting their functions to the storage and retrieval of assets and learning objects and the aggregation, or assembly, of learning objects into courses. Others include some of the same functions as an LMS, including learner administration, content-launching, and progress-tracking capabilities. Any such LMS-style functionality is subject to the relevant specifications.

The specifications that may be relevant for the content management functions of an LCMS are the following:

- AICC CMI Specification — Clearly, if you are using an LCMS to assemble learning objects into course structures for import into an AICC-conformant LMS, the LCMS must be capable of producing AICC-conformant content packages.
- SCORM Content Aggregation Model — If you have decided to adopt the SCORM learning object technology for your content, you will certainly want to make sure that an LCMS is capable of producing SCORM-conformant content packages.

Assessment Systems

If you are considering the purchase of a system for developing, presenting, or managing the results of test items and assessments, the relevant specification is the IMS QTI specification. The IMS does not provide any certification or self-testing tools for its specifications. Instead, it requires vendors claiming conformance to provide detailed statements about which portions of the specification their products support. In essence, no particular components of the specification are required, so you must look at the vendor statements to determine whether the product will meet your needs. This arrangement is, of course, less than ideal in assuring interoperability between different assessment components. If and when the ADL adopts portions of QTI into the SCORM, it will likely provide better methods of ensuring conformance. See Chapters 7 and 12 for more details on QTI conformance.

As with the SCORM, it is essential to check which version of the specification a product supports. QTI is a new and rapidly developing specification, so there are major differences between versions.

Shopping for Standards-Conformant E-Learning Components before You Start

Preparation is the key to a successful e-learning purchase. If you have not already done so, clearly define your requirements. Step back and take a long hard look at the "big picture." Consider why your organization needs to build or extend an e-learning infrastructure and what doing so is expected to achieve both in the short and long term. As LMS vendors, we often receive request-for-procurement documents that list every conceivable function and feature that an LMS might provide. In the majority of cases such a shotgun approach merely indicates that the purchaser does not really know what would be useful and is listing everything just in case. This approach is fine if the purchaser has limitless time and money, but would you really want to pay for a top-of-the-line luxury car when a bicycle would be perfectly adequate? Consider how important it is that your components are standards conformant and that they can interact with one another. Consider how portable and future-proof they need to be. Chapter 2 listed a few situations in which standards conformance may be irrelevant. In almost all other situations, it is vital. Finally, figure out which standards apply to your planned e-learning infrastructure and make conformance to those standards a key requirement.

Managing Vendors

Do your standards homework before you talk to vendors. Be clear about the certifications and conformance tests that are available for the standards you are concerned about. Read the relevant chapters of this book and check its associated Web site (http://www.elearning-standards.com) for more information. Vendors are generally an honest bunch, but their levels of knowledge about standards vary tremendously, especially among salespeople. I once heard a vendor's representative claim their LMS to be AICC certified when the product had not even been submitted to the AICC for certification tests. There was no intention to be dishonest; the product actually was conformant and eventually became certified, but the information given at the time was incorrect. Always check with the relevant standards body for confirmation that a product is certified.

Also remember that both the specifications and the products themselves change over time. For example, products have to be recertified by the AICC every 2 years. If a product is close to the end of its 2-year period, it may not have been tested against the latest version of the CMI specification. Check the testing report to see exactly what version of the specification the product was tested against. On the other side of the coin, a vendor is not required to recertify its product when it releases an upgraded version. Although it is unlikely that the developers of a previously certified product will purposely deviate from the standards, the addition of new features can sometimes disable older functionality. The listings on the AICC Web site indicate which version was tested; if the current version is different, it would be wise to ask for a demonstration of continued conformance.

Similarly, conformance to SCORM version 1.1 is quite different from conformance to SCORM version 1.2. Be sure to ask vendors to which version their product conforms.

In the absence of certification to a standard, always insist on seeing some test results data, a demonstration of conformance, or both. For example, ask LMS vendors to demonstrate their products by launching and tracking a SCORM-conformant learning object or importing an AICC-conformant course. If a vendor refuses or seems reluctant to do this, move on.

Another good idea, particularly in the case of LMS and LCMS vendors, is to ask what type of support they provide for helping you to set up or develop standards-conformant courseware on their systems. Ask whether they charge for this help and how much. The authors are aware of at least two well-known vendors who charge heavily for this kind of support. One charges $1,500 per day for support; the other offers a standards-conformant course template for the hefty price tag of $10,000. Clearly, you need to be aware of such costs before making a purchase decision.

Conclusion

In this chapter we have looked briefly at the choices available and at the decisions to be made before purchasing or developing e-learning components. On the basis of this information, you should have a good idea of the e-learning standards that are relevant to your current situation or that may become relevant for you in the future. The remaining chapters of this book offer further information on those standards. Chapters 4 through 7 present a high-level view of the standards specifications. Chapters 8 through 12 have more in-depth information that is mainly of interest to courseware developers.

4

Standards for Interoperable Data Tracking

Introduction

Beginning with this chapter, we narrow our focus to the individual specifications for each of four key aspects of e-learning: data tracking, meta-data, course packaging and interchange, and assessment. This chapter provides an introduction to standards-based interoperable data tracking. Proper communication of data between learning objects (LOs) and the learning management system (LMS) is the most critical part of an effective e-learning implementation. Our experience as consultants indicates that it is also the source of the most confusion and frustration.

This chapter opens with an overview of the mechanics of data tracking, explained in terms of the traditional correspondence course. It goes on to compare and contrast data tracking using two different standards-based communication schemes, as put forth in the AICC CMI and SCORM specifications, including the pros and cons of each. It also includes details on what is involved in AICC certification and SCORM conformance self-testing.

The Mechanics of Data Tracking

The Learning Object

This chapter focuses on the LO and its relationship with the LMS. LOs are directly launched and tracked by the LMS and are the smallest chunks of learning that the LMS knows about. The student enters an LO under control of the LMS, typically by selecting it from a menu. When the student finishes the LO, control of the learning experience is passed back to the LMS. Typically the LMS displays the menu again. Some LMSs may be able to automatically launch the next LO in a predefined sequence.

Internally, an LO can be extremely simple or highly complex. The ideal is for LOs to be small and tightly focused, but this is a recommendation only, not a requirement of the specifications. It is permissible, although not advisable, for an LO to include a large hierarchy of topics and subtopics. However, no matter how complex an LO may be, the LMS can track only one set of data for it.

The Components of Data Tracking

Before we begin to look at data tracking in the e-learning world, let's pause to consider an older form of distance education, the correspondence course. Here is how you might go about signing up for and completing such a course. We assume here that you are already an established student with the Learn-A-Lot Correspondence School.

1. You look through the latest Learn-A-Lot catalog and apply for their course on butterfly collecting. Learn-A-Lot mails the course materials to you along with contact information for Joe Monarch, who will be your mentor for the course. Meanwhile, the Learn-A-Lot records administrator sets up a file in which to maintain your course results.
2. Per the standard Learn-A-Lot procedure, you immediately send a letter to Joe notifying him that you have received your materials and are starting the course. You then work your way through the course, sending each assignment to Joe as you complete it. Joe grades your assignments and sends you feedback on them. When you reach the end of the materials, you send in your final exam and inform Joe that you have completed the course.
3. All student records are kept in a standard format. Each time Joe receives one of your assignments, he fills out a form with the results in the required format and sends it to the records department, where it is added to your file. When he sends them the form for your final exam, the records department computes your final grade and marks your file as completed.

Notice that there are three major components involved in the correspondence school course: starting the course, communicating results, and maintaining records. These same basic components apply to e-learning. (See Figure 4.1.) An e-learning system must include the following:

1. A means to *launch* an LO under the control of the LMS
2. A *method of communication* for transferring data between the LO and the LMS
3. A *data model* that standardizes the names and format of the data elements to be tracked

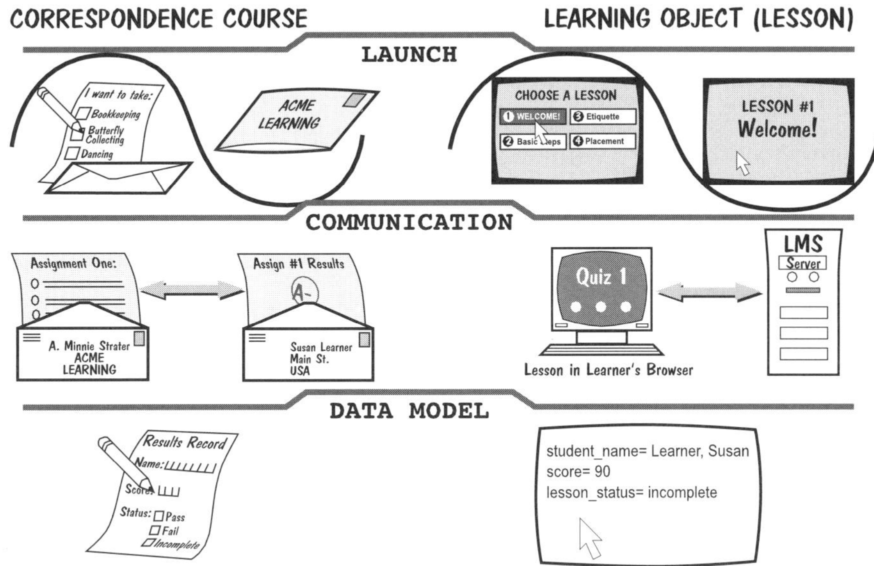

FIGURE 4.1
The components of e-learning.

To implement interoperable data tracking, each of three components must have some degree of standardization. To this end, the standards bodies have developed two alternate methods for data exchange: the Application Program Interface (API) and the HTTP-based AICC CMI Protocol (HACP).

The API Specification

The API is the more recently developed and more rapidly advancing of the two data exchange methods. It is included in both the AICC CMI and the SCORM specifications. As we will see, portions of this method are derived from the HACP method.

The following is a high-level description of the launch, communication, and data model components of the API data exchange method.

Launching an LO

The API launch mechanism defines a standardized way for the LMS to deliver an LO. The LMS must provide the following launch functions:

1. Determine which LO is to be launched.

2. On the student's computer, open a special browser window that provides a standard communication interface with the LMS. This interface, which is supplied as part of the LMS, is called the *API adapter.*
3. Provide the Web address (URL) of the LO's first page.[1]

Figure 4.2 illustrates these functions.

The means by which these functions are accomplished are left to the designers of the LMS. For example, many LMSs allow the learner to select the LO to be launched from a menu. Others may offer the option of automatically choosing and launching the appropriate LO.

Only the LMS is allowed to launch an LO, and the student may have only one LO open at a time. When the student exits an LO, control must be passed back to the LMS. (See Figure 4.3.) In most current LMSs, the student is then

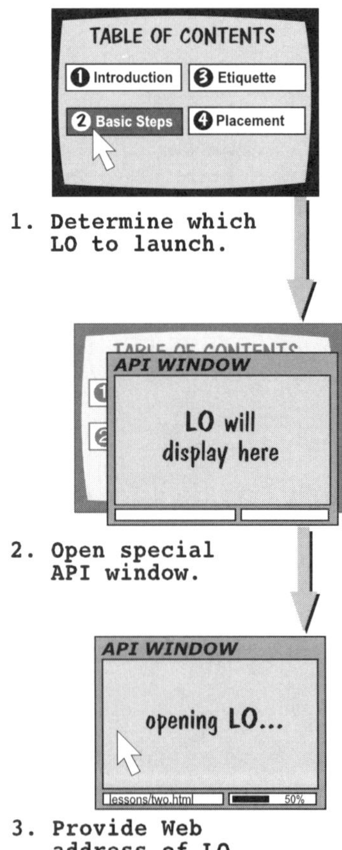

FIGURE 4.2
API launch functions.

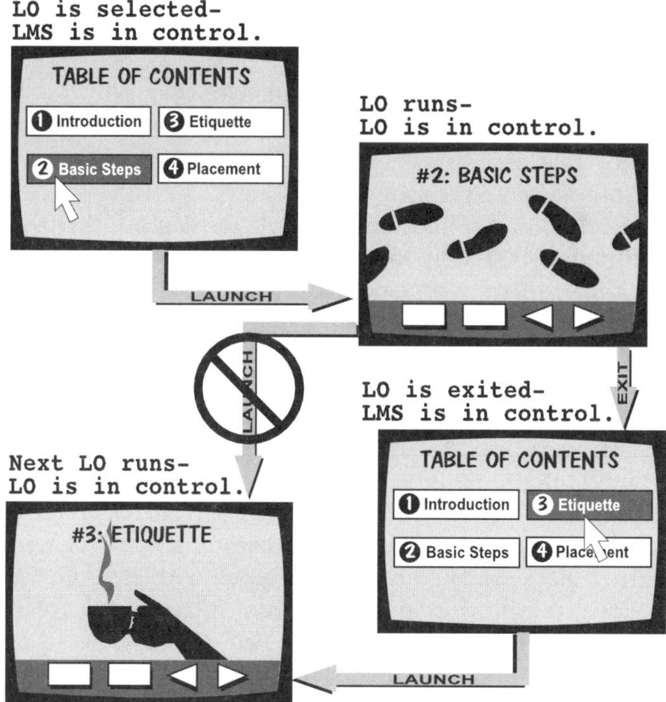

FIGURE 4.3
Flow of control betw\een the LMS and learning objects.

returned to an LMS-generated menu to select another LO. However, some LMSs may automatically launch the next appropriate LO based on sequential or adaptive criteria.

Communication between the LO and the LMS

The API provides the mechanism by which the LMS and an LO "talk" to each other. The API defined in the AICC and SCORM specifications is designed to be simple and flexible. It consists of a small set of function calls that are issued by the LO and responded to by the LMS. The calls are made in JavaScript, a programming language that is built into virtually all modern Web browsers.

The launch of an LO by the LMS can be compared with the situation of a child being sent off to visit relatives for an unspecified period of time. "Call us as soon as you get there," the parents tell the child. "And call us again when you're ready to come home. Oh, and if you need anything or want to tell us what you've been doing, you can call us in between."

When the child arrives at the destination, his first obligation is to find a telephone and call home. In the same way, when a LO reaches its destination (the student's browser window), it must find the API and use it to call the LMS. Once the LO locates the API, it must "phone home" to let the LMS know it has "arrived safely." To accomplish this, it calls the JavaScript function *LMSInitialize.* The call is received by the API, which passes it on to the LMS. When the call reaches the LMS, an ongoing communication session is established, and the LO can proceed in whatever manner its authors have chosen.

Continuing our child-on-vacation analogy, we can see that the child has only one additional obligation: to notify his parents when he is ready to end the trip. The same is true of a standards-based LO. The only other function that it is required to call is *LMSFinish,* which closes the communication session and allows the LO to proceed with its shutdown activities.

Looking at our analogy once more, we see that the parents suggested that the child might want to call them in the middle of his stay. The API communication interface provides two more calls that correspond to the two reasons the child might call home — because he needs something or because he wants to tell his parents something. *LMSGetValue* asks the LMS for a specific piece of information, such as the learner's name or the total time that the learner has spent in previous sessions with the LO. *LMSSetValue* sends the LMS a specific piece of information, such as the learner's score or the elapsed time in the current learning session. See Figure 4.4 for an illustration of an API communication session.

FIGURE 4.4
An API communication session.

The Data Model

A data model formally defines a set of data that an LMS can track. Many different data models are possible, and the API is designed to be independent of any specific model. As of this writing, only one data model, the AICC CMI data model, has been adopted into the specifications. It was chosen because it is well defined and has been successfully implemented by a substantial base of LMSs and courseware. New data models are being developed and will be added to the specifications in the future. However, it is likely that the CMI model will remain the predominant model for some time to come.

The AICC and ADL groups have worked together to refine the AICC's original CMI data model for use in the API environment. However, the ADL ultimately adopted a significantly reduced set of data elements into the SCORM, whereas the AICC chose to maintain the entire set.

If you look at the specification documents, you will see that even the reduced set of data elements is quite extensive. Fortunately, most of the elements are optional. A conforming LMS is required to support only a small core set of elements, which are the same in both specifications:

- Student ID — Typically the learner's log-in name
- Student name — The complete name of the learner
- Lesson location — A "bookmark" that allows the learner to enter a partially completed LO at the point that she last exited
- Credit — "Yes" or "no" indicator of whether the learner is taking the LO for credit
- Lesson status — Indicator of the learner's current progress in the LO, for example, not started, incomplete, failed, passed
- Previous entry — "Yes" or "no" indicator of whether the learner has attempted the LO before
- Score — Numeric result from activities and tests in the LO, typically expressed as a percentage
- Total time — Accumulated time from all LO sessions, as calculated and maintained by the LMS
- Session time — Time spent in a given session, as reported by the LO
- Exit data — Indicator of how or why the learner exited from the LO
- Suspend data — Information that a partially completed LO may need to store for use when the learner returns to complete it, such as the learner's responses to an already-completed exercise
- Launch data — Special information that an LO may need right after it launches, such as the location of an external file containing content updates[2]

Unlike an LMS, an LO is not required by the specifications to use any data elements at all. However, ignoring all the data elements tends to make the entire LMS concept somewhat irrelevant. Most LOs at least report a score or status and a session time.

The HACP Data Exchange Specification

HACP was the original data exchange method developed by the AICC. It is still in widespread use, but has not been adopted into the SCORM.

The following is a high-level description of the launch, communication, and data model components of the AICC HACP data exchange specification.

Launching an LO

The HACP launch mechanism differs somewhat from the API mechanism. A HACP-based LMS must provide the following launch functions:

1. Determine which LO is to be launched
2. Send the following information to the student's browser:
   - The Web address (URL) of the LO's first page
   - A session ID that allows the LMS to distinguish this particular learning session from others that it may be managing at the same time
   - A return address with which the browser will communicate to exchange tracking data
   - Any LO-specific information that may be required to successfully complete the launch[3]

Figure 4.5 illustrates these functions. The designers of the LMS may use any desired method to provide the required launch functions.

As in the API specification, only the LMS is allowed to launch an LO, and a learner can have only one LO open at a time. Control must be passed back to the LMS when the student exits an LO.

Communication between the LO and the LMS

In the API section, we compared the launch of an LO with sending a child on vacation. In contrast, launching an LO in HACP is more like sending a secret agent into the field. "Here are your orders," her superior tells her, "We've provided you with a phone number and a mission ID. When you

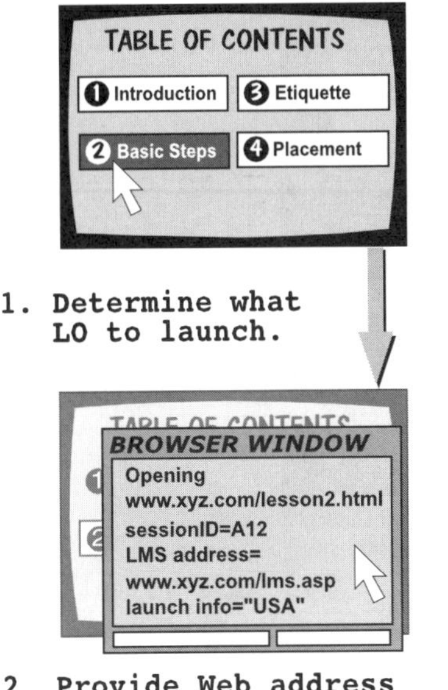

FIGURE 4.5
HACP launch functions.

reach your assigned destination, you can use that information to contact the computer at headquarters. The computer will send back a coded file with all the information we have on your assignment. If you learn anything new, you can send a message using the same code. And finally, even if you don't contact us for anything else, you must inform us when you have completed your mission."

The agent arrives at her destination, enters the agency computer's number on her handheld device, and logs in using her mission ID. The computer immediately sends her a file of information, which she carefully decodes to find out what she needs to know before proceeding with her mission. Similarly, an LO using HACP initiates communication with the LMS by sending a *GetParam* command to the return-address URL that was provided in the launch line. When the LMS receives the command, it sends back a complete set of current data about the student and the LO. These data arrive in one long string from which the LO must extract the individual values it needs.

Continuing with our secret-agent analogy, we see that the agent's orders include two additional responsibilities: to send back new data if there is anything to report and to inform headquarters when her mission is completed. In the HACP session, the LO sends data to the LMS using the command *PutParam.* The data must be sent in an exacting format that the LO is responsible for generating. Finally, the LO must send an *ExitAU* command to end the communication session. See Figure 4.6 for an illustration of a HACP communication session.

FIGURE 4.6
A HACP communication session.

The Data Model

The HACP specification uses the AICC's original CMI data model, which was originally developed to exchange data via files on a local area network. Like the API data model, it contains an enormous number of defined data elements, most of which are optional. Only the elements listed below are required for an LMS to conform to the specification. Most of these elements are defined exactly like their API counterparts. Only those that differ significantly from the API version are defined here:

- Student ID
- Student name
- Credit
- Lesson location
- Lesson status — Indicator of the learner's current progress in the LO, for example, not started, incomplete, failed, passed. The value may include a secondary "flag" value that indicates either whether or not the student has attempted the lesson before or how and why the student last exited from the lesson. This flag serves essentially the same purpose as the *Previous entry* and *Exit data* elements in the API data model.
- Score
- Time — Depending on its context, either the total time the student that has spent in the LO (value received from the LMS) or elapsed time in a given learning session (value sent to the LMS). In the API version, this element has been split into *Session time* and *Total time* to make it less confusing.
- Core lesson data — Information that a partially completed LO may need to store for use when the student returns to complete it. This element is equivalent to the *Suspend data* element in the API model.
- Core vendor data — Special information that an LO may need right after it launches. This element is equivalent to the *Launch Data* element in the API data model.[4]

As in the API version, an LO is not obligated to use any data elements, but most will at least report a score or lesson status and a time.

Optional Data Model Elements

Both the API and HACP data models include numerous optional elements, such as tracking by individual objectives or interactions and support for customization of lessons based on a learner's performance, preferences, or both. Both data models organize their elements into groups. The following generalized descriptions of the data groups apply to both data models. Significant differences between the sets of data elements in the AICC and SCORM data models are noted in the descriptions.

- Core — This group contains the required data elements described in earlier sections of this chapter. In addition to the required elements, it contains an optional element called *lesson mode* that provides for browsing and reviewing of LOs. It also includes an option for the LO to report the maximum and minimum scores that the learner could have attained.

- Comments — This group allows brief, free-form text comments to be passed between the LO and the LMS. The LMS can send a comment from a manager or administrator to be displayed to the learner. The LO can record and send a comment from the learner.
- Evaluation — This group provides a mechanism for recording detailed information about the learner's experience, such as multiple learner comments, responses to individual interactions, and the path taken through the content. This information is typically collected for the purpose of evaluating the effectiveness of the LO. This group is not included in the SCORM data set.
- Objectives — This group records score and status information for individually identified learning objectives.
- Student data — The name of this group is somewhat misleading. The LMS uses it to provide data that controls the learning experience, such as mastery (minimum passing) score, time limit, and action to be taken by the LO if the time limit is exceeded. The mastery score, which is one of the more commonly implemented optional elements, is set in the LMS. If a mastery score is available, the LMS will use it to calculate pass–fail status, overriding any status set locally by the LO. In the AICC data set, this group also contains elements that allow tracking of individual score, time, and status for multiple attempts to complete an LO during a single session.
- Student demographics — This group provides background information about the learner. The information can be used by the LO to customize the learner's experience. This group is not included in the SCORM data set.
- Student preferences — This group allows the learner to set preferences for the presentation of LOs. It includes settings for appearance, sound, language, and the like. Preference information set in an LO is used if the learner returns to the same LO; it may also be provided as initial preferences for other LOs. The AICC data set contains more elements than does the SCORM set.[4, 5]

Unfortunately, LMS support for most of the optional elements is patchy. Be sure to ask prospective LMS vendors about their current support and future plans for optional elements that are of interest to your organization.

API vs. HACP: Pros, Cons, and "Gotchas"

The API and HACP data exchange methods each have their own pros and cons. Each also has one major "gotcha" that precludes its use in certain environments. Some LMSs offer both methods, so it may not be necessary to commit to one or the other. Still, it is useful to compare their strengths and weaknesses.

The following are key issues to consider if one must choose between the API and HACP methods. Table 4.1 provides a summary of the pros and cons described here:

- Standards compliance — The API conforms to both the AICC and SCORM specifications. HACP is not a part of the SCORM specification.
- Certification available — As of this writing, formal certification is available only for HACP. One can trust that the HACP components of an AICC-certified product have been independently tested, whereas one has only the vendor's word that an API interface meets the standard. Once API certification becomes available, this advantage should disappear quickly.
- Track record — The API method is significantly newer than HACP and represents a considerably greater departure from the original LAN-based AICC mechanism on which both are based. As a result, current API implementations have the potential to be more trouble prone than implementations based on the more thoroughly tested HACP method.

TABLE 4.1

API Compared with HACP

Characteristic	API	HACP
Standards compliance	AICC, SCORM	AICC
Certification available	No	Yes
Track record	Shorter	Longer
Robustness	Good	Better
Potential for growth	More	Less
Likelihood of significant changes to specification in the near future	More	Less
Implemented base (learning management systems and courseware)	Narrower	Broader
Easy to use for courseware development	Yes	No
Potential problems with firewalls and browser security features	Yes	No
Works with content on any server	No	Yes
Fully compatible with HTML and Javascript lessons	Yes	No

- Robustness — HACP is a direct communication link between the LMS and the LO. Because it has no intermediary software like the API, there is less that can go wrong in the transmission of data.
- Potential for growth — Because of its acceptance outside the AICC, we expect the API to progress more rapidly and see significantly wider adoption in the future than HACP. However, we believe that HACP is likely to enjoy continued support for some time because of a sizeable installed base and some significant limitations in current API implementations.
- Likelihood of significant specification changes — The API is still new enough that significant changes may be expected in the short term. In particular, new data models are already being developed. HACP, on the other hand, has been in place for several years and has developed a large user base. As a result, it is not likely to change radically in the future.
- Implemented base — Because it is the older of the two methods, HACP is currently better supported than the API. Not all standards-based LMSs have adopted the API yet, and there is a sizeable existing base of well-tested HACP courseware. Once certification becomes available for the API, we expect to see this lead disappear fairly quickly.
- Ease of use — From the standpoint of the content developer, the API is far easier to use than HACP. Most of the communication complexity is handled by the API itself. The author needs only to learn a few straightforward function calls and develop an understanding of the content elements to be tracked. HACP, on the other hand, places the entire burden of composing and deciphering data messages on the LO. The structure of these messages is complex, and the LO must include special routines to extract data from incoming messages and build messages to contain outgoing data. A few authoring packages provide tools to simplify building these routines, although some of them have significant limitations. There are also sample LOs available that can be used as shells for new LOs with similar structure and tracking requirements. Without such tools and samples, many developers find HACP difficult to work with. The Web site for this book, http://www.elearning-standards.com, has some code samples available for download.
- Potential problems with firewalls and browser security features — Although the API can be implemented in many ways, a significant number of LMS vendors implement it as a Java applet that runs in the student's browser. Unfortunately, Java applets tend to be seen as security risks. Many firewalls block them entirely, and some

organizations configure their employees' browsers to disable support for Java. In contrast, HACP does not require Java applets or other questionable program code to be run on the user's computer. Data is transferred directly between the LMS and the LO in the form of plain-text messages. As a result, HACP incurs no problems with firewalls and browser security features. (Note that there are non-Java implementations of the API available. If this is an issue for your organization, be sure to bring it up with prospective vendors.)

- Works with content on any server — The "gotcha" for the API is its inability to use LOs that are located on a server in a different domain from that of the LMS. The problem results from security features built into Internet Explorer and is not an issue with Netscape browsers. The bottom line here is that if your LMS is located on a server at, for example, http://www.MyDomain.com, it cannot communicate with LOs that are located on a server at http://www.MyOtherDomain.com. This limitation is under study by SCORM development committees, and there will eventually be a solution. In the meantime, if you cannot restrict your students' choice of browsers or store your learning content in the same domain as your LMS, you will need use HACP instead of the API. For a more technical explanation of this problem, see Chapter 9.
- Fully compatible with HTML plus JavaScript LOs — The "gotcha" for HACP is its inability to establish two-way communication with LOs developed in HTML plus JavaScript, the native languages of Web pages. The HTML–JavaScript combination is a popular choice for developing LOs because they are relatively easy and inexpensive to produce and update. Also, file sizes can be kept small for use over slow dial-up modems, and users are not required to download and install special plug-ins for their browsers. Unfortunately, although JavaScript (the programming language built into most Web browsers) can readily send data to the LMS in the required HACP format, it cannot receive the HACP messages that the LMS returns. Essentially, an LO developed in HTML plus JavaScript is "deaf" in regard to the LMS. Some of the ramifications of this limitation include the following:
    - Inability to use bookmarking when a student reenters a partially completed LO
    - Inability to customize the learning experience based on the student's current status or whether the LO is being taken for credit
    - Inability to correctly compute the student's status in certain instances

Certification and Self-Testing

As of this writing, certification for the API is not yet available through either AICC or ADL. ADL has released test suites for self-testing against SCORM versions 1.1 and 1.2. However, it has not yet designated the independent test labs that will be required for official certification testing. Once official testing is in place, AICC is expected to adopt the SCORM testing into its own certification processes.

For HACP, the AICC offers formal certification for Web-based LMSs, LOs, authoring tools, and other related entities.

In addition to the data-tracking and interoperability requirements that we have discussed in this chapter, the AICC method also defines a course interchange format used for transferring the structure of multilesson courses between LMSs. Details of course interchange are covered in Chapter 6, but it is important to note here that certification of an LMS or a course includes this component.

In relation to the tracking and interoperability requirements, AICC certification indicates the following:

- An AICC-certified LMS is able to launch an AICC-compliant LO and send and receive data using the HACP method. It supports all required data elements in the exact manner described by the specification.
- An AICC-certified LO (AU) can receive and correctly interpret the launch line and establish a communication session with the LMS. It is able to send and receive data in accordance with the HACP method. It may use none, any, or all of the required data elements, and it uses those elements in the exact manner described by the specification.
- An AICC-certified courseware development tool gives the author the capability of creating LOs that can pass the LO certification tests. When listing certified products, the AICC subdivides this general category into authoring, courseware generation, and assessment tools.

Certification testing is conducted by independent test laboratories using test suite software developed by the AICC. Certified products are listed on the AICC Web site and are authorized to display the "AICC-Certified" logo.[6]

The AICC also offers vendors the opportunity to claim AICC compliance and to display the "Designed to AICC Guidelines" logo. This logo indicates that the vendor has paid a fee to the AICC and vouches for the fact that its software meets AICC guidelines. The vendor may have tested the software using the AICC Test Suite, which is a self-test version of the certification tests. However, there is no guarantee that any kind of testing has been conducted.

Conclusion

Understanding and correctly using the standards-based methods for communicating tracking data between LOs and LMSs is critical to a successful e-learning implementation. Unfortunately, it can also be confusing. In this chapter, we have presented a high-level discussion of the issues involved, including the pros and cons of the HACP and API data exchange methods. We have also provided comparative information on the data exchange methods as an aid to decision making. Fortunately, it may not be necessary to commit to one or the other of the protocols when choosing an LMS; a number of vendors have implemented or are in the process of implementing both HACP and the API.

In the next chapter we will discuss methods to make LOs self-describing and easy to share via catalogs, databases, and search engines.

References

1. Dodds, P., Ed., *Sharable Content Object Reference Model (SCORM): The SCORM Run-Time Environment*, version 1.2.. Advanced Distributed Learning, 2001, section 3.2. Available at: http://www.adlnet.org.
2. Dodds, P., Ed., *Sharable Content Object Reference Model (SCORM): The SCORM Run-Time Environment*, version 1.2. Advanced Distributed Learning, 2001, section 3.4.2. Available at: http://www.adlnet.org.
3. AICC CMI Subcommittee (Hyde, J., chair), *CMI Guidelines for Interoperability*, revision 3.5, Appendix A. AICC, 2001, section A.2. Available at: http://www.aicc.org.
4. AICC CMI Subcommittee (Hyde, J., chair), *CMI Guidelines for Interoperability*, revision 3.5. AICC, 2001, sections 5.1–5.2. Available at: http://www.aicc.org.
5. Dodds, P., Ed., *Sharable Content Object Reference Model (SCORM): The SCORM Run-Time Environment*, version 1.2. Advanced Distributed Learning, 2001, section 3.4. Available at: http://www.adlnet.org.
6. AICC CMI Subcommittee (Hyde, J., chair), *AICC/CMI Certification Testing Procedures*, revision 1.5. AICC, 2000, section 2.0. Available at: http://www.aicc.org.

5

Standards for Self-Describing Learning Objects

Introduction

The previous chapter began our tour through the specific areas of e-learning that are covered by the standards. We learned about the inner workings of communication between lessons and management systems. With this foundation in place, we can begin to look at how LOs and other learning content can be shared between users. Most of this chapter will focus on a standard format for providing what might be called directory information about LOs. This information, formally termed *meta-data,* describes LOs so that others can easily locate them and determine their potential usefulness for a given purpose.

This chapter is closely tied to the next one, which addresses standards for describing the structure of a course in a way that can be directly imported into an LMS. This chapter lays the foundation for what follows by describing the various types of data objects and how they work together in creating the structure of a course. It also introduces Extensible Markup Language (XML), an industry-standard markup language for encoding structured data to be used via the Internet and other distributed applications. The standards that will be discussed in this and the next two chapters all use XML to encode data.

Self-Description and Sharability

One of the major purposes for providing LO meta-data is to help make the LO sharable. The interoperability standards described in the previous chapter are the foundation of sharability, allowing any conforming LMS to work with any conforming LO. But there are other requirements that must also be met before an LO can be easily shared on the kind of global level envisioned by the standards bodies.

Constructing Courses from Sharable Components

One key aspect of sharability involves the ability to group individual learning components in different ways to create larger composite chunks of learning. You can use a given LO in as many composite learning components as you wish. These composite components, often referred to as *blocks,* can be grouped in the same way.

Some LMSs allow you to import or define individual LOs and then use them to build courses within the administrative interface. Others may require you to create the course structure externally and provide the LMS with special import files. Either way, however, the standards require LOs to be sharable between courses. For example, an LO about basic telephone courtesy that was originally developed as part of a new-employee course for a call center might find its way into other courses aimed at administrative assistants and perhaps even executives. (See Figure 5.1.)

A key implication of this ability to mix and match LOs is the fact that the source of the individual LOs in a course does not matter. As we saw in Chapter 1, you might customize an off-the-shelf course about Microsoft Excel by replacing one LO with a commercially produced LO from a different source. You could then add a newly developed LO specific to your own organization. Taking this idea to its logical conclusion, you might choose to construct a course in which every LO comes from a different source.

FIGURE 5.1
Interchangeable learning objects.

You Can't Share It Unless People Can Find It

In the Excel example, you were seeking to improve on an off-the-shelf course by replacing one of its LOs with a better one. How might you locate that replacement LO? Figure 5.2 shows two possibilities.

In today's e-learning environment, you would probably search through one or more catalogs of LOs. A comprehensive search would likely require you to locate and search numerous catalogs from both individual vendors and resellers offering selections of courseware from various sources. You would probably also use Internet search engines to locate sites with relevant online LOs. Such a search could take days to complete.

Suppose, instead, that you have access to a single gigantic online catalog offering all the best standards-based courseware available throughout the world. Suppose further that each listing in this catalog contains a reliable

FIGURE 5.2
Searching for courseware.

set of basic information about the courseware. Can you see how much more efficient your search would be? This is the standards bodies' ultimate vision for self-describing, sharable learning content. Their goal is to have large, searchable repositories from which organizations can select LOs to construct their e-learning curricula.

This rather utopian vision of global access to quality LOs will probably not replace proprietary courseware catalogs and custom development any time soon. However, the standards lay the groundwork for large-scale discovery and sharing of LOs by standardizing the information used to describe them. The remainder of this chapter focuses on the standards that define the format and content of this descriptive information.

Meta-Data — How LOs Become Self-Describing

To facilitate the ability to find and share LOs, various standards groups have worked together to define a consistent set of meta-data to be provided for each LO. We will focus here on the version of meta-data found in the SCORM specification, which is derived from the IMS Learning Object Meta-Data (LOM) specification.

By definition, meta-data is data about data. The meta-data for an LO includes such information as its title and description, its price and terms of use, and the location from which it can be downloaded or accessed online. The meta-data is not physically part of the LO itself; rather, it comprises a separate document that is designed to travel with the LO. A copy of this document is also intended to be placed online, where it can be accessed by catalogs and special search utilities.

XML — The Language of Meta-Data

XML is a powerful and flexible industry standard for communicating structured information. It was developed by the World Wide Web Consortium as a means of sharing information via the Internet. However, it has begun to catch on for many non-Internet applications as well.

Why XML?

With the exception of the data-tracking mechanisms, the major e-learning standards are all XML based. The AICC and ADL are even giving serious consideration to developing a data-tracking protocol using an extension of XML. The learning-standards bodies chose XML for a number of reasons:

- It conveys both the information itself and the structure or significance of that information.
- It can be written, read, and understood by ordinary people, not just programmers and computers.
- It transfers data in plain-text format, which can be used by applications on any operating system.
- It has broad and growing industry support, so it is likely to remain a viable standard for the foreseeable future.

An XML Primer

XML is used for documents that contain structured information. Structured information combines informational content such as text and pictures with an indication of the meaning or purpose of that information. For example, a description of a book could contain the name "Tom Jones" as a piece of information. Out of context, the name is ambiguous. It could be the book's title, main character, biographical subject, or author. Only by looking at the structure of the book's description could we determine the appropriate meaning.

As a markup language, XML is a cousin to Hypertext Markup Language (HTML). Like HTML, it uses pairs of *tags* that are placed like bookends around sections of text in a document. (See Figure 5.3.) These tags provide information about the text they enclose. There are two primary differences between HTML and XML markup:

- HTML focuses primarily on the appearance of text and other information as displayed in a browser. XML focuses on the purpose or meaning of information.
- HTML is limited to a single set of predefined tags. XML allows tags to be defined by users.

FIGURE 5.3
XML tags.

Let's look at an example of XML in action. Here is an XML description of the novel *Tom Jones* by Henry Fielding. (In this and all future XML code examples, the line numbers are provided for convenience in discussing the code. They are not part of the actual XML and *must not* be included in a real XML document.)

```
01  <book>
02      <full_title>The History of Tom Jones, A
    Foundling</full_title>
03      <author>
04          <name>Fielding, Henry</name>
05          <birthplace>Glastonbury, England</
    birthplace>
06          <birthyear>1707</birthyear>
07      </author>
08      <first_publication_date>1749<
    first_publication_date>
09      <characters>
10          <character>
11              <name>Tom Jones</name>
12              <description>Hero of the story
    </description>
13          </character>
14          <character>
15              <name>Sophia Western</name>
16              <description>Hero's true love
    </description>
17          </character>
18      </characters>
19      <plot_summary>An orphan boy experiences
    many adventures and love affairs while growing
    up in eighteenth-century England.</plot_summary>
20  </book>
```

This example demonstrates several key features of XML:

- Each piece of information is preceded by a tag with the form *<tagname>* and followed by a tag with the form *</tagname>*.
- Tag names are meaningful; they indicate what kind of information the tag should contain.
- Tagged items can be nested inside other tagged items to provide increased detail. In lines 03–07 of this example, the author's name, birthplace, and birth year are contained within the main *<author>* *</author>* tags. A pair of tags that contains other tagged items is called, logically enough, a *container* item.
- Multiple items of the same type can be included within a container item. In lines 09–18 of this example, there are two *<character>* items within the *<characters>* container.

- The same tag name can be used in different contexts to mean different things. In this example, the *<name>* tag is used to indicate both the author's name (line 04) and the names of the characters (lines 11 and 15). There is no confusion between the two because they are used inside different containers.
- The same XML structure can be used to describe any other book by a single author. It could also be easily modified to accommodate books by multiple authors.

One other thing to notice is that, except for the format and placement of the tags and the general nesting structure, everything else in this example is arbitrary. We could have used different names for the tags, grouped the information in a different way, or included different information altogether. As a human reader, you can understand the example fairly easily. But if we planned to submit the example as an entry in an online catalog that you were developing, we would all have to agree on the tag names and structure, as well as on what types of information are to be included. This is where standards come in.

SCORM Meta-Data

Meta-data is one of two components of the SCORM Content Aggregation Model. The second component, which involves defining the structure of courses, is discussed in Chapter 6.

Meta-data models are defined for learning content at all levels of the SCORM hierarchy. (See Figure 5.4.) However, the specifications do not currently require meta-data to be supplied for any of them. The only requirement is that meta-data, if it exists at all, must conform to the specification.

Why Bother with Meta-Data?

If meta-data is optional, why bother with it? Especially if you develop in-house courseware, creating meta-data adds to the time and cost involved. Depending on your situation, you may want to ignore this standard for the time being. However, there are several good reasons to create standard meta-data.

- It is an excellent tool for documenting LOs created within your own organization.
- It provides an effective organizational system for your entire library of standards-based LOs.

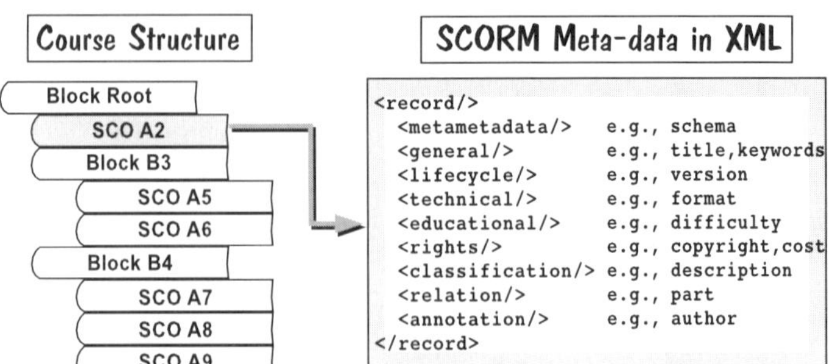

FIGURE 5.4
A Sharable Content Object Meta-data. (Adapted from Kause, L., *ADL/SCORM Structure and Meta-Data Files*. Paper presented at EuroTaac 2002 Conference, Edinburgh, Scotland, March 2002, slide 31.)

- If you plan to sell LOs created by your organization, providing meta-data will make it easier for potential buyers to locate and evaluate them.
- Eventually meta-data will probably be required at certain levels in the content hierarchy. If you develop courseware, creating the meta-data now will likely prove more efficient than having to go back and create it later.
- The IMS and ADL are currently developing specifications for a mechanism by which an LMS can automatically select and launch SCOs based on defined selection criteria. These criteria will most likely be based, at least in part, on meta-data.

A Simplified Example of Meta-Data

The following is a simplified example of meta-data for a sharable content object (SCO). It includes a single entry for each mandatory meta-data category and element. It is not a valid meta-data document as it stands. In simplifying it, we have left out a number of specialized tags that are required by the specification. See Chapter 10 for a complete, annotated example of SCO meta-data. Once again, the line numbers are not part of the XML.

```
01  <lom>
02      <general>
03          <title>Pie Crust Techniques</title>
04          <catalogentry>
05              <catalog>Catalog of Culinary Art
    Courses</catalog>
06              <entry>p-006</entry>
07          </catalogentry>
08          <description>How to make a pie crust
    <description>
09          <keyword>pie</keyword>
10      </general>
11      <lifecycle>
12          <version>2.0</version>
13          <status>Final</status>
14      </lifecycle>
15      <metametadata>
16          <metadatascheme>ADL SCORM 1.2<
    metadatascheme>
17      </metametadata>
18      <technical>
19          <format>text/HTML</format>
20          <location>pie101.htm</location>
21      </technical>
22      <rights>
23          <cost>yes</cost>
24          <copyrightandotherrestrictions>yes
    <copyrightandotherrestrictions>
25      </rights>
26      <classification>
27          <purpose>Educational Objective</purpose>
28          <description>This SCO will give the student
    a basic understanding of the pie crust-making process.
    </description>
29          <keyword>cooking basics</keyword>
30      </classification>
31  </lom>
```

In this example, the individual data elements are the pairs of tags that have actual text between them, such as *<title>Pie Crust Techniques</title>* in line 03. These elements are grouped into categories as indicated by the outer container elements, such as the *<general>* – *</general>* pair in lines 02 and 10.

Required Meta-Data Elements

If a meta-data file is provided for a SCO or a content aggregation, it is required to include the categories and elements listed below. Some, but not all, of the listed categories and elements are also required in meta-data for an asset. We will use the term *learning component* (or just *component*) as a generic term that encompasses both SCOs and content aggregations:

- General (category) — Information about the learning component as a whole
  - Title (element) — A name for the component
  - Catalog entry (subcategory) — Information that defines a listing within a known cataloging system; this system may be a major online database or nothing more elaborate than the collection of learning components developed by your organization
    - Catalog (element) — Name of the catalog
    - Entry (element) — ID of the catalog entry
  - Description (element) — A text description of the component's content
  - Keyword (element) — A keyword or phrase describing the component; typically several different keyword elements will be included
- Lifecycle (category) — Information about the component's history and current state of development
  - Version (element) — The version or edition of the component
  - Status (element) — The current state of development for the component, such as "draft" or "final"
- Metametadata (category) — Information about the meta-data document itself
  - Meta-data scheme (element) — Name and version of the specification on which the meta-data are based
- Technical (category) — Information about the technical requirements needed to use the learning component
  - Format (element) — The data type of the component, which can be used to determine the software needed to access it
  - Location (element) — The information needed to locate the actual component, such as a URL
- Rights (category) — Information about cost, copyrights, and terms of use
  - Cost (element) — Whether or not payment is required for use of the component; the data in the element will be either "yes" or "no"

  - Copyright and other restrictions (element) — Whether or not the component is copyrighted or subject to other use restrictions; the data in the element will be either "yes" or "no"
- Classification (category) — Information on how the component fits into some known classification system; the same component may have more than one classification
  - Purpose (element) — The type or purpose of the classification, such as "educational objective" or "skill level"
  - Description (element) — A text description of the component in relation to the classification purpose
  - Keyword (element) — A keyword or phrase that describes the object in relation to the classification purpose[1]

Certification and Self-Testing

There is no certification available for meta-data as of this writing. As noted in Chapter 4, ADL does not yet have any certification in place. Even when it becomes available, the first version of SCORM certification is not expected to include meta-data. See the Web site for this book, http://www.elearning-standards.com, for updates on the status of certification.

ADL does offer self-test suites for versions 1.1 and 1.2 of the SCORM. These allow developers to confirm their own conformance with the SCORM specification. Both versions include validation tests for meta-data.

The Downside of the Specification — Trying to Allow for Everything

The IMS, and to a slightly lesser extent the ADL, have a far-ranging vision for the standards that they are developing. They want to allow for all possible contingencies, both now and in the future. Here are some examples.

- There is a provision for including the same elements several times in a meta-data document, each in a different language.
- Just in case the broad range of optional meta-data elements does not quite meet a developer's needs, a specification for defining extensions to the meta-data model is available.

- There is a provision for developing new meta-data models that can be referenced as add-ons to the existing model.

The result of all this built-in flexibility is that the specification documents are long and complex. It is a good bet that most users will stick to the basics and avoid the extra complications.

Conclusion

In this chapter we have shown how meta-data can provide a self-description component for LOs and aggregations. By providing key information in a standardized way, meta-data helps make learning components sharable. We have also introduced XML and seen how it is used for writing meta-data. In the next chapter, we will look at the SCORM and AICC specifications for communicating the hierarchical structure of a course.

Reference

1. Dodds, P., Ed., *Sharable Content Object Reference Model (SCORM): The SCORM Content Aggregation Model*, version 1.2. Advanced Distributed Learning, 2001, sections 2.2.2 and 2.2.4.4. Available at: http://www.adlnet.org.

6

Standards for Importing and Exporting Entire Courses

Introduction

In the last chapter we learned how meta-data helps make LOs and aggregations self-describing for efficient sharing and reuse. But for courses and other structured content aggregations, meta-data is only part of the reusability story. There must also be a standard mechanism for describing the structure and certain key behaviors of the aggregation. With such descriptive information available, entire courses can be imported directly into a standards-based LMS.

In this chapter we will see how the AICC CMI and SCORM specifications define course structure for the purpose of transferring courses between LMSs.

Portable Courses

Courses can be made portable by packaging their component parts with a set of directions for reassembling and using them, much like many of today's consumer products. (See Figure 6.1.) The "instruction sheet" or *interchange files* for a course must contain information on its structure, content, and learning requirements. If the structure and content of the interchange files are standardized, a conforming LMS can read them and recreate the original course structure.

A conforming LMS must be able to export the appropriate interchange files for any course in its database. However, not all LMSs allow you to build a new course. Some require all courses to be imported, meaning that you may have to create the necessary interchange files for yourself.

The AICC and SCORM specifications define similar sets of information needed to recreate a course in an LMS. There is considerable overlap between

FIGURE 6.1
Assembling a course.

the two. As we shall see, however, each specification also includes certain information unique to its philosophy of course construction.

Common Course Structure Information

The following types of information appear in both specifications.

- The version number of the specification that was used to create the course
- A unique identifier for the overall course itself and for each component, used to set up the structural relationships between the components
- A title for the overall course and for each of its structural components (i.e., blocks and LOs, but not assets)
- A text description of the overall course and each of its structural components
- An identifying label assigned to the course and each of its structural components by its original developer
- A description of the complete course structure, including whether and how its components should be grouped and the order in which they should appear on course menus in the LMS

- Specific information about each LO required for launch and for determining appropriate content behavior. Only the first of these (file location) is required by the specifications:
  - The location of the file to be launched by the LMS, either as a relative path from the location of the interchange and structure files or as a complete URL
  - Any special parameters that must be included in the command line when the file is launched
  - The maximum time allowed to complete the LO
  - The action to be taken when the time limit is reached
  - The mastery score
  - Any special information that the LO will need once it is launched

Two Specifications, Two Philosophies

As in other areas, the AICC and the SCORM have somewhat different philosophies. These philosophies strongly influence their implementations of course interchange, as shown in Figure 6.2.

The SCORM is concerned with global sharing of all types of content. It uses an XML file called a *manifest* to describe any content to be transported between learning systems. Such content may be a single SCO or asset, an unstructured collection of SCOs, assets, and other learning resources, or a structured content aggregation (a course or block). The manifest file for a content aggregation package is a specialized version of the general

FIGURE 6.2
Course interchange methods.

content package manifest. It describes the aggregation's components, structure, and special behaviors. It may also reference the meta-data associated with the individual components of the aggregation. A SCORM content aggregation manifest can include multiple variations of the course's structure.[1]

The AICC specification is focused more tightly on the course itself. It uses a set of text files designed to describe the course structure, components, and special behaviors as efficiently as possible. Because there is no meta-data directly associated with AICC blocks and AUs, the AICC files also have provisions to include information about the content provider and the authoring tools that were used to create the content. Unlike the SCORM, the AICC specification does not address methods of packaging unstructured collections of content components.[2]

The SCORM Content Packaging Model

As mentioned above, the SCORM includes two types of packaging specification:

- Content package — One or more reusable assets, SCOs, or aggregations collected for transfer between learning systems
- Content aggregation package — A structured group of learning components that may include any combination of assets, SCOs, and content aggregations, typically equivalent to a course (see Figure 6.3)

Both types of packages require a manifest file, which serves as a descriptive packing list for the included items. This file must be named "imsmanifest.xml" and must be located at the root (outermost level) of the distribution medium (e.g., .zip file, download directory, CD-ROM). The package may or may not include the physical content files and any associated meta-data files. The manifest provides URLs to the locations of any external content and meta-data files.

The Structure of a Manifest

The general structure of a SCORM manifest file is illustrated in the outline below. Italicized items in pointed brackets are the actual XML tags used in the manifest. The listed elements were chosen to give a feel for the type of information that can be included in a course manifest. For a more complete list and description of the individual manifest data elements, see Chapter 11.

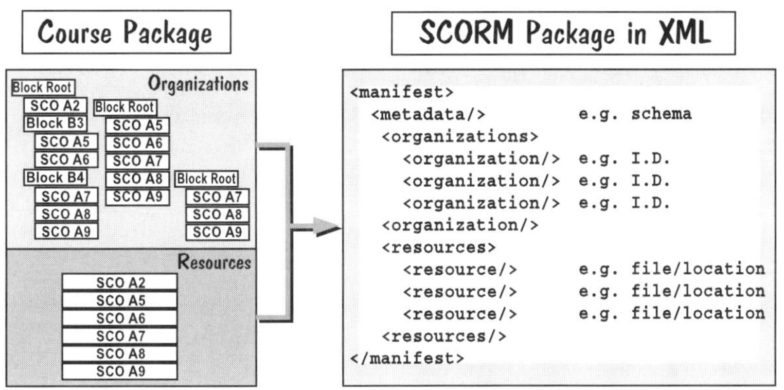

FIGURE 6.3
A SCORM content aggregation package. (Adapted from Kause, L., *ADL/SCORM Structure and Meta-Data Files,* slide 31. Paper presented at EuroTaac 2002 Conference, Edinburgh, Scotland, March 2002.)

- *<manifest>* — Outer container element that includes everything else
  - *<metadata>* — Container element for meta-data that describes the overall package; this container is often left empty.
  - *<organizations>* — Container element for one or more organizational structures. It must be left empty for content packages, which by definition have no organizational structure. For content aggregation packages, it must contain at least one *<organization>* element.
    - *<organization>** — Description of the structure and special behaviors of a specific course; more than one *<organization>* can be defined for the same content aggregation, each representing a different path through the content.
      - *<title>* — Title of the organization (course), typically displayed to learners by the LMS
      - *<adl:description>* — Description of the organization, which may include a content summary, purpose, scope, and so on; the LMS may display the description to learners.
      - *<item>* — Container element for information about a SCO or block that forms part of the overall organization; most organizations have multiple item elements, which may be nested to represent the block-and-SCO structure of the course. Any type of *<item>* element may include the following information:

* Note the subtle difference in spelling between the main *<organizations>* tag and its subsidiary *<organization>* tags. Mixing up the two tag names will result in an unusable manifest. The same applies to the *<resources>* and *<resource>* tags.

        - A unique (within the package) identifier that can be referenced by other elements
        - A flag to indicate whether or not the item will be displayed by the LMS on course menus
        - The title of the block or SCO as it will be displayed by the LMS on course menus
        - A description of the block or SCO that the LMS can display to learners
        - Any prerequisites for the block or SCO

    An *<item>* element describing a SCO may include the following information:

        - A reference to a *<resource>* element that in turn provides the URL to the start-up file for the SCO
        - Any time limit for the SCO, with instructions for what to do if the limit is exceeded
        - The maximum score for the SCO
        - The minimum passing score for the SCO
        - Any initialization information that may be needed by the SCO

- *<resources>* — Container element for a list of the individual SCO and asset files contained in the package.
    - *<resource>* — Container element for descriptive and location information about a specific content file; most packages include multiple resources. Information for a *<resource>* may include the following:
        - A unique (within the package) identifier that can be referenced by other elements
        - A description of the type of resource
        - A URL to the entry point of the resource
        - An indicator of whether the resource is a SCO or an asset
        - References to other resources upon which this resource depends[3]

A Complete Content Package

A complete content package represents a unit of reusable learning content of any type or size. It may be as small and simple as a single asset or as large and complex as an entire curriculum. Whatever its size and complexity, it must contain all the information needed to correctly deploy its content in a compatible learning environment.

A complete content package must contain a single top-level manifest. This manifest may contain one or more nested submanifests that describe smaller units of learning included in the package. Typically a package will also contain the physical files referenced in the manifest. However, a manifest may reference files anywhere on the Internet (or an intranet), so it is possible for a single manifest file to make up the entire physical content of a package.

The SCORM suggests, but does not require, the use of a package interchange file (PIF) for transporting content packages between systems. A PIF comprises the entire set of manifest and content files in a single archive-formatted file, such as a .zip, .jar, .cab, or .tar file. These files retain the exact directory (file and folder) structure of their contents, allowing them to travel without fear of accidental rearrangement of the files so that the referenced links to them become broken. Archive file formats also typically compress data to minimize download times.[4]

The AICC Course Interchange Files

The AICC method for course interchange was developed before XML came into widespread use. So, the AICC defined its own set of files, called course interchange files (CIF), to instruct an LMS in how to recreate a course. There are seven files, of which four are necessary to assemble even the simplest course. The other three files add more advanced functionality, such as prerequisites, special completion requirements, and relationships to instructional objectives.

The CIF files are formatted in plain text. Each is designated by a filename extension that relates to its purpose. These files can be viewed and edited in a simple text editor such as Microsoft Notepad. The four required files are as follows:

- The Course (*.crs)* file contains information about the course as a whole, listed simply as pairs of keywords and their values. The information in this file includes the following:
  - The creator of the course
  - An identifying label assigned to the course by its creator
  - The primary authoring tool used to create the course
  - The title of the course
  - The version of the AICC specification to which the course conforms
  - The maximum number of AUs a given learner may maintain in a partially completed state
  - The total number of AUs in the course
  - The total number of blocks in the course

- The *Descriptor (.des)* file provides specific information for each individual AU and block included in the course. This information includes the following:
  - A unique (within the course) identifier that is referenced by the other files
  - The title of the block or AU as it will be displayed by the LMS on course menus
  - A description of the block or AU that the LMS can display to learners
- The AU *(.au)** file contains all the information needed to properly launch and track each AU. The information that can be provided for each AU (much of which is optional) includes the following:
  - The identifier assigned to it in the Descriptor file
  - The URL to the starting file for the AU
  - Any time limit for the AU, with instructions for what to do if the limit is exceeded
  - The maximum score for the AU
  - The primary authoring tool used to create the AU
  - The minimum passing score for the AU
  - Any information that should be contained in the *Core vendor* data element. This information may be needed for the AU to run correctly.
  - A password that the LMS can use to authenticate the AU
- The Course Structure *(.cst)* file spells out the block and AU structure of the course.

See Chapter 11 for an annotated example of each of these CIFs.[5]

The Launching and Sequencing of LOs

The requirement that the LMS control the launch of LOs has left something of a void when it comes to influencing the sequence in which learning content is presented. This lack of control is one of the biggest hurdles for courseware design.

* The *.au* extension used for this file can be somewhat confusing in a Microsoft Windows environment. It is a standard extension for a sound clip file. Windows machines will typically assign the file a sound-related icon (picture of a speaker) and will attempt to play it in a media player if you double-click the file's icon. The best way to open an AU file for viewing or editing is with your text editor's "Open" command.

In theory, sequencing possibilities are almost endless. An LMS might allow the learner to choose freely among available LOs. It might enforce a rigidly designed sequence in which each item is a prerequisite to the next. It could select and automatically present the next LO on the fly, basing its selection on any available data about the learner and her previous interactions with the learning content. Or it could mix and match different sequencing methods to suit the learner's preferences or the nature of different parts of the content. In current practice, however, the capabilities are far more limited.

Sequencing is intimately tied to the ability of an LMS to automatically launch LOs without learner intervention. Many LMSs can only launch an LO when the learner selects it from a menu. Under this arrangement, there is really only one way to influence the order in which the learner experiences the contents of a course. If prerequisites are imposed on an individual LO, the LMS can block the learner from entering it until those prerequisites have been completed.

An LMS that can automatically launch LOs clears the way for a much broader spectrum of sequencing possibilities. It also requires a mechanism to specify sequencing rules that the LMS can use to select the appropriate LO at any given point. This is where things get difficult.

Beyond the simplest case — a single specified order of delivery — sequencing is very complicated to implement. The AICC CMI specification offers some relatively primitive ways to define sequencing based on prerequisites and completion requirements. The SCORM 1.2 specification lays some groundwork for sequencing but does not address it directly. However, at the time of this writing the first public draft of the *IMS Simple Sequencing Specification* has just become available. The ADL plans to incorporate simple sequencing into SCORM 1.3.

Today's Capabilities

As we have just explained, the specifications do not yet fully address sequencing. The AICC CMI specification includes a system for defining prerequisites from which some sequencing information can be inferred. It also provides a means of specifying completion requirements for various course components. These completion requirements may optionally include certain sequencing information. The SCORM has incorporated the AICC's prerequisite system, but not its completion requirements, preferring instead to wait for the IMS specification.

Prerequisites

The AICC defines prerequisites in an optional *Prerequisites (.pre)* course interchange file. This file specifies which AUs or blocks must be completed before the learner may enter a specified AU or block, as illustrated in Figure 6.4. If optional objectives tracking is implemented, objectives may also be used as prerequisites.

FIGURE 6.4
Prerequisites.

The AICC system includes a scripting language that allows developers to define complex prerequisites such as "the learner must have completed Block 1 and passed any two of AUs 4, 5, 6, or 7 but must not have completed Block 3." All prerequisites are based directly or indirectly on the value of the lesson status parameter. By default, a block is considered completed if all its components are completed or passed.[6]

The SCORM currently uses the AICC-developed scripting language to define prerequisites but leaves open the possibility of alternative methods to be developed in the future. It incorporates prerequisites into the course manifest file. SCOs and block-level content aggregations can be used as prerequisites. Like an AICC block, a content aggregation is considered completed if all its components are completed or passed.

See Chapter 11 for sample files containing prerequisites and for details about the prerequisite scripting language.

Completion Requirements

The AICC specification includes another optional course interchange file, *Completion Requirements (.cmp)*. You can use this file to instruct the LMS to do any or all of the following, as illustrated in Figure 6.5:

- Set the lesson status of an AU based on specified criteria, such as passing a different AU or combination of AUs. You could use this capability to allow learners to "test out of" (skip based on other test results) an AU.

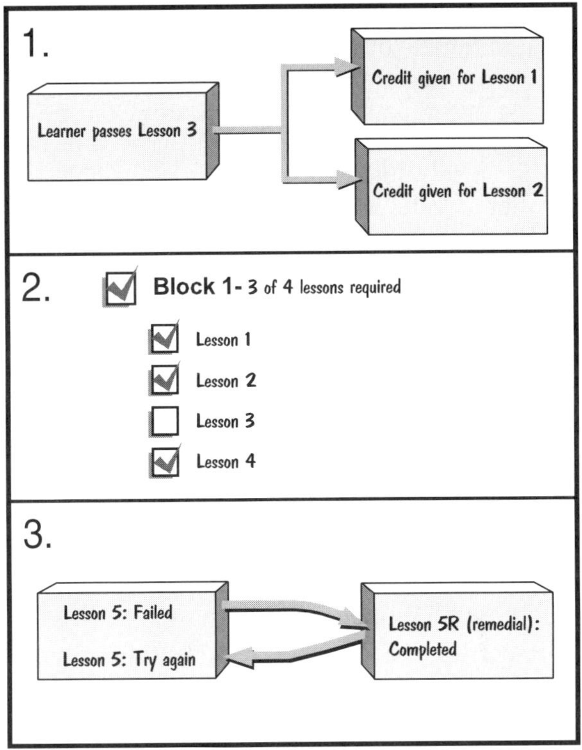

FIGURE 6.5
Completion requirement examples.

- Set the completion status of an instructional block based on specified criteria, such as passing or completing a subset of its components. One could use this capability to allow learners to choose one of several approaches to experiencing the block's content.
- Automatically branch to a specified AU based on specified criteria, such as failing a given AU. As an added option, an AU can be specified to which learners will be returned after completing the branch. One could use this capability to allow branching to a remedial AU and then returning to the main content track. Note, however, that branching instructions are useful only if the LMS can automatically launch AUs. Many LMSs do not have this capability.

The criteria for completion requirements are specified using the same scripting language as prerequisites. Like prerequisites, completion requirements can be based only on AU or block status. This limits their sequencing capabilities significantly. Branching based on such factors as score, time, or learner characteristics or preferences is not possible.[7]

The SCORM isvisible Attribute

Automated lesson launch is of particular concern in the SCORM community because of its emphasis on single-topic SCOs. The need to return to an LMS menu after every page or two of content can be disruptive and annoying.

In preparation for a fully fledged sequencing specification, the SCORM Content Aggregation Model includes an attribute named *isvisible*. This attribute, which can be optionally specified for each *<item>* element in a manifest, instructs the LMS to display or hide the element's title. If it is not specified, its value defaults to "true," which allows the item to appear on LMS menus. If its value is set to "false," the item will not appear (see Figure 6.6). This attribute can be used to hide the little SCOs that make up a larger chunk of learning (perhaps equivalent to a traditional lesson) that appears on the learner's menu.

If auto-launching is available, the learner can select a visible item, and the LMS will automatically launch its hidden components in the required sequence. However, until a sequencing specification is in place, there is little that can be done with this capability. Even the simplest fixed-order approach is marginal. There is no specified way to tell the LMS which LOs are to be auto-launched and which are to be learner selected. Although this information can be inferred from the value of *isvisible*, the attribute is not really intended for this purpose.[8]

Auto-Launch Availability

The specifications leave it up to LMS vendors to decide whether they will offer automatic launch capabilities. At the time of this writing, the lack of a robust sequencing specification has discouraged vendors from implementing auto-launch or has forced them to use proprietary methods that may have to be radically changed to conform with the specifications that are just now. emerging.

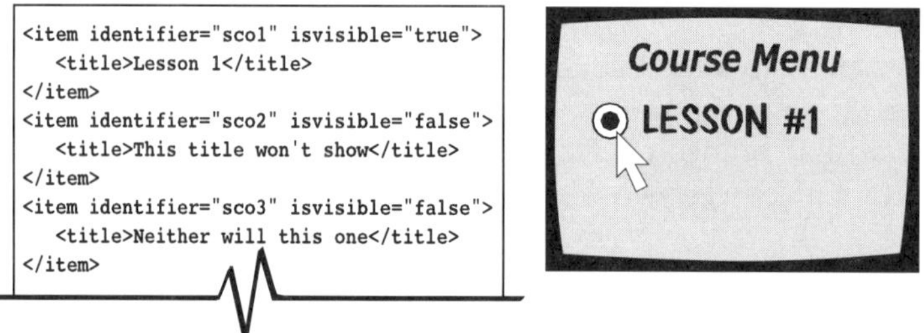
<item identifier="sco1" isvisible="true">
<title>Lesson 1</title>
</item>
<item identifier="sco2" isvisible="false">
<title>This title won't show</title>
</item>
<item identifier="sco3" isvisible="false">
<title>Neither will this one</title>
</item>
Course Menu
LESSON #1

FIGURE 6.6
The SCORM *isvisible* attribute.

Looking Ahead

As mentioned above, the IMS released its first public draft of the *Simple Sequencing Specification* on May 13, 2002. The ADL has announced that it plans to release an Application Profile for sequencing in the near future. This document will provide guidelines for using the IMS specification in SCORM environments. Simple sequencing will also be incorporated into version 1.3 of the SCORM.

As its name suggests, the Simple Sequencing Specification focuses on relatively simple sequencing scenarios. It includes the following:

- A behavior model that describes the process that an LMS should follow to determine which SCO to launch and when to launch it
- A definition model that details the information, controls, and rules needed to describe the desired sequencing behavior
- A tracking-status model that defines and explains how to compute the status information used in sequencing decisions

From the standpoint of an LMS developer, there is a good deal that is new in this specification. It is likely to take some time before sequencing support at the LMS level becomes widely available. In the meantime, the specifications will continue to evolve, offering increasing functionality and flexibility. See the Web site for this book, http://www.elearning-standards.com, for updated information on the progress of the sequencing specifications.

Certification and Self-Testing

The AICC has defined four levels of course interchange complexity:

- Level 1 includes only the four required interchange files, as described above.
- Level 2 allows prerequisites and completion requirements based on single elements only.
- Level 3 is split into two parts, either or both of which may be supported by a conforming LMS.
  - Level 3A allows complex prerequisites and completion requirements using the scripting language described in the specification.
  - Level 3B allows learning objectives to be defined in relation to elements of the course and used as prerequisites, completion requirements, or both.[9]

At the time of this writing, the AICC Test Suite and certification process address only level 1 course interchange. No testing is available for prerequisites, completion requirements, or objectives. This means, unfortunately, that one will not be able to count on total compatibility between LMSs and courseware that support these higher interchange levels. Among other problems, it is quite possible for an LMS to support only part of the requirements for one of these levels. For example, an LMS could support prerequisites but not completion requirements, making it effectively "level 1 plus." Be sure to ask for a demonstration and a reasonable assurance of technical support if considering an LMS that claims to support objectives, prerequisites, or completion requirements.

The SCORM 1.2 Conformance Test Suite includes all current content and content aggregation packaging requirements. An LMS that claims SCORM 1.2 conformance should be able to extract and correctly use all the structural and behavior information from a course manifest. It should also be able to export a conforming manifest document for a course that was constructed or modified in the LMS.

Conclusion

In this chapter we have seen how the structure and, to some degree, the behavior of courses can be documented in manifests and course interchange files. Thanks to standards, these files can be used by any conforming LMS to reconstruct the course to the original designer's specifications. In the next chapter we will apply the idea of standards-based structure files to a different area in the e-learning arena: tests and test questions.

References

1. Dodds, P., Ed., *Sharable Content Object Reference Model (SCORM): The SCORM Content Aggregation Model,* version 1.2. Advanced Distributed Learning, 2001, section 2.1.1. Available at: http://www.adlnet.org.
2. AICC CMI Subcommittee (Hyde, J., chair), *CMI Guidelines for Interoperability,* revision 3.5. AICC, 2001, section 6.0.1. Available at: http://www.aicc.org.
3. Dodds, P., Ed., *Sharable Content Object Reference Model (SCORM): The SCORM Content Aggregation Model,* version 1.2. Advanced Distributed Learning, 2001, section 2.3.4. Available at: http://www.adlnet.org.
4. Dodds, P., Ed., *Sharable Content Object Reference Model (SCORM): The SCORM Content Aggregation Model,* version 1.2. Advanced Distributed Learning, 2001, section 2.3.3.2. Available at: http://www.adlnet.org.
5. AICC CMI Subcommittee (Hyde, J., chair), *CMI Guidelines for Interoperability,* revision 3.5. AICC, 2001, sections 6.1–6.4. Available at: http://www.aicc.org.

6. AICC CMI Subcommittee (Hyde, J., chair), *CMI Guidelines for Interoperability*, revision 3.5. AICC, 2001, section 6.6. Available at: http://www.aicc.org.
7. AICC CMI Subcommittee (Hyde, J., chair), *CMI Guidelines for Interoperability*, revision 3.5. AICC, 2001, section 6.7. Available at: http://www.aicc.org.
8. Dodds, P., Ed., *Sharable Content Object Reference Model (SCORM): The SCORM Content Aggregation Model*, version 1.2. Advanced Distributed Learning, 2001, section 2.3.5.3.1. Available at: http://www.adlnet.org.
9. AICC CMI Subcommittee (Hyde, J., chair), *CMI Guidelines for Interoperability*, revision 3.5. AICC, 2001, section 6.0.3. Available at: http://www.aicc.org.

7

Standards for Tests and Test Questions

Introduction

The three previous chapters have concerned themselves with the two major specifications that define relationships between learning content and learning management systems. In this chapter we will step aside slightly to discuss a somewhat more specialized specification. The IMS Question & Test Interoperability specification, or QTI, details a method for sharing test questions and/or complete tests and reporting their associated results.

QTI is a large and complex specification that has attracted interest around the world. Although it has not yet been widely implemented, it is making inroads in many areas. Assessment systems such as Questionmark Perception have added or are in the process of adding the ability to import and export test questions in QTI format alongside those in their native formats. Some authoring tools, such as Macromedia Authorware, have added limited QTI import and export support in their latest versions. LMS vendors are also taking a close look at the specification with a view to integrating it. Finally, the ADL is considering incorporating some or all of the QTI specification into a future version of the SCORM.

This chapter will introduce the basic concepts of QTI and attempt to convey a sense of this specification's potential in the e-learning community.

Why a Separate Specification?

Testing of all types can be easily included in conventional learning objects, of course. In fact, it is not unusual for a course to include one or more test-only learning objects. So why did the IMS see the need for a separate specification?

The QTI model is designed for more than just presenting a test within an LMS. It can be used to store and transport entire libraries of individual test questions, structured groups of questions, and complete tests. Part of its purpose is to archive testing content in a standardized, neutral format that can be mapped to other formats now and in the future.

Question and Test Interoperability

The QTI takes content interoperability to a level beyond that of the other specifications by eliminating the need for separate physical content files. Instead of referencing a test file developed in a tool such as Authorware or ToolBook Instructor, the QTI document simply provides a standardized description of the content, presentation style, and behavior of the test and its individual questions. It relies on the end user to provide software that can translate this description and present the test as its authors intended.

How Is QTI Being Used Today?

At the time of this writing, there are few fully developed QTI assessment products on the market. None of them can handle the full range of QTI item types, and most are still based on the version 1.1 specification. Many of the products handle only individual items. Some have merely added QTI import and export as a secondary option to their own native item format.

There are a number of QTI products in development, however, and interest in the specification is growing.

The IMS Question and Test Interoperability Models

The QTI specification includes the following two main components:

- The Assessment-Section-Item (ASI) Information Model, which provides the actual test question content, response processing, sequencing of presentation, and overall test scoring
- The Results-Reporting Information Model, which provides a standard method for long-term storage of results and their use in a variety of contexts

These components are specified in several individual specification documents, as illustrated in Figure 7.1. Chapter 12 discusses the specific content that appears in some of these documents. The ASI component can be implemented separately, allowing the use of alternative results reporting mechanisms (or no results reporting at all). The Results-Reporting component was added to the specification with the release of version 1.2.

The ASI Information Model

The ASI specification defines the data elements used to describe the appearance and organization of individual questions (items), structured groups of questions (sections), and entire tests (assessments), along with unstructured

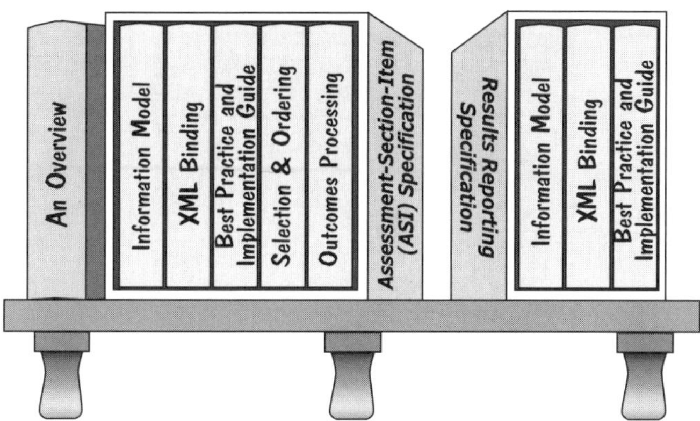

FIGURE 7.1
IMS Question and Test Interoperability specification documents.

"packages" of QTI components called *object banks.* It includes elements that control processing of the learner's responses to individual items. In addition, it provides a mechanism for creating rules that allow an assessment system to do as follows:

- Select test items and sections from an object bank and present them in a specified sequence
- Compute overall scores and other results (outcomes) for sections and assessments

This section will focus on the main ASI information model and its expression in Extensible Markup Language (XML). See Chapter 12 for information on selection, sequencing, and processing outcomes.

The ASI Hierarchy

The information model defines a structural hierarchy that is conceptually similar to the SCORM content packaging structure. This hierarchy is illustrated in Figure 7.2. The basic data objects are the following:

- Item — The smallest independent unit that can be exchanged using QTI. It contains all the information needed to display a single question, process the learner's response, and provide hints, solutions, and feedback as required. (Within their respective hierarchies, an item is analogous to an SCO.)
- Section — A group of zero or more items or other sections. Sections are simply grouping devices, with no particular characteristics of their own. Used in conjunction with selection and sequencing rules, these can help control the order in which test

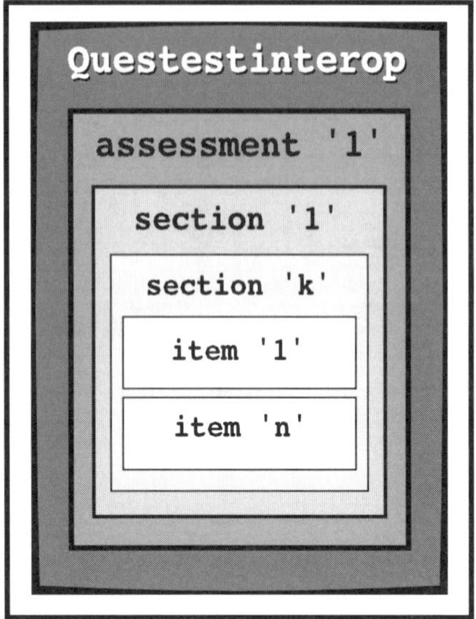

FIGURE 7.2
QTI structural hierarchy.

questions are presented to learners. (A section is analogous to a block-level content aggregation.)

- Assessment — An organized group of one or more sections, typically representing a complete test. An assessment contains all the information needed to present the test questions to the student in either a preset or variable order and to produce an aggregate score from the individual items. (An assessment is roughly analogous to a course-level content aggregation.)
- Object bank — A searchable collection of items or sections bundled together with no implied organization, designed for transporting content between systems. Object banks can also function as databases of test objects from which assessments can be constructed. (An object bank is roughly analogous to a content package, although it provides a bit broader functionality.)

An assessment must contain at least one section and may not include any loose items. A section may contain other sections or individual items, or it may be empty. An object bank may contain any combination of sections and individual items. It must include meta-data that enables its contents to be searched. Section, assessment, and databank documents may contain the actual data for the individual items and sections within them, or they may reference these objects in external documents.[1]

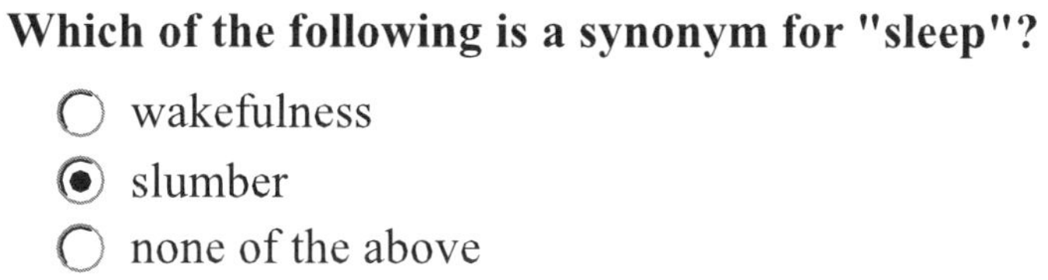

Which of the following is a synonym for "sleep"?

◯ wakefulness

◉ slumber

◯ none of the above

FIGURE 7.3
QTI test question — typical rendering.

A Simple Example of an Item

The excerpt shown below is a QTI XML representation of a single multiple-choice test item. When this item is presented to a learner, the first two answers can appear in either order, whereas the "none of the above" answer always remains in the final position. The question has only one correct answer and no time limit.

The example describes only how the question will look when displayed to the learner. Figure 7.3 shows a typical rendering of the question, with the answer choices shuffled. Response processing, which includes indicating the correct response and specifying appropriate feedback, would need to be added before the question could be used in an actual test.

The text for the question portion (stem) of the item is presented in line 06. The answer choices can be found in lines 13, 20, and 27. Keep in mind that the line numbers are not part of the actual XML document.

```
01  <item title = "Multiple Choice Example" ident =
    "Unique_EX001">
02      <qticomment>This is a simple multiple choice
    example. The rendering is a standard radio button
    style. No response processing is incorporated.
        </qticomment>
03      <presentation label = "Example001">
04          <flow>
05              <material>
06                  <mattext>Which of the following
    is a synonym for "sleep"?</mattext>
07              </material>
08              <response_lid ident = "MCa_01"
    rcardinality = "Single" rtiming = "Yes">
09                  <render_choice shuffle = "Yes">
10                      <flow_label>
11                          <response_label ident =
    "A">
12                              <material>
```

```
                              <mattext>slumber</mattext>
                          </material>
                      </response_label>
                  </flow_label>
                  <flow_label>
                      <response_label ident = "B">
                          <material>
                              <mattext>wakefulness</mattext>
                          </material>
                      </response_label>
                  </flow_label>
                  <flow_label>
                      <response_label ident = "C" rshuffle = "No">
                          <material>
                              <mattext>none of the above</mattext>
                          </material>
                      </response_label>
                  </flow_label>
              </render_choice>
          </response_lid>
      </flow>
  </presentation>
</item>
```

Available Test Item Types

The QTI specification currently includes items of the following types, many with several variations.

- True–false — The correct answer is one of two opposing choices.
- Multiple choice — One and only one choice is correct.
- Multiple response — One or more choices make up the correct answer.
- Image hot spot — The correct answer is a location on a graphic image.
- Fill in the blank — The learner types in text or numbers. This category of item may include short-answer or even essay questions, although response processing for these types will generally require some level of human intervention.
- Select text — The learner must identify a specific string of text presented in some larger context such as a paragraph or list.

- Slider — The learner moves a slider to choose a number within a given range.
- Drag and drop — The learner drags objects to predefined locations or places them in a specific order.

Additional question types are expected to be added in future versions of the specification.[2]

Item-Level Response Processing

In addition to formatting and displaying a test item, a complete QTI item description must include information on how to judge and respond to the learner's response.

Response-processing information provided for an item may include the following:

- Identification of the correct answers
- A conditional test used to determine the correctness of the learner's response
- Instructions for setting a score variable based on the learner's response
- Feedback text for the overall item
- Feedback text for individual response options
- Text for hints that can be displayed to the learner[3]

Results Reporting

As mentioned above, the Results-Reporting Specification was added to QTI in version 1.2. It provides a means of recording assessment results at various levels of detail for such purposes as archival storage, statistical analysis, and interfacing with an LMS.

A Simple Example of Results Reporting

The following XML sample contains summary results for a single individual on a single exam. From this document we can learn that Tom Sawyer (Social Security number 222-33-4444) completed the exam on February 6, 2003. It took 1 hour and 23 minutes for him to finish. His score was 82, which gave him a grade of B. He exceeded the minimum passing score and grade of 60 and D, respectively (see Figure 7.4). Appendix A, Listing 7.1, shows this report as it would appear in actual use, without the line numbers.

```
<qti_result_report>
    <result>
        <context>
            <name>Tom Sawyer</name>
            <generic_identifier>
                <type_label>SSN</type_label>
                <identifier_string>
DoL:222334444A</identifier_string>
            </generic_identifier>
            <date>
                <type_label>Exam</type_label>
                <datetime>2003-02-06T00:00:00
</datetime>
            </date>
        </context>
        <summary_result>
            <type_label>Assessment
</type_label>
            <generic_identifier>
                <type_label>Assessment Id
<type_label>
                <identifier_string>WeTest:33-184
<identifier_string>
            </generic_identifier>
            <date>
                <type_label>Exam</type_label>
                <datetime>2003-02-06T00:00:00
<datetime>
            </date>
            <status>
                <status_value>Complete
<status_value>
            </status>
            <duration>P0Y0M0DT1H23M0S</duration>
            <score varname = "SCORE" vartype =
"Integer">
                <score_value>82</score_value>
                <score_min>0</score_min>
                <score_max>100</score_max>
                <score_cut>60</score_cut>
            </score>
            <grade members = "A,B,C,D,F" varname =
"GRADE">
                <grade_value>B</grade_value>
                <grade_cut>D</grade_cut>
            </grade>
        </summary_result>
    </result>
</qti_result_report>
```

FIGURE 7.4
QTI summary results.

The Data Model

The Results-Reporting Information Model defines four types of reportable results.

- Summary result — An overall result for a single attempt at a single evaluation (i.e., an assessment, section, or item)
- Assessment result — Detailed result information for a single attempt at a specific assessment
- Section result — Detailed result information for a single attempt at a specific section
- Item result — Detailed result information for a single attempt at a specific item

Summary result reports, such as the example in the previous section, are stand-alone documents that do not reflect the structure of the underlying evaluation. The other three types of results can be nested to represent the complete structure of the evaluation being reported on.[4]

The Downside — Trying To Be Too Comprehensive

Like most of the specifications, QTI aspires to address every possible situation that could arise in actual use. This results in hundreds of complicated specification pages, with the promise (or threat) of many more to be added in future versions. Furthermore, as one can tell by the sample XML excerpts presented in this chapter, a document or group of documents containing a typical real-world assessment is immense.

IMS has recognized these issues to some degree and has provided a stand-alone specification for a bare minimum system called QTI Lite. This specification is restricted to defining individual multiple-choice items with a single correct answer. It does not address sections or assessments. QTI Lite will certainly have its uses, but the leap between it and the full specification is quite large. Perhaps other reduced subsets of the specification will eventually be developed by IMS or other interested parties.

Looking Ahead

Throughout the QTI documents, IMS has spelled out expansion plans for version 2.0 of the specification. Much of the work will be in the areas of selection and ordering, outcomes processing, and results reporting. However, it is also likely that we will see new item types.

ADL is looking at the QTI, especially the Results-Reporting component, for possible future incorporation into the SCORM.

Establishing Conformance

Unlike AICC and ADL, IMS does not involve itself in certification or self-testing. It relies instead on detailed disclosure by vendors. Any vendor claiming any level of QTI conformance is supposed to provide two documents, a conformance summary and an interoperability statement, which detail the specification features that are supported. Templates for these documents are provided in the specification. The conformance summary is the simpler of the two documents and should provide enough information to make informed purchase decisions. The specifications state that vendors claiming conformance must provide a conformance summary in response to a reasonable request from a prospective customer. A sample conformance summary is shown in Table 7.1.

TABLE 7.1

Sample Conformance Summary

Feature	Conformance Summary (Version 1.2) Publish (Export, Data)	Accept (Import, Display)	Repackage Feature
Object-bank level support	N	N	N
Assessment level support	N	N	N
Section level support	N	N	N
Items supported	N	Y	N
Metadata	N	Y	N
Question types	N	Y	N
Multiple choice	—	Y	—
Drag and drop	—	N	—
Fill-in-the-blank	—	Y	—
Image hot spot	—	Y	—
Objectives and rubric	N	Y	N
Flow	N	Y	N
Response processing	N	Y	N
Feedback	N	Y	N
Hints and solutions	N	Y	N
Material content	N	Y	N
Text	N	Y	N
Emphasized text	N	Y	N
Image	N	Y	N
Video	N	N	N
Audio	N	N	N
Other	N	N	N

Source: From Smythe, C., Shepherd, E., Brewer, L., and Lay, S. *IMS Question & Test Interoperability: ASI Best Practice & Implementation Guide,* final specification, version 1.2, Table 10.1. IMS Global Consortium, February 2002, © IMS Global Learning Consortium, Inc. Available at http://www.imsproject.org.

Vendors may choose to implement any desired subset of the full range of QTI-specified features. They may also choose to support those features in any one or more of the following modes:

- Publish — Can export an XML document that includes the given feature
- Accept — Can use and, if appropriate, display the given feature or element in imported QTI content

- Repackage — Can import (but not necessarily use) QTI XML documents, combine data from them, and export the combination as a new document[5]

Because a vendor can claim QTI conformance based on a very limited subset of the specification (such as accepting simple multiple-choice items), carefully study the conformance summary to ensure that the product will meet your needs.

Conclusion

Assessment plays at least as important a role in e-learning as it does in conventional classroom learning. The IMS QTI specification brings this critical learning component to the forefront. In this chapter we have barely scratched the surface of the current and future capabilities of QTI. For those who are interested in developing their own QTI-conformant assessments, we will revisit the specification in greater detail in Chapter 12.

This chapter completes Part 1 of this book. In it, we have provided an overview of e-learning and the major standards and specifications that support it. We have offered advice on selecting, purchasing, and deploying standards-conformant learning management systems, courseware, and other system components. Although we have introduced key elements of the major specifications, we have dealt mainly with high-level concepts rather than details.

Whereas Part 1 was intended for all readers, Part 2 narrows the focus to those who will be directly involved in developing standards-conformant learning content, including courseware developers, programmers, instructional designers, and training managers. Chapter 8 provides some general guidelines for creating standards-conformant courseware. The remaining chapters discuss the details of the major specifications and how they apply to creating learning and assessment content.

References

1. Smythe, C., Shepherd, E., Brewer, L., and Lay, S., *IMS Question & Test Interoperability: ASI Information Model Specification,* final specification, version 1.2. IMS Global Consortium, 2002, section 4. Available at: http://www.imsproject.org.
2. Smythe, C., Shepherd, E., Brewer, L., and Lay, S., *IMS Question & Test Interoperability: ASI Information Model Specification,* final specification, version 1.2. IMS Global Consortium, 2002, section 3.2. Available at: http://www.imsproject.org.

3. Smythe, C., Shepherd, E., Brewer, L., and Lay, S., *IMS Question & Test Interoperability: ASI Information Model Specification,* final specification, version 1.2. IMS Global Consortium, 2002, section 5.4. Available at: http://www.imsproject.org.
4. Smythe, C., Shepherd, E., Brewer, L., and Lay, S., *IMS Question & Test Interoperability: Results Reporting Information Model,* final specification, version 1.2. IMS Global Consortium, 2002, section 3. Available at: http://www.imsproject.org.
5. Smythe, C., Shepherd, E., Brewer, L., and Lay, S., *IMS Question & Test Interoperability: ASI Best Practice & Implementation Guide,* final specification, version 1.2. IMS Global Consortium, 2002, section 10. Available at: http://www.imsproject.org.

Part 2

A Guide for Designers and Developers

8

Working with Standards: How to Author Standards-Based Content

Introduction

This chapter will offer some practical advice about the things to consider before starting development of standards-conformant e-learning content. We will discuss data that can be saved in and retrieved from your LMS, what to do with that data within each LO, how to cope with nonstandard data elements, and how to control navigation through courses. Next, we will take a look at future-proofing content to help keep it up-to-date with evolving standards. Finally, we will provide specific information about locating and using the specification documents themselves.

Planning Your Standards-Based Content

What Data Do You Want to Track?

Before you dive headlong into developing content, you should address some fundamental design issues. First of all, you need to figure out exactly what data you want to track. This will depend on things such as the objectives of your e-learning initiative and the requirements of your organization. However, before you can do that, you must check exactly what data elements your LMS will support.

Understanding What Data Your LMS Supports

Both the AICC CMI specification and the SCORM Run-Time Environment specification contain a data model. These two data models are similar. The differences between them are discussed in Chapter 9. All conformant LMSs are required to support a set of core data elements. These are listed in

Chapter 4 and described in detail in Chapter 9. The rest of the elements in the data models are optional.

Some of the core data elements, such as *student ID* and *student name,* are provided by the LMS and cannot be changed by the LO. Other items, such as *lesson score, lesson location* (bookmark), and *lesson status,* can be set by the LO. When a learner exits from an LO, the LMS stores the data that it has received from the LO. If the user later initiates another session with the same LO, the LO can read the values from the last session, update them, and send them back to the LMS for storage at the end of the session.

Using Optional Data Elements

As we have mentioned, there are a significant number of optional data elements defined in the AICC and SCORM data models. These are summarized in Chapter 4. The SCORM version 1.2 data model is based on the AICC CMI specification data model but has a reduced set of optional data items. Although these data elements are optional, an LMS that offers tracking for any of them is required to implement them in conformance with the specifications.

Suppose, for example, you would like to use the optional *mastery score* data element. This element enables an administrator to set up a passing score value within the LMS. IF a value is set, the LMS ignores any status sent from the LO and calculates the status for itself. If the element is available, the LO can request its value from the LMS and test it against the lesson score to judge whether the learner has passed.

If you decide use optional data elements in your LO, consider how it might affect that LO's portability. If the content is likely to be used with more than one LMS, there is no guarantee that all the LMSs will support the same set of optional elements. One way to guarantee portability is to avoid optional elements altogether. Another way is to build logic into LOs that checks to see whether an LMS supports a particular optional data element and then takes the appropriate action based on the element's availability. Keep in mind that this method will not work if content is developed in Hypertext Markup Language (HTML) for use with an HTTP-based AICC CMI Protocol (HACP) interface because information cannot be received from the LMS.

Testing for Optional Elements

The method that is used to test for an optional element depends on whether the API or HACP is used to communicate with the LMS. The following general directions should help the reader think about how the LO might be structured. For further details, see Chapter 9 and the relevant specification documents. Using one of the following methods will allow an LO's tracking capability to adapt to the LMS that it is running in or future-proof it in readiness for future enhancements to the existing LMS.

When the API Is Used to Communicate with the LMS

There are two ways to determine the availability of optional data elements using the API. Each group of data elements, as described in Chapter 4, has a special element that uses the ending "._children." Issuing an *LMSGetValue API* call with one of these elements returns a list of the supported data elements in the given group. For example, *LMSGetValue(cmi.core._children)* would return all the elements in the "core" group that are supported by the LMS. This proactive approach is particularly useful for those who want to check for several different data elements in the same group. On the other hand, one can safely issue an *LMSGetValue* or *LMSSetValue* for the desired element. If the element is not supported, the LMS will set an error code of 401. The LO can check for this error code, as explained in Chapter 9, and respond appropriately.

When HACP Is Used to Communicate with the LMS

Issue a *GetParam* call and check for the appropriate keyword in the set of data returned from the LMS. If the keyword is not there, it is not supported. If you try to send an unsupported data element from a LO, a correctly designed LMS will simply ignore it. So the LO is probably safe to send any data but should not explicitly "promise" the student anything. For instance, it should not tell the student that future LOs will use preference settings from the current LO.

Unsupported Data Elements

For those who want to track data about the LO that is not included in the AICC and SCORM data models, there is a required data element specifically designed for that purpose. It is called *Suspend_Data* in the API data model and *Core_Lesson* in the HACP data model. For simplicity, we will refer to this element as *suspend data* for the rest of this section.

Suspend data is a field in which you can enter up to 4096 characters of data about the LO that you may want to use in future sessions. The LO writes data to this field and sends to the LMS, which stores it exactly as received. The data can then be retrieved by the LO at the beginning of the next session. Any data that you wish can be stored in this field. The only limitation is that the data must be transferred between the LO and the LMS as an ASCII string. It is up to the LO to build the string and send it to the LMS. After retrieving the string from the LMS, the LO must parse it to extract the required information.

Example of Using Unsupported Data

A typical example in which you might take advantage of the *suspend data* element is with an LO that is divided into several topics, each with its own quiz. You may want to track the learner's progress in each topic. Because the LO is the smallest piece of learning content that can be launched and tracked by an LMS and only one score can be tracked for the lesson, you must devise your own topic-based tracking scheme. To track a score for each topic, you can program your LO to store each topic score in a string variable. The format that you use for this string is up to you and may be influenced by the authoring tool you are using. The LMS simply stores the string between sessions. When developing in Authorware, for example, it is effective to store a carriage return symbol ("\r") after each value you store in the string. So if you have five topics to track and the user has taken the quiz for the topics 1 through 3, your string might look like this:

83\r92\r79\r\r\r

This string tells the LO (and us) that the learner has scored 85, 92, and 79 in topics 1 through 3. Then, if in the next session the user scores 95 for the quiz in topic 5, the string will look like this:

83\r92\r79\r\r95\r

A similar scheme can be used with other authoring tools, but the most effective delimiter symbol to separate the topics may be different.

The variables in which the LO maintains the topic scores must be initialized with any default values at the beginning of each session. Then the *suspend data* must be requested from the LMS. If it is the first time that this learner has launched that particular LO, the *suspend data* string will be null and should be ignored. If there are already values written in the string from a previous session, the string must be parsed (picked apart) to extract the individual topic scores. These values can be used to control lesson behavior, such as by displaying a list of passed and failed topics. To accomplish this update the values of the variable as the learner progresses through the topics. Then use the variables to rebuild the string when you are ready to send it back to the LMS at the end of the session, or as often as you feel is appropriate.

When Should Data Be Sent to the LMS?

One concern that developers frequently have when designing standards-conformant lessons is deciding at what points in the LO and how frequently they should send data back to the LMS. In an ideal world, the answer would be that the LO should send data only once, when the learner completes or exits it. However, there are several circumstances in which the learner's session can be ended unexpectedly, such as the following:

- The network connection is lost.
- The client's computer crashes.
- The learner forgets to exit the LO and a time-out occurs.

- The learner takes too long to complete the LO and a time-out occurs.

Concern about losing data due to such occurrences may suggest that you should send data very frequently. But there are limits to how often data can be sent without impacting bandwidth and server performance.

To strike a balance between securing the data and over-burdening the network, consider the following:

- *How critical is the data?* Data elements such as a lesson score should probably be sent immediately, whereas time in lesson may not be considered so critical.
- *What data elements are you tracking?* If you are keeping a bookmark (*lesson location*), does this need to be updated in the LMS for each new screen accessed by the learner, or is it acceptable for the bookmark to be accurate to within a few screens of the learner's location when the connection was lost?
- *How many database hits can you afford?* If you are pressed for server capacity, you may want to minimize the number of data transfers.

It is also important to consider how the data is sent from the LO. The exact mechanics for exchanging data between LO and LMS vary depending on the authoring tools and the communications method (API or HACP) being used. However, generally, you will be saving data in local variables within the lesson and then issuing one or more function calls to upload the data to the LMS. Provided that the upload is successful, the data then will be safely stored in the LMS.

Clearly, an upload should be done immediately if any of the data that is designated as critical is updated in the lesson. This may include events such as the following:

- A final quiz score is calculated.
- The lesson's status changes, such as from incomplete to complete, failed to passed, and so on.
- A lesson objective is completed.

Data items that you do not regard as critical or that are constantly changing, for example *lesson location* or *time in session*, can be uploaded as frequently as you feel is appropriate.

In the case of the API, some LMSs cache (temporarily store) data locally until an *LMSCommit* function call is issued to upload the cached data to the LMS. If this is the case, be aware that the data is not "safe" until the *LMSCommit* call has been issued. See Chapter 9 for more details on using *LMSCommit*.

Although the HACP specification does not address data caching, some authoring tools that use HACP have their own routines to simulate caching.

Data is held locally (usually within the LO) until the LO executes an explicit instruction to upload it. For example, Authorware LOs may build the HACP data string internally and use a function called *CMIFlush* to trigger the upload. In this case, data is also unsecured until the upload has taken place.

Abnormal terminations are a special case. Both the API and HACP depend on a special function call to terminate the session. If the session ends without issuing this call, for example because the network connection is broken, the behavior will vary from one LMS to another. Typically the LMS will not pick up the data from the most recent *PutParam* or *LMSCommit* call until the next time that the student starts a session with that lesson.

This means that the data from the terminated session will be temporarily unavailable. This can lead to inaccuracies in student progress reports until the next session takes place.

Intracourse Navigation and Content Chunking

One of today's biggest challenges for standards-based course development is the tug-of-war between the relatively primitive options for navigation between the components of a course and the ideal of small, tightly focused, repurposable LOs. As discussed in Chapter 6, the difficulty revolves around the closely intertwined issues of automatic lesson launch and sequencing of learning content. The *IMS Simple Sequencing Specification* holds a good deal of promise in alleviating this situation. At the time of writing, this specification has just been published as a public draft and is being fast-tracked for adoption into the SCORM. It will almost certainly undergo some modifications before inclusion in the SCORM. After that, it is likely to take a year or more before the sequencing capabilities are widely implemented. In the meantime, it is necessary to find compromise solutions.

How Current LMSs Control Navigation

One of the most significant changes in approach that courseware developers will encounter is how a standards-conformant LMS handles navigation between lessons or LOs. Traditional CBT courses control their own interlesson navigation, typically by offering a main menu from which the learners can select lessons. The menu is fully under the control of the courseware designer; it can dictate the learner's path through the material or allow total freedom to skip around. As we saw in Chapter 4, however, in a standards-conformant learning environment, the equivalent of the main menu resides within the LMS. When the learner selects a lesson (LO) from this menu, the LO is launched by the LMS and takes control of the learning experience. When the learner exits the LO, control is returned to the LMS.

As illustrated in Chapter 4, Figure 4.3, only the LMS is allowed to launch an LO. This method of operation enables the LMS to track and store data for each LO independently. Although this arrangement requires that the LMS control the launch of each LO, it does not necessarily require learner involvement in that launch. However, as we saw in Chapter 6, today's standards-conformant systems offer few, if any, other options.

For LMSs that have implemented only the minimum course interchange requirements of AICC or SCORM, the only available options for navigating between LOs are learner controlled (requiring the learner to select each LO from the main menu) or automatic launch in a fixed sequence. Because the actual mechanism to be used for automatic launch is not defined in the specifications, it can be problematic, and many LMSs have not implemented any auto-launch capabilities. Thus, learner-controlled navigation is the more widely implemented of these options.

Content Chunking and Navigation

Limited navigational control is one of the biggest stumbling blocks for developers using today's e-learning standards. In particular, it impacts decisions regarding the appropriate length of LOs. Obviously, if you build LOs that are context independent and map onto a single learning concept or objective, it could take thousands of them to construct an average-sized course. It would be utterly impractical for the learner to have to return to the course menu in the LMS after each small piece of content is completed. On the other hand, if your LMS can automatically launch the content in the desired sequence, use of smaller LOs is much more feasible. Of course, if designing courseware for use on multiple LMSs, you need to assume the lowest common denominator, learner-controlled navigation.

Navigation is one of several factors that will affect decisions on how to break up and organize lesson content. Here are some key considerations.

- With learner-controlled navigation, an LO essentially equates to what the learner perceives as a lesson.
- If auto-launching is available, what the student sees as a lesson may consist of many LOs. This is particularly true if the SCORM *isvisible* attribute is used to hide the LOs that will be launched automatically, as described in Chapter 6.
- In a learner-controlled navigation environment, the learner has to choose each LO from the menu in the LMS. Clearly it would be impractical to offer the learner hundreds of choices, so individual LOs need to be large enough to keep the menu manageable.
- An LO is the smallest chunk of learning that can be tracked independently, and it can have only one score and one status. The more content the LOs cover, the less detailed that tracking will be.
- Current instructional design philosophy suggests that the learner should be able to complete a lesson (whether a single LO or an automated sequence of LOs) in a single sitting or a maximum of 20 minutes.

- If developing LOs in HTML using the HACP communication method, remember that data communication is one way, as discussed in Chapter 4. Because the LO cannot retrieve data posted in previous sessions from the LMS, each LO should be short enough to be completed in a single sitting.

Advanced Sequencing and Navigation Features

As mentioned in Chapter 4, several sequence and navigation-related features are available at higher levels of AICC course interchange — objectives, prerequisites, and completion requirements. The SCORM also currently supports prerequisites. You may want to design your courseware to take advantage of them if you are lucky enough to have an LMS that supports them.

Objectives Tracking

An AICC-conformant LMS that supports one of the higher levels of course interchange can track status and other data about individual objectives that are mapped to the LOs in a course. Status in a given objective can be used as a lesson prerequisite or special completion requirement, as we will see shortly. It is expected that the ADL will eventually incorporate some form of objectives tracking into the SCORM as well. Even if your LMS does not currently support objectives tracking, you may want to develop and maintain a mapping of objectives to LOs for potential future use.

If you are developing for multiple AICC-based LMSs, you can safely include objectives in the course interchange files. A conforming LMS that does not support the necessary interchange level will simply ignore the information. Within lessons, you can handle objectives tracking just as you would any other optional data elements.

Prerequisites

Prerequisites, which are supported by both the AICC and SCORM specifications, specify an order in which learners are permitted to access lessons. Only an LMS that supports the optional higher levels of AICC course interchange is required to provide prerequisite support, whereas any SCORM-conformant LMS is required to do so.

The prerequisite rules, which are based on the status of LOs or objectives (AICC only), are set up directly in the LMS or passed to it when a course is imported. The LMS uses these rules to control the learners' path through the lessons, typically by blocking the launch of lessons for which the prerequisites have not been met. Chapter 11 includes details and examples of the use of prerequisites.

When setting up your course structure, it is a good idea to list any prerequisites in the lesson descriptions. Even if your LMS doesn't support prerequisites, the descriptions will serve as suggestions to help guide learners through your material. It is also safe to include prerequisite information in AICC course interchange files designed for multiple LMSs. If they are not supported, the LMS will ignore them.

Completion Requirements

Completion requirements, available at the higher levels of AICC course interchange, provide the most advanced standards-based mechanisms available at the time of this writing for controlling the path of a learner through a course. If you are fortunate enough to be developing courseware for an LMS that supports completion requirements, you will be able to enable the automatic completion of LOs or objectives based on the completion of other lessons or objectives. For example, suppose you build a course that includes a preassessment LO. You can set a completion requirement for each of the first five LOs in the course that automatically sets their status to "completed" if the learner passes the preassessment. Or, if a course has 10 lessons, you may require that only 8 of them must be completed for the whole course to be considered complete. The same type of logic can be applied to objectives if the LMS supports them.

At the highest course interchange level, the AICC CMI specification provides some auto-sequencing capabilities in conjunction with completion requirements. If your LMS supports this level of interchange and also has automatic launch capability, a completion requirement can indicate the next LO to be launched and, if desired, another LO after that. So, for example, you could instruct the LMS to divert a learner to a remedial or enrichment LO, then send the learner back into the "main" learning sequence. Chapter 11 includes more details and examples on specifying completion requirements.

Planning for Remediation

In certain learning contexts, it is important to be able to provide remedial content for slower learners. Obviously the navigational and auto-launching capabilities of your LMS will play a large role in how this is achieved. Let's consider a remediation example and see how it can be handled with varying degrees of LMS support.

In our example, the learning content for a particular concept is being developed at three different levels:

- Normal level, which presents the concept at a level appropriate to what you consider your "average" audience
- Remedial level 1, which presents the concept with fewer assumptions of preexisting knowledge
- Remedial level 2, which presents the concept assuming no preexisting knowledge

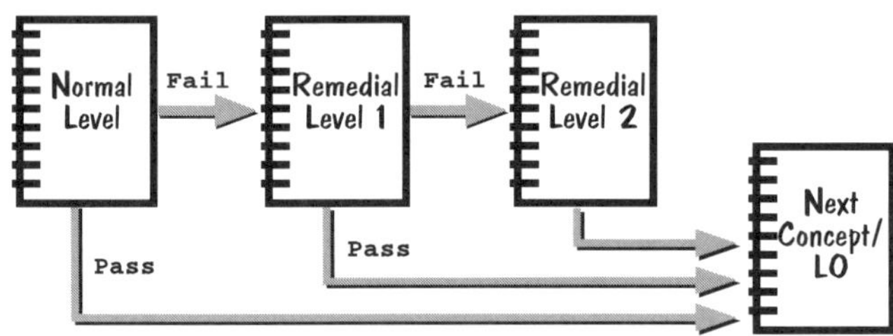

FIGURE 8.1
Remedial pathing.

The learner paths through this content are shown in Figure 8.1. All learners begin with the normal level. If they pass this level they move on to another concept. If they fail the normal level, they are forced to complete remedial level 1. If they fail remedial level 1, they must complete remedial level 2. For the purpose of this example, we will assume that all learners pass level 2.

If your LMS does not have automatic launch capabilities and does not support completion requirements, remediation is best handled inside a single LO. Using the programming capabilities of your authoring tool, you can use variables to track the learner's results at each content level and branch to the appropriate sections of content as required. How the lesson does this is up to you; the standards do not address what goes on inside an LO. However, if you segregate the three levels into clear-cut modules (for example, by placing them on separate frameworks in Authorware), you lay the groundwork for easily turning them into separate LOs when improved LMS capabilities become available.

If your LMS supports prerequisites and completion requirements, you may want to place each level of the content in a separate LO. Even if your LMS cannot launch LOs automatically, you can force the user to take the desired remedial path by using the following scheme:

- Set up a prerequisite sequence in which each LO is a prerequisite to the next on the list, as follows: *normal–remedial 1–remedial 2*–LO for next concept
- Set up the following completion requirements:
  - If *normal* is passed, set the status of *remedial 1* to "passed."
  - If *remedial 1* is passed, set the status of *remedial 2* to"passed."

With this setup, the learner is initially required to pass through all three content and remediation levels before being allowed to continue with the LO for the next concept. However, as soon as the learner passes one of the levels, the completion requirements kick in and set the LO status for the remaining levels to "passed." The prerequisite for the LO containing the next concept is met, and the learner is now free to choose it from the menu.

The best situation of all is when your LMS can automatically launch LOs based on completion requirements. You can then automate the whole process by setting up completion requirements to do the following:

- If *normal* is failed, launch *remedial 1*.
- If *remedial 1* is failed, launch *remedial 2*.
- If *normal* or *remedial 1* or *remedial 2* is passed, launch LO for next concept.

Keeping an Eye on the Future

As you have already seen, e-learning standards are currently something of a moving target. Inevitably, as today's specifications are put into more intensive practical use around the world, they will be modified and refined based on the practicalities of real-world experience. The rigorous process leading up to their approval as accredited standards will also introduce refinements and enhancements. However, this is not a reason to avoid developing to the current specifications. The overall direction toward which the standards are developing is fairly clear. Also, the groups developing the specifications are committed to providing an efficient upgrade path when they make significant changes.

The best way to future-proof learning content is to design with the future in mind. Although some later rework is inevitable, there are a number of steps that can be taken to minimize the required effort. Here are some suggestions:

- *Plan for LOs.* Although you may still be producing your courses using the classic lesson paradigm, you can plan ahead by creating each lesson as a set of semi-independent learning modules. Make each module as small and as self-contained as possible, both in content and in program structure. This will make it easier to convert your content to an LO environment later on. For example, if you are developing in Authorware, set up each module as a single page on a framework so that it can be easily extracted and set in its own navigational framework later.
- *Set up rich data tracking.* Even if your current LMS does not support the optional data elements in the AICC or SCORM data model, you can still set up variables to track any elements that you think may be desirable in the future. For example, both data models provide optional interaction (question) level tracking. Go ahead and program the appropriate HACP or API calls to make use of these capabilities. You can comment them out in your code or use

a variable to switch the calls on or off at the beginning of each piece. Better still; use the method that we described earlier to check for availability of optional elements. Then when an upgraded version of your LMS (or a newly purchased LMS) makes tracking for these elements available, you can take advantage of them with minimal changes to your content.

- *Create meta-data files.* Even if you don't plan to share your content, meta-data will probably eventually become necessary to take advantage of projected standards developments. For example, flexible methods for selecting and sequencing LOs to meet different needs may make use of certain meta-data elements. Creating and maintaining standards-compliant XML meta-data files for your content is not a big deal if you develop these at the same time as you develop the content, and you may even find it immediately useful for your own organizational purposes. By getting into the XML habit, you can save a lot of retrofitting time later when you wish to take advantage of new developments in the specifications. Chapter 10 discusses several tools that provide assistance in creating meta-data.
- *Store test questions in QTI format.* One of the major purposes of the QTI specification is to provide a neutral format for storing test questions. If your organization does a significant amount of testing, it could be advantageous to use this format to organize and store banks of items for future use. Several tools are available that can export QTI items.
- *Set up external media assets* (images, text, sound bites, multimedia). Keep your media external to the content or in libraries if possible. That way it will be easier to set up each piece of media as a SCORM asset later on.

Using the Specification Documents

The next four chapters contain references to the ADL/SCORM, AICC, and IMS specifications, which can be obtained from the Web sites of their respective organizations. This book's Web site provides current version information for each of these specifications, as well as direct links to each of the specification documents.

Often more than one version of each specification is available. Determining which version to use can be tricky. If you are developing courseware for a specific LMS, you should use the most recent specification version that it supports. If you are developing courseware for use with multiple LMSs, you may want to program it to support multiple versions. The version supported by the LMS can be obtained by a lesson at runtime, so you can use internal branching logic to provide multiversion support when needed.

As a general rule, don't try to read any of the specifications straight through. They are designed for reference, not sustained reading. Besides, only relatively small portions of the documents are relevant to the task of developing lessons.

The various specification documents can be found as follows.

SCORM Specifications

- Web site: http://www.adlnet.org
- Main document files:
  - *The SCORM Runtime Environment*
  - *The SCORM Content Aggregation Model*
- Versions: 1.1 or higher
- Useful related files
  - *The SCORM Overview*
  - *SCORM Version 1.2 Addendums* (contains some critical corrections for v1.2)
  - *IMS Global Learning Consortium, Inc. Learning Resource Meta-data Specification Version 1.2.1 XML XSD* (the XML Schema used as the controlling document for v1.2. XML Schemas are explained in Chapter 10)
- Notes: As of this writing, the most recent version of the SCORM is 1.2, which was last updated in October 2001. You may find the following version information useful:
  - The Runtime Model did not change significantly between versions 1.1 and 1.2.
  - In version 1.1 of the Content Aggregation Model, the meta-data section is considerably less detailed. The information model elements are for the most part the same, but less information is supplied for each of them. There is no explanation of the XML binding, but several XML examples are provided. The XML for version 1.1 references a DTD rather than an XML Schema. With version 1.2, the IMS Learning Resource Meta-Data Information Model was incorporated into the SCORM. Essentially the specification is a specialized application of the IMS model to the specific context of SCORM-conforming environments.
  - The SCORM version 1.2 Content Packaging Model represents a significant departure from the way version 1.1 handled course interchange. Version 1.1 did not address content packaging. Instead, it defined a Content Structure Format Information Model. Content structure format (CSF) files are quite different from the content structure information contained in a Manifest file. You may want to produce both CSF files as well as manifests to maintain backward compatibility.

AICC Specification

- Web site: http://www.aicc.org
- Document file: *CMI001 — CMI Guidelines for Interoperability*
- Versions: 2.0 or higher for HACP, 3.0 or higher for API
- Notes: The AICC specification was originally developed for file-based, rather than Web-based, management. As a result, the Web-based portions of the specification appear in appendices. You will often need to jump back and forth between the appendices and the main document chapters to get all the information you need.
  - The HACP specification was introduced in version 2.0, where it is presented as Appendix A. The appendix describes only the changes to the original file-based specification that are needed to track data in a Web-based environment. Most of the launch and communication information appears in this appendix, but the content model details are specified in section 5 of the main document. There have been significant changes to the data model across versions, so it is important to ask your LMS vendor which versions are supported.
  - The API specification was introduced in version 3.0, where it is presented as Appendix B. Version 3.5 matches the SCORM 1.1 specification. For the API interface, the SCORM specification is easier to read and follow than the AICC specification, so we recommend that you use it as your primary resource.
- The Course Interchange Files format (CIF) is specified in section 8 of the document. It was last updated in version 3.0.

IMS Specifications

Meta-Data Specification

- Web site: http://www.imsproject.org
- Main document file: *IMS Learning Resources Meta-Data Information Model*
- Versions: 1.1 or higher
- Notes: As of this writing, the most recent finalized version is 1.2.1, which was last updated in September 2001. Version 1.2.2, which contains error corrections primarily to the Schema, is in public beta at the time of this writing and will probably be finalized by the time this book reaches print.

QTI Specification

- Web site: http://www.imsproject.org
- Main document files:
  - *IMS Question & Test Interoperability: ASI Information Model Specification*
  - *IMS Question & Test Interoperability: Results Reporting Information Model*
- Versions: 1.0 or higher
- Notes: As of this writing, the most recent version is final version 1.2, which was last updated in February 2002. The QTI specification documents are difficult to work with, for several reasons.
  - They are extremely long, with much of their length taken up by extensive examples. Unfortunately, both the main text and the examples contain some ambiguities and errors.
  - The layout of the data object descriptions and XML binding is awkward to use, although to be fair, the format is probably the best possible in a printed document. The difficulty lies in the fact that many elements and attributes are repeated frequently throughout the model. For example, *<material>* elements occur everywhere something is to be displayed to the learner, and a significant number of elements have *label* attributes. To avoid redundancy, these elements and attributes are described in detail only once, with all other uses of them providing only the cross-reference. Although this is logical, it forces constant jumping between pages until you become adequately familiar with the frequently used items.

9

Creating Interoperable Learning Objects

Introduction

This chapter considers the use of data-tracking standards in LO development. It is written with the assumption that you have already read Chapter 4. It provides additional detail on how the API and HACP data exchange methods address LO launch, communication, and data models. It also includes more technical information about the biggest limitations of the two methods. Finally, it offers solutions to some of the most common problems courseware developers encounter in using the standards.

The material in this chapter is designed as an "entry ramp" to the specification documents, which are large, cumbersome, and sometimes difficult to understand. Ultimately you will need to refer to the actual specifications, but this chapter should prepare you to use them efficiently.

Although there are a number of examples of actual code presented in the text and tables of this chapter, they are somewhat limited. The Web site associated with this book, http://www.elearning-standards.com, contains more samples, as well as explanations of how to use them with various authoring tools.

The API Data Exchange Method

As we saw in Chapter 4, there are three components to data tracking, a launch process, a communication method, and a data model. In this section we focus on how these three components are defined for the API method, and how LOs operate within them. We also provide additional explanation on the cross-domain problem that limits today's implementations of the API method.

Launching an LO

When using the API method, launching an LO is fairly straightforward (at least from the point of view of the LO). The definition record for each LO includes a URL to the LO's opening file. The LMS uses the stored URL to open the file in the learner's browser. At the same time, it makes an API adapter available to the LO. The API adapter, which consists of a small program running in a browser window, can be thought of as a translation service. It allows the LO to communicate data using a simple, standardized "language" while translating to and from whatever data format and communication protocol the LMS requires. Courseware developers can ignore what goes on between the API adapter and the LMS. They need only see to it that their LOs can find and communicate with the API adapter.

For an LO to find the API adapter, the LMS must launch it in a location that has one of two specific types of relationship to the window that contains the API adapter code. (See Figure 9.1.)

1. The window containing the API adapter may contain a frame or subframe in which the LO is launched. The frame containing the LO can be nested several levels deep if the LMS design requires it.
2. The window containing the API adapter can open a new window for the LO, or open an intermediate window that in turn opens the LO window. If the LMS design requires it, a chain of several windows can be opened.

The method by which the LO locates the API adapter is explained in the following section.

Communication between the LO and the LMS

Once the LMS has launched the LO, it is the LO's responsibility to locate the API adapter. As we saw in the previous section of this chapter, the LMS makes the API adapter available at a location where the LO can use a simple JavaScript routine to find it. Both the AICC and SCORM specifications contain sample routines that can be used verbatim or adapted to suit your courseware. You can find these routines at the following locations in the specification documents:

- AICC: CMI001 — *CMI Guidelines for Interoperability,* Appendix B, Section B.2.3.1
- SCORM: *The SCORM Runtime Environment*, Section 3.3.6.1

Once the LO finds the API adapter, it communicates with it using a set of standard JavaScript functions. Altogether there are eight API functions, including three error-handling functions and one function that controls the

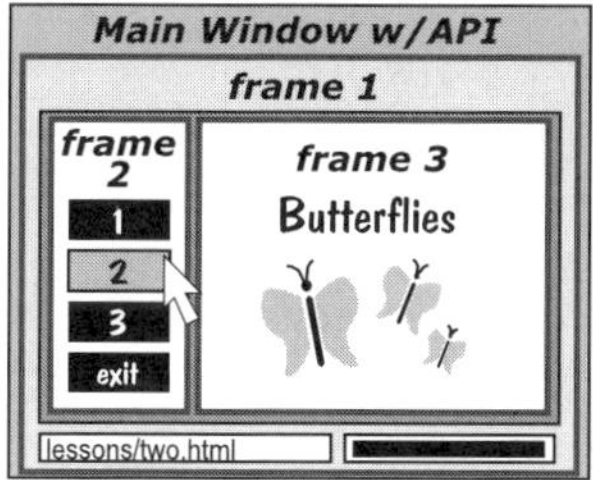

1. Frame 2 needs to find the API. It looks at the parent frame- frame 1. The API is not there, so it looks at its parent's parent- the main window. It finds the API there.

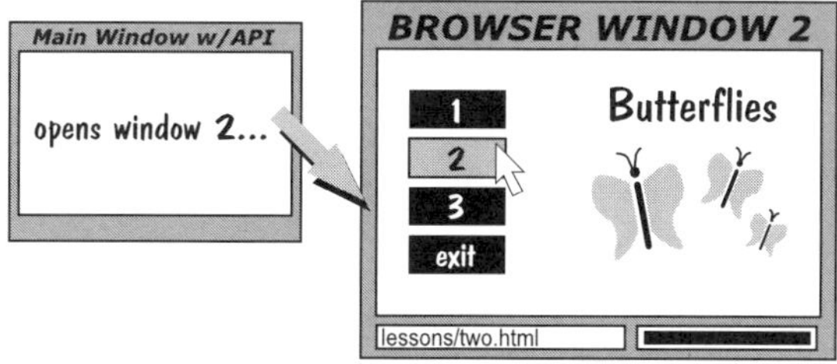

2. Window 2 needs to find the API. It looks for a parent but doesn't find one because it's all one frame. So, it looks for the window that opened it- window 1. It finds the API there.

FIGURE 9.1
Finding the API.

points at which data is passed from the API adapter to the LMS. Table 9.1 provides details about the format, purpose, and correct usage of the API function calls, along with examples of their use.

All API function names are case sensitive — they must be capitalized exactly as shown in the specifications. All parameters (items within the parentheses after the function name) are strings and must be surrounded by double quotation marks. They are also case sensitive and must be typed in all lowercase.

As you can see from Table 9.1, the LMS returns a value for every call it receives. For functions that do not request specific information, the value is either "true" if the call was successfully received and processed or "false" if there was a problem. (Of course, a major problem may keep the LMS from responding at

TABLE 9.1
API Function Calls

Name (Syntax)	Description	Parameters and Return Values	Example[a]
LMSInitialize ("")	Initiates communication between the lesson and the LMS	Parameter: empty string (""); return value: "true" or "false"	var result = LMSInitialize ("");
LMSFinish ("")	Ends communication between the lesson and the LMS; no function calls except LMSGetLastError will be processed after a successful call to LMS Finish	Parameter: empty string (""); return value: "true" or "false"	var result = LMSFinish ("");
LMSGetValue (data_element)	Retrieves the value of a specified data element from the LMS	Parameter: name of the data element; return value: a string containing the value of the specified data element, if available, or an empty string ("")	var credit = LMSGetValue ("cmi.core.credit");
LMSSetValue (data_element,value)	Sends a value for a given data element to the LMS	Parameters: (1) name of the data element and (2) value to be assigned to that element; return value: "true" or "false"	var result = LMSSetValue("cmi.core.session_time", "00:17:12");
LMSCommit ("")	Forces the API to send any cached (accumulated) values to the LMS (an API may be programmed to cache values received from LMSSetValue calls in order to reduce network traffic.)	Parameter: empty string (""); return value: "true" or "false"	var result = LMSCommit ("");
LMSGetLastError ()	Retrieves a code indicating what, if any, error occurred on the previous API call; allowable error values are defined in the specifications	Parameter: none; return value: string containing a numeric error code	var errorcode = LMSGetLastError();
LMSGetErrorString (error_number)	Retrieves a text string describing the error specified by the given number; error string values are defined in the specifications	Parameter: error code number; return value: string containing a predefined error message	var errormsg = LMSGetErrorString ("403");

LMSGetDiagnostic (error_number) or LMSGetDiagnostic ("")	Retrieves a text string that contains an error message provided by the LMS vendor, which may be more useful or user-friendly than the predefined error string	Parameter: either (1) the error code number or (2) an empty string (""); return value: string containing the vendor-defined error message for (1) the given error number or (2) the most recent error. This may be an empty string if the vendor has not provided diagnostic text.	var moreinfo1 = LMSGetDiagnostic ("403"); var moreinfo2 = LMSGetDiagnostic ("");

Source: All data from AICC CMI Subcommittee (Hyde, J., chair), *CMI Guidelines for Interoperability,* Appendix B, revision 3.5. AICC, 2001, section B.3. Available at: http://www.aicc.org.

[a]In actual practice, these calls must be placed on a single line, without carriage returns. They have been word-wrapped here to fit in the available space.

all.) An empty string returned in response to an *LMSGetValue* call may indicate an error, or it may be a legitimate value. A well-designed LO should check all returned values and provide appropriate error processing.

Notice that we have said very little about what happens between the API adapter and the LMS. The purpose of the API is to shield the courseware developers from the technical details of communicating with the LMS. Therefore the specifications address only what happens on the LO side of the API adapter. The designers of the LMS may use any method that they choose for data transfer to and from the API adapter.[1]

The API Data Model

The data model consists of a hierarchical set of data elements. These elements are the parameters that are used in *LMSGetValue( )* and *LMSSetValue( )* function calls. Dot notation is used to identify a specific element in the hierarchy, as illustrated in Figure 9.2.

All element names begin with a designation of the data model, in this case, "cmi." When new data models are adopted, each will have its own designation. Element names must be all lowercase, and they must not contain any spaces or any special characters other than the dot (period) and underscore.

Table 9.2 gives details about the data elements that an LMS is required to support, along with a few useful optional data elements. See the specification documents for information on the remaining optional data elements.

The obligations of an LMS with regard to the data model are as follows:

- Implement all required data elements exactly as specified in the model.
- If an optional element is supported, implement it exactly as specified in the model.
- Provide a list of all supported data elements in a given data group in response to an *LMSGetValue(cmi.[name of group]._children)* call.
- If an optional element is not supported, set a special error code (401) if the element is requested or set by an LO.[2]

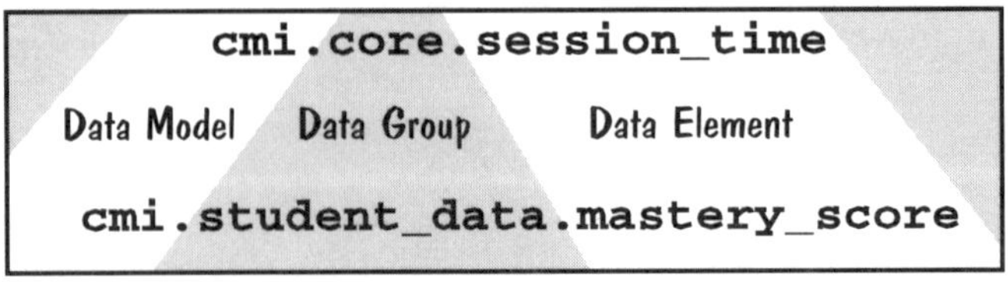

```
cmi.core.session_time
Data Model   Data Group   Data Element
cmi.student_data.mastery_score
```

FIGURE 9.2
Dot notation.

TABLE 9.2

API Data Elements

Element Name	Description and Usage Notes	Get[a]	Set[b]
cmi.[any group]._children	A special data element used to determine which elements in the given group are supported by the LMS. For example, *LMSGetValue(cmi.student_data._children)* would return a list of the supported data elements, if any, in the optional *student_data* group.	X	
cmi.core.student_id	A unique identifier for the learner, often the learner's log-in ID. This value is not often used by lessons.	X	
cmi.core.student_name	The learner's full name, in "last_name, first_name middle_initial" format. Example value: "Student, Joseph P."	X	
cmi.core.credit	Indicates whether or not the learner is taking the LO (either an AU or a SCO) for credit. This information could be used to control what the LO displays. For example, quizzes might be hidden in no-credit mode. This value is also used in determining lesson status. Allowed values: "credit," "no-credit"	X	
cmi.core.lesson_location	The location at which the learner last exited the LO. It is intended for use as a bookmark. When an LO is first launched, the LMS initializes this value to an empty string (""). The LO can set a new value when the learner exits and read it back in when the learner returns. The format and interpretation of the value is up to the LO.	X	X
cmi.core.lesson_status	The learner's current status in the LO. When the learner enters the LO for the first time, the LMS initializes the value to "not attempted." Normally the LO updates the learner's status when the learner exits. Allowed values are the following: • "passed" — Used when the LO produces a score • "failed" — Used when the LO produces a score • "completed" — Used when the LO is taken for credit but does not produce a score • "incomplete" — Used when the LO is taken for credit and the learner exits without completing it • "browsed" — Used in conjunction with the optional *cmi.core.lesson_mode* data element. If lesson_mode is implemented, the learner may have the option to browse a learning object before officially beginning it. A status of "browsed" can be used to indicate that the learner has done so. • "not attempted" — Used only by the LMS as the initial status value	X	X

(*continued*)

TABLE 9.2 (continued)

API Data Elements

Element Name	Description and Usage Notes	Get[a]	Set[b]
cmi.core.entry	Indicates whether the learner has previously entered the LO. The LO might use this information to determine what is displayed to the learner. The value is in part determined by the value of the *cmi.core.exit* element. See the description of that element for more details. Allowed values are the following: • "ab-initio" — The learner has never before entered the LO. • "resume" — The learner is reentering the LO from a suspended (partially finished) state. This value is set only if the lesson set the *cmi.core.exit* value to "suspend." • "" (an empty string) — The learner is reentering an LO for which *cmi.core.exit* was not set to "suspend." This may occur if the LO does not set *cmi.core.exit* or if the learner reenters an already completed LO.	X	
cmi.core.score.raw	An indication of the learner's performance in the LO. It may be a cumulative score based on exercises in the LO, a percentage correct on the final test, a count of the objectives completed, or any other value that makes sense in the context of the LO's design. The value must be between 0 and 100, so it must be adjusted if it falls outside the range (e.g., if there are 150 test questions or a right-minus-wrong scoring scheme yields a negative result). Typically it will represent a percentage. An empty string ("") must be used to indicate that there is no score to be reported, as opposed to a score of "0." It is important to enforce this distinction. If the LMS implements the optional *mastery_score* element, setting the score to "0" when there is no score to be reported may cause the LMS to erroneously assign a lesson status of "failed."	X	X
cmi.core.total_time	The accumulated time of all the learner's sessions in the LO. This value is calculated by the LMS and is typically used for generating administrative reports. An LO might display it to the learner or use it as a criterion for controlling the learner's path through the course. Required format, with lowercase letters indicating optional digits: *hhHH:MM:SS.ss*	X	
cmi.core.session_time	The elapsed time spent by a learner in a single session. This value is calculated and reported by the LO and is used by the LMS to calculate *total_time.* Required format, with lowercase letters indicating optional digits: *hhHH:MM:SS.ss*		X

(*continued*)

TABLE 9.2 (continued)

API Data Elements

Element Name	Description and Usage Notes	Get[a]	Set[b]
cmi.core.exit	Indicates how or why the learner last left the LO. The LMS can use this information to set the value of *cmi.core.entry* and to perform certain other actions. Allowed values are the following: • "time-out" — Indicates that too much time elapsed in the session, as determined by the LO. • "suspend" — Indicates that the learner exited the LO with the intent of completing it later; this value tells the LMS to set *cmi.core.entry* to "resume" the next time the learner enters the LO. • "logout" — Tells the LMS to automatically log the learner out of the course. Normally a learner is returned to the course menu or sent directly to the next LO in the course after completing an LO; setting *cmi.core.exit* to "logout" allows the learner to log out of the course from within the LO. • "" (an empty string) — Indicates that the learner exited the LO normally.		X
cmi.core.lesson_mode	The value of *cmi.core.lesson_mode* indicates the LO behavior that the learner desires after launch. It can be set to one of the following values: • "browse" — The learner wants to preview the content without taking it for a grade or completion credit. The LO may return a *cmi.core.lesson_status* of "browsed" to the LMS. Any other score or status information sent by the LO should be ignored. • "normal" — The learner wants to take the LO for a grade or completion credit. This is the default mode, equivalent to the standard behavior of the LO if *cmi.core.lesson_mode* is not supported or has not been set. • "review" — The learner has already received a grade or completion credit for the LO and wishes to review the content. The LO can use the value of *lesson_mode* to set special behaviors. For example, tests or quizzes might be hidden in browse mode.	X	
cmi.suspend_data	A storage place for data generated within a session that will be needed when the learner returns to the LO later. It can hold up to 4096 characters of ASCII text that can be read back in by the LO the next time it is launched. A few possible uses are the following: • Recording the responses that a learner makes to specific interactions so that they can be already filled in if the learner revisits them in a subsequent session • In an LO with flexible navigation, recording which sections the learner has visited so that they can be checked off on a menu	X	X

(continued)

TABLE 9.2 (continued)

API Data Elements

Element Name	Description and Usage Notes	Get[a]	Set[b]
cmi.suspend_data	• Recording the location of a file that was dynamically generated from within the LO; this could be used in the event that the LO needs to store more than 4096 characters of information *(continued)*	X	X
cmi.launch_data	A storage place for special data required every time a LO is launched. Without this data, the LO may not run correctly. This data (up to 4096 ASCII characters) is included in the LO definition maintained in the LMS. Possible uses include the following: • The location of an external file from which frequently updated content can be loaded into the LO at runtime • A contact e-mail address or phone number that is different for each organization that uses the LO • The locations of external graphics files (such as logos) that allow each company to customize the appearance of the LO	X	
cmi.student_data. mastery_score	A minimum passing score that is set in the LMS. If a mastery score exists, the LMS will compare any score sent by the LO to the mastery score and set the LO's status accordingly. Any status set independently by the LO is ignored. Therefore, it is useful for the LO to use the value of *cmi.student_data.mastery_score,* if it exists, to calculate status internally and provide feedback to the learner. If there is no mastery score, the LO is responsible for setting the status.	X	

Source: All data from AICC CMI Subcommittee (Hyde, J., chair), *CMI Guidelines for Interoperability,* Appendix B, revision 3.5. AICC, 2001, section B.3. Available at: http://www.aicc.org.

[a] An "X" in the Get column indicates that the element's value can be retrieved by the LO using the *LMSGetValue*( ) call.

[b] An "X" in the Set column indicates that the LO can set the element's value using the *LMSSetValue*( ) call.

If you are creating an LO for use with standards-certified LMSs, keep the following points in mind:

- You can count on support for all required data elements.
- You may be able to count on certain specific optional elements if you are creating the LO for exclusive use with a specific LMS. The LMS vendor will be able to tell you which optional elements are available. You should still proceed with caution. Although the specifications require optional elements to conform if they are used, the conformance self-test available at the time of this writing does not

test for them. As a result, it is possible for an apparently conformant LMS to implement optional elements in a nonconforming way.

- If your LO may be run under more than one LMS, you cannot rely on support for optional data elements. The data model offers various ways to determine whether a given element is supported by the LMS. As discussed in Chapter 8, you can add logic to your LO that tests for the desired elements and uses them when they are available but does not "break" if the elements are not supported.
- Your LO must send data values that meet the specifications. All data elements have a maximum length. Some data elements (such as *cmi.core.session_time*) have a specified format. Others have a range or list of allowable values. For example, *cmi.core.score.raw* must fall between 0 and 100, and *cmi.core.exit* must be one of four specific values.
- All values are passed back and forth as strings of characters. Your LO must be able to convert values that should be interpreted as numbers (such as *cmi.core.score.raw*) or other special data types as needed.
- Your LO must process data elements in a meaningful way. This requires that you thoroughly understand the purpose and specified usage of each data element you use, as well as any relationships it has with other data elements.

The Cross-Domain Problem

As explained in Chapter 4, the biggest issue for API implementations involves security precautions present in Microsoft Internet Explorer.

As we have seen, the LO content typically resides in a frame within the browser window that contains the API adapter. The LO communicates with the API adapter using JavaScript, a programming language that can be interpreted by the browser. The JavaScript in the LO sends messages across the boundary of its own frame to communicate with the API adapter in the outer frame (window).

Unfortunately, browser manufacturers see a potential breach of security in allowing program code in one frame to have direct access to another frame. Microsoft Internet Explorer resolves this concern by implementing the so-called "same origin rule." This rule does not allow JavaScript to communicate between frames unless both frames originate in the same domain (see Figure 9.3).

Netscape browsers use a different security mechanism that does not interfere with the necessary communication between the LO and the API adapter.

The HACP Data Exchange Method

The HACP exchange method includes the same three components as the API method. In this section we provide detail on how these components

FIGURE 9.3
The cross-domain problem.

function and how to create LOs that work with them. We also provide technical details on the inability of HTML-based courseware to receive data from the LMS.

Launching an LO

When an LMS launches an LO using the HACP method, it incorporates all the launch information that must be sent to the learner's browser into a single URL command line known as a *launch line*. A sample launch line with its component parts labeled is shown in Figure 9.4. The LMS assembles the launch line using a combination of values that are available within the system or created on the fly. The URL of the LO file is stored in the definition of the LO. The *session ID* is a unique value that the LMS generates on demand when the LO is selected for launch. The *return address* is the URL of the script the LMS uses to communicate with LOs, which is predefined in the system. In addition to these three required pieces of data, the launch line can also include optional Web launch parameters that are stored in the LO definition. If used, these parameters are added to the end of the launch line, separated from the other values by an ampersand character ("&").

When an LO starts up, it must capture the parameters from the launch line and store their values in local variables for use in communicating with the LMS later. This seems straightforward, but there is one complication. Blank spaces, many punctuation marks, and a number of other so-called special characters confuse a browser if they appear in the parameters portion of a URL command line (the part that comes after the question mark). To resolve this problem, the offending characters are replaced with a coded equivalent. In Figure 9.4, for example, colons have been replaced by "%3A," and forward slashes by "%2F." As you can see, this URL encoding makes the data more difficult for humans to read. It also requires LOs to be able to decode the parameters to use them properly.[3]

Communication between the LO and the LMS

HACP communication between an LMS and an LO is accomplished by HTTP messages traveling between the Web server and the learner's browser. There are two types of messages.

- *Request messages* are sent from the learner's browser, using the HTTP "POST" method. Most authoring tools provide a straightforward way to set up and send such messages.
- *Response messages* are sent from the LMS's Web server in response to request messages.

The message data for both types of messages comprises a set of parameters that follows a format convention called *name–value pairs.* A name–value pair looks like an equation: *name = value.* The name side of this equation is the name of the parameter, and the value side of the pair contains the value of the parameter. For example, the name–value pair *session_id = demo478* indicates that the value of the session ID is demo478.

The value of the parameter *aicc_data* is itself a series of name–value pairs, each one representing an element from the data model. You can think of these parameters as representing data fields in the LMS's database record for the learner. The parameter name is equivalent to the title of the data field, and the value represents the content that is or will be stored in that field. For example, the name–value pair *student_name=Martin, Linda K.* indicates that there is a field in the learner's record called *student_name* and that the field contains the information *Martin, Linda K.**

FIGURE 9.4
The HACP launch line.

* The way that a given LMS actually stores the AICC data internally is not dictated by the specification and may be somewhat different from our conceptual notion of it. However, from the point of view of an LO, the LMS functions as though it is storing the data in this manner.

Request Messages

A request message takes the form of a series of name–value pairs, separated by ampersand (&) characters. Table 9.3 describes the purpose and usage of the parameters that may be included in a request message. The message must conform to the following usage rules.

- Name–value pairs may appear in any order.
- The value side of each pair must be URL encoded.
- Parameter names are not case sensitive, as illustrated by the examples in Table 9.3.
- If an optional parameter is not used, both the name and the value for that parameter must be omitted from the message.

TABLE 9.3

HACP Request Message Parameters

Parameter Name	Required?	Value	Example
command	Yes	A valid HACP command as described in Table 4.5	command = getparam
version	Yes	The version of the AICC specification to which the lesson is written	version = 3.0
session_id	Yes	The unique session identifier that was passed to the lesson in the launch line	session_id = jsmith489
AU_password	No	A string of characters that enables the learning management system to authenticate the lesson	AU_PASSWORD = SpecsRGood
AICC_Data	Yes	Data elements from the content model, expressed as name–value pairs; when used with some commands, such as *GetParam* and *ExitAU*, the value side of this pair may be left blank. Because the data element name–value pairs are themselves part of a value, they must be completely URL encoded.	AICC_data=[core]%0D%0Alesson_location%3Dend%0D%0Alesson_status%3Dpass%0D%0Ascore%3D87%0D%0Atime%3D00:23:15[a]

Source: All data from AICC CMI Subcommittee (Hyde, J., chair), *CMI Guidelines for Interoperability*, Appendix A, revision 3.5. AICC, 2001, section A.5.1. Available at: http://www.aicc.org.

[a]This entry is all one line that has been word-wrapped to fit in the table. The URL encoding can be translated as follows: %0D, carriage return; %0A, line feed; %3D, equals sign (=).

Some typical request messages are shown below. Note that there are no spaces in any of these messages. Long lines have been wrapped and indented to fit on the page.

EXAMPLE 9.1 REQUESTING DATA FROM THE LMS

```
Command=getParam&Version=3.5&session_id=demo478&AICC_Data=
```

EXAMPLE 9.2 SENDING DATA TO THE LMS WITH PROPER URL ENCODING

```
command=PutParam&ver-
    sion=3.5&session_ID=demo478&AICC_data=[core]%0D%0Alesson_
    location%3Dend%0D%0Alesson_status%3Dpass%0D%0Ascore
    %3D87%0D%0Atime%3D00:23:15
```

In the example above, the following URL-encoded replacements for special characters have been made:

- %0D — the nonprinting "carriage return" character
- %0A — the nonprinting "line feed" character
- %3D — the "=" character

HACP Commands

Table 9.4 describes the three command values that an LMS is required to support. As in the API method, an LO is not required to use all the commands. A conformant LO must issue an *ExitAU* command, but the other two commands are optional. However, unless the LO sends at least one *PutParam,* the LMS has no data to record and may treat the session as having never occurred. The specification supports a number of other commands that are optional for both the LMS and the LO. See the specification document for details.

Response Messages

The format of response messages is rigorously defined so that an LO can extract the data it requires. The message takes the form of a series of name–value pairs. Each pair is separated by a combination of two special nonprinting characters, *carriage return* (CR) and *line feed* (LF), in that order. The message must conform to the following usage rules:

- Name–value pairs may appear in any order, except that *AICC_data,* if it appears, must be the last name–value pair.
- The value side of each pair must be plain text (not URL encoded). This is a major difference between request and response messages.
- Parameter names are not case sensitive, as illustrated by the examples in Table 9.5.

TABLE 9.4
HACP Commands

Command	Function	Usage Considerations
GetParam	Gets input data from the LMS	*GetParam* will typically be the first command a lesson sends. The lesson may use it again later in the lesson if desired. The response from the LMS will differ depending on which version of the AICC specification is in effect. In version 2.x, the response to *GetParam* will be the same throughout a session, regardless of data sent by *PutParam* commands. In version 3.x, the response will reflect changes made by the most recent *PutParam* command if one has been issued.
PutParam	Sends output parameter data to the LMS	Although the specifications do not require it, a lesson should issue this command at least once during a session. Using multiple *PutParam* commands to post data at key points in a lesson can help guard against loss of data if the connection is dropped. Each time that a *PutParam* is issued, new values for data elements overwrite their previous counterparts. Data elements that are not changed retain their existing values. At the completion of a session, the LMS will permanently save the session data as it stands after the final *PutParam*.
ExitAU	Ends a lesson session	Every lesson is required to issue an *ExitAU* command. Because it ends the communication session, it must be the last command in the lesson.

Note: HACP, Hypertext Transfer Protocol–Based Aviation Industry CBT Committee (AICC) Computer-Managed Instruction Protocol; LMS, learning management system. *Source:* All data from AICC CMI Subcommittee (Hyde, J., chair), *CMI Guidelines for Interoperability*, Appendix A, revision 3.5. AICC, 2001, section A.6.2. Available at: http://www.aicc.org.

- If an optional parameter is to be omitted, both its name and value must be omitted from the message.
- Extra white-space characters (Space, Tab) are allowed before and after the name, equal sign, and value in a name–value pair.
- The value portion of a name–value pair is defined as beginning with the first non-white-space character after the equal sign. Except in the case of the *AICC_data* parameter, the value ends with the last non-white-space character before the next CR–LF combination.
- The value of the *AICC_data* parameter, which contains embedded CR–LF combinations, ends with the last character in the message.

TABLE 9.5

HACP Response Message Parameters

Parameter Name	Required?	Value	Example[a]
error	Yes	A valid AICC error number. See the specification document for details.	error=1<CR–LF>
error_text	No	The AICC error description that corresponds to the error number. See the specification document for details.	Error_description = Invalid Command<CR–LF>
version	No	The version of the AICC specification being used.	VERSION = 3.0.2<CR–LF>
AICC_Data	Only in response to a *GetParam* command	Data elements from the content model, expressed as name–value pairs. All data elements supported by the LMS must be included, whether or not they currently have an associated value.	AICC_data= [core] student_id=ktsmith student_name=Smith, Kathryn T. output_file= credit=c lesson_location= lesson_status=n,a path= score= time=00:00:00 lesson_mode=s [core_vendor] [core_lesson]

Source: All data from AICC CMI Subcommittee (Hyde, J., chair), *CMI Guidelines for Interoperability*, Appendix A, revision 3.5. AICC, 2001, section A.5.2. Available at: http://www.aicc.org.

[a]<CR–LF> is used throughout the Example column to represent the combination of characters required to separate the name–value pairs, except in the bottommost entry, in which the <CR–LF> terminator for each line in this example has been omitted to save space.

A typical response message is shown below. The nonprinting CR–LF combination that separates each name–value pair is not shown in this example:

Table 9.5 describes the purpose and usage of the parameters that may be included in a response message, along with additional examples. The next section, "The Data Model," provides a more detailed explanation of the *AICC_data* parameter.[4]

```
Error = 0
error_text = successful
version = 2.0
aicc_data = [core]
Student_ID = B1781
Student_Name = Twist, Oliver
Credit = C
Lesson_Location =
Lesson_Mode = Sequential
Lesson_Status = Not Attempted
path =
Score =
Time = 00:00:00
[Core_Vendor]

[Core_Lesson]
```

The Data Model

The data model consists of a hierarchical set of data elements. These elements make up the value portion of the *AICC_data* parameter, where they appear as name–value pairs. Individual elements are organized into groups, the names of which appear inside square brackets in the *AICC_data* value. The elements within a given group may be listed in any order. Figure 9.5 illustrates the use of groups in an *AICC_data* value.

Element names are often referred to as *keywords* in the AICC specifications. They are not case sensitive, but they must be spelled exactly as specified and may not include any spaces.

Table 9.6 gives details about and examples of the data elements that a HACP-based LMS is required to support. It also includes two frequently used optional elements. For details on other optional elements, see the specification document.

Most of the key points about creating LOs that were listed in the discussion of the API data model also apply in relation to the HACP data model. They are summarized below for your convenience. Refer back to "The API Data Model" subsection in the "The API Data Exchange Method" section for further details:

- You can count on support for all required data elements.
- If you are developing for a single LMS, it may support optional data elements that you can use.
- If you are developing for multiple LMSs, you cannot rely on support for any optional elements, but you can program your LO to take advantage of them if they are available.
- Your LO must send data values that conform to the data model.

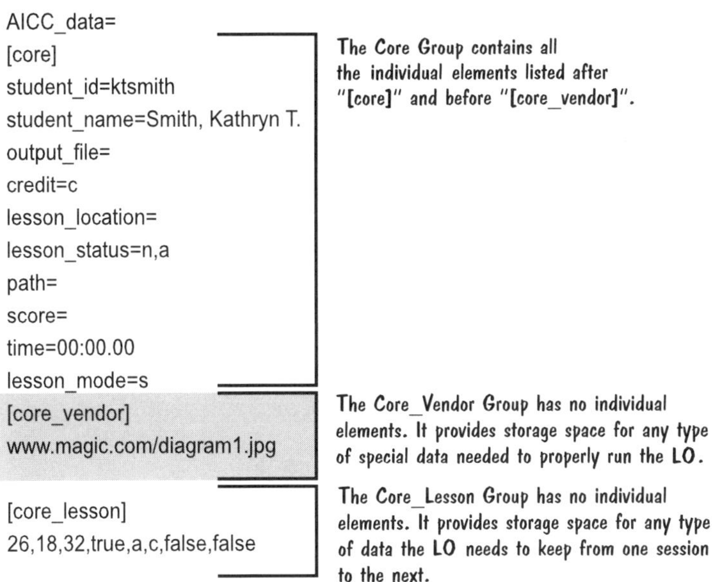

FIGURE 9.5
Use of groups in the AICC_data parameter.

- Your LO must be able to convert text values that should be interpreted as numbers (such as *score*) or other special data types as needed.
- Your LO is responsible for processing data elements in a meaningful way.

A HACP environment imposes two additional requirements on your LO:

- Your LO must be able to parse response messages to extract the data received from the LMS.
- Your LO must be able to build correctly formatted request messages, including URL encoding.

The HTML Communication Problem

As discussed in Chapter 4, HACP's biggest weakness is its inability to establish two-way communication with HTML plus JavaScript LOs. The problem results from the fact that HACP messages are sent by the LMS in plain text, not HTML. JavaScript, the programming component of standard Web pages, cannot extract data from input that does not have some HTML content.

Obviously, the best solution to this problem is to avoid it, either by using an authoring tool that produces plug-in or Java-based LOs or by using the API communication method. However, in many situations neither of these

TABLE 9.6
HACP Data Elements

Element Name (Keyword)	Description and Usage Notes	Examples[a]
[Core] Group		
student_id	A unique identifier for the learner, often the learner's log-in ID. *This value cannot be changed by the AU.*	student_id=jimmy76 <CR-LF>
student_name	The learner's full official name, in "last_name,first_name middle_initial" format. *This value cannot be changed by the AU.*	student_name=Johnson,Susan B.<CR-LF>
Credit	Indicates whether or not the learner is taking the AU for credit. This information could be used to control what the AU displays. For example, quizzes might be hidden in no-credit mode. This value is also used in determining lesson status. Allowed values: "credit" or "c"/"no-credit" or "n." Only the first character of the value is significant, and capitalization does not matter. *This value cannot be changed by the AU.*	Credit = c<CR-LF> credit=No-Credit<CR-LF>
lesson_location	The location at which the learner last exited the AU. It is intended for use as a bookmark. The AU can set a value when the learner exits and read it back in when the learner returns to the AU. The format and interpretation of the value is up to the AU.	Plain-text example: lesson_location=p24<CR-LF> URL-encoded equivalent: lesson_location%3Dp24%0D%0A
lesson_status	The learner's current status in the AU; when the learner enters the AU for the first time, the LMS initializes the value to "not attempted" or "n." Normally the AU determines the learner's status. Allowed values are as follows: • "passed" or "p" — Used when the AU produces a score • "failed" or "f" — Used when the AU produces a score • "completed" or "c" — Used when the AU is taken for credit but does not produce a score • "incomplete" or "i" — Used when the AU is taken for credit and the learner exits without completing it	Plain-text example: lesson_status=passed<CR-LF> URL-encoded equivalent: lesson_status%3Dpassed%0D%0A

	• "browsed" or "b" — Used in conjunction with the optional *lesson_mode* data element. If *lesson_mode* is implemented, the learner may have the option to browse an AU before officially beginning it. A status of "browsed" can be used to indicate that the learner has done so. • "not attempted" — Used only by the LMS as the initial status value In addition to the values shown above, a status may include a second, flag value separated from the main status by a comma. Two sets of flags are available, one to be set by the LMS and the other by the AU. Flag values set by the LMS are the following: • "ab initio" or "a" — The learner has never before entered the AU. • "resume" or "r" — The learner is reentering the AU from a suspended (partially completed) state. This value is set only if the AU set a *suspend* flag when it last exited. Flag values set by the AU are the following: • "time-out" or "t" — Indicates that too much time elapsed in the session, as determined by the AU • "suspend" or "s" — Indicates that the learner exited the AU with the intent to complete it later; the LMS resets the flag to "resume" when the learner reenters the AU. • "logout" or "l" — Tells the LMS to automatically log the learner out of the course; otherwise, when learners complete an AU, they are returned to the course menu or sent directly to the next AU in the course. Setting the "logout" flag allows the learner to log out of the course from within the AU. For all status and flag values, only the first letter is significant, and capitalization does not matter.	Example using a flag: lesson_status=n,a
Path	Parameter used for file-based LMS systems. It is not applicable to Web-based LMSs and will not contain a value. However, its name will be included in the complete *AICC_data* string sent in response to a *GetParam* command. *This value cannot be changed by the AU.*	N/A

(*continued*)

TABLE 9.6 (continued)

HACP Data Elements

Element Name (Keyword)	Description and Usage Notes	Examples[a]
score	An indication of the learner's performance in the AU; score is computed by the AU and can be based on any system that makes sense to the AU designer. In versions 2.x of the specifications, score must be a single integer number. However, in versions 3.x, it can be a single decimal (floating-point) number, or it can be followed by one or two optional values, a maximum and a minimum possible score in that order, separated by commas. The AU should not report a score until the learner has completed all scored interactions. If the LMS implements the optional *mastery_score* element, reporting a partial score or setting the score to "0" when there is no score to be reported may cause the LMS to erroneously assign a status of "failed" to the learner.	Plain-text version 2.x example: score=70<CR-LF> URL-encoded equivalent: score%3D70%0D%0A Plain-text version 3.x example: score=70,120,0<CR-LF> URL-encoded equivalent: score%3D70,120,0%0D%0A
time	The nature of this value depends on whether it is being sent by the LMS or the AU. When the LMS sends a time in response to a *GetParam*, it represents the accumulated time of all the learner's sessions in the AU. When the AU posts a time in a *PutParam*, it represents the elapsed time spent by the learner in the current AU session. The required time format, with lowercase letters indicating optional digits, is *HH:MM:SS* for specification versions 2.x and *hhHH:MM:SS.s* for versions 3.x.	Plain-text example: time=00:47:32<CR-LF> URL-encoded example: time%3D00%3A47%3A32%0D%0A

lesson_mode (optional element)	The value of *lesson_mode* indicates the AU behavior the learner desires after launch. An LMS that supports this element may include one of the following modes in its response string: • "browse" or "b" — The learner wants to preview the content without taking it for a grade or completion credit. The AU may return a *lesson_status* of "browsed" to the LMS. Any other score or status information sent by the AU should be ignored. • "normal" or "n" The learner wants to take the AU for a grade or completion credit. This is the default mode, equivalent to the standard behavior of the AU if *lesson_mode* is not supported or has not been set. • "review" or "r" The learner has already received a grade or completion credit for the AU and wishes to review the content. The AU can use the value of *lesson_mode* to set special behaviors. For example, tests or quizzes might be hidden in browse mode. For all *lesson_mode* values, only the first letter is significant, and capitalization does not matter. This value cannot be changed by the AU.	lesson_mode=b lesson_mode=Review
[Core_Lesson] Group		
	This group, which does not contain any individual data elements, provides a storage place for data generated within an AU session that will be needed when the learner returns to the AU later. It can hold up to 4096 characters of ASCII text that can be read back in by the AU the next time it is launched. A few possible uses are: • Recording the responses a learner makes to specific interactions so that they can be already filled in if the learner revisits them in a subsequent session. • In an AU with flexible navigation, recording which sections the learner has visited so that they can be checked off on a menu. • Recording the location of a file that was dynamically generated from within the AU. This could be used in the event that the AU needs to store more than 4096 characters of information.	(any developer-defined string)

(*continued*)

TABLE 9.6 (continued)

HACP Data Elements

Element Name (Keyword)	Description and Usage Notes	Examples[a]
[Core_Vendor] Group		
	This group, which does not contain any individual data elements, provides a storage place for special data required every time that an AU is launched. Without this data, the AU may not run correctly. This data (up to 4096 ASCII characters) is included in the AU definition that is maintained in the LMS. Possible uses include the following: • The location of an external file from which frequently updated content can be loaded into the AU at run time. • A contact e-mail address or phone number that is different for each organization that uses the AU. • The locations of external graphics files (such as logos) that allow each company to customize the appearance of the AU. *This value cannot be changed by the AU.*	(any developer-defined string)
[Student_Data] Group[b]		
mastery_score (optional element)	A minimum passing score that is set in the LMS. If a mastery score exists, the LMS will compare any score sent by the AU to the mastery score and set AU's status accordingly. Any status set independently by the AU is ignored. Therefore, it is useful for the AU to use the value of *mastery_score*, if it exists, to calculate status internally and provide feedback to the learner. If there is no mastery score, the AU is responsible for setting the status. *This value cannot be changed by the AU.*	mastery_score=50 Mastery_Score=80

Source: All data from AICC CMI Subcommittee (Hyde, J., chair), *CMI Guidelines for Interoperability*, revision 3.5. AICC, 2001, sections 5.1 and 5.2. Available at: http://www.aicc.org.

[a]Values that can be changed by the AU via a *PutParam* command are shown in both plain text and URL encoding.

[b]This is an optional group containing several data elements, only one of which we describe here. See the specification for explanations of the other elements in the group.

solutions is an option. If you must develop HTML content for a HACP interface, here are some things to watch out for:

- You cannot get a value for *lesson_location*, so there is no way to automatically return a learner to a previous exit point in the LO. The best alternatives are to keep individual LOs quite short or provide flexible navigation within the LO.
- You cannot customize the learning experience based on *lesson_status* or *credit*. Be sure the content of your LO is appropriate for all learners under all circumstances.
- *Mastery_score*, which is among the most frequently implemented optional AICC data elements, can prevent you from providing accurate pass–fail feedback to the learner. If a mastery score is set in the LMS, the LMS will use it to calculate the learner's status, overriding any status that is calculated in the LO itself. With two-way communication, this is not a problem because the *mastery_score* value is sent in response to a *getparam* request and can be used for the LO's calculations. When the LO cannot access this value, however, the learner could be in for a surprise. If it is possible to ensure that the LMS administrator does not set a mastery score or sets the same score as your LO uses, you may be able to safely provide pass–fail feedback. However, if you do not have this level of control over LMS administration, it may be better to avoid giving such feedback.

Common Development Problems and Solutions

In HACP, How Do I Know What the *time* Data Element Refers To?

As described in Table 9.6, the HACP data model uses the same data element name, *time*, to represent both the elapsed time for a given LO session and the total time a learner has spent working on an LO, which may include several sessions. Obviously this can be rather confusing. The API data model uses two separate data elements, *cmi.core.session_time* and *cmi.core.total_time*, which clarifies things considerably.

When using HACP, the key thing to remember is that the LMS knows about prior sessions and the LO may not. So, when the LMS sends a time to the LO, it includes all prior sessions; in other words, it is a total time. The LO, on the other hand, is expected to account for the current session only. So the time it should send back to the LMS is the elapsed time for that session. The following list of "do's and don'ts" should help you keep track of time in your LO.

- DON'T save the value for *time* that the LMS sends unless your LO will actually make use of it.
- DO use separate local variables in your LO for the total time and the session time, assuming you need the total time at all. Use variable names that make the meaning of the values clear.
- DO keep track of the entire elapsed time for each session. Start the timer as soon as the LO is launched, and calculate the elapsed time when the learner exits.
- DO send back only the time spent in the current session. DON'T add in the time you received from the LMS.

How Do I Send and Receive Time Values?

Another time-related source of confusion is the required format for time values. As noted in the tables above, the basic format is HH:MM:SS. All the digits in this format are required and must be padded with leading zeros where necessary. Do not try to get away with sending the LMS a value in seconds. If your authoring tool does not automatically track time in hours, minutes, and seconds, you will have to find or program a routine to make the conversion. Note that the most recent specification versions have added some optional digits to allow for extremely long time periods and extremely precise tracking.

How Do I Calculate Lesson Status?

Determining the learner's lesson (LO) status is probably the single most complicated tracking task. In both the HACP and API data models there are six possible statuses plus several optional entry and exit values or flags to further confuse the issue. Worse yet, status is impacted by the values of other data elements. The following steps will help guide you through the muddle. You may want to send the status value to the LMS each time it changes. This provides protection in case of a dropped connection, but at the expense of creating more traffic on the network. Note that this sequence can be used with the data models for both the API and HACP. When naming a data element, we list both versions in the following format: *HACP name/API name.*

1. Find out whether your target LMS(s) support the optional *lesson_mode/cmi.core.lesson_mode* data element.
2. Find out whether your target LMS(s) support the optional *mastery_score/cmi.core.mastery_score* data element.
3. Decide whether your LO will assign a "pass" or "fail" upon completion or whether the LO will simply be recorded as completed. Also decide what criteria will be used to determine when the learner has completed the LO and whether the learner has passed or failed.

4. As soon as the LO starts, get and save the values for the following data elements from the LMS:
   - *credit/cmi.core.credit*
   - *lesson_mode/cmi.core.lesson_mode* (if applicable)
   - *mastery_score/cmi.core.mastery_score* (if applicable)
5. If *lesson_mode / cmi.core.lesson_mode* is supported, check for a value of "browse" or "b." Browse mode gives the learner an opportunity to preview the LO without officially "taking" it. Set *lesson_status/cmi.core.lesson_status* to "browsed." Skip the remaining steps; a status of "browsed" will not change during the session.
6. If the value of *credit/cmi.core.credit* is "no-credit" or "n," skip the remaining steps. Status should not be changed in no-credit mode.
7. If the learner is taking the LO for credit, set *lesson_status/cmi.core.lesson_status* to "incomplete" as soon as the learner officially starts the LO. You may want to defer changing the status until the learner has actually begun to view instructional content. The status should not change again until the learner meets the completion criteria.

The remaining steps are used to set the status after the learner meets the criteria for completion.

8. If the LO is not designed to report a pass–fail, set *lesson_status/cmi.core.lesson_status* to "completed."
9. If the LO is designed to report a pass–fail, status will depend on the specific criteria for passing and whether or not there is a mastery score set in the LMS:
   - If the criteria for passing depend on something other than a numeric score, set *lesson_status/cmi.core.lesson_status* to "pass" or "fail" as appropriate. Avoid setting *score/cmi.core.score.raw* to a numeric value (including "0") in case a mastery score has been set in the LMS.
   - If *mastery_score/cmi.student_data.mastery_score* exists and contains a numeric value, treat it as the minimum passing score and set *lesson_status/cmi.core.lesson_status* accordingly. Although the LMS will set the final status itself when there is a mastery score, it is usually good form to have the LO calculate it so that it can be reported to the learner.
   - If *mastery_score/cmi.student_data.mastery_score* does not exist or contains an empty string, set *lesson_status/cmi.core.lesson_status* based on the LO's internal passing score.

I Set *lesson_status/cmi.core.lesson_status* to "Incomplete," but the LMS Shows a Status of "Failed." Why?

This typically occurs when a mastery score is set in the LMS. If the LO sends back a partial score or a score of 0, the LMS will compare that score with the mastery score and override the status set by the LO. For this reason, do not send a numeric score until the student has completed the LO.

If you need to keep track of a partial score, use the *[Core_Lesson]* (HACP) or *cmi.suspend_data* (API) data element to store the value and read it back when the LO is resumed.

What If a Learner Launches an LO That She's Already Passed?

There are several possible outcomes when a learner returns to a previously completed LO.

- The learner essentially starts from scratch, with the LO overwriting previous results.
- The learner reviews the LO with no impact on previous results.
- The LO selectively overwrites previous results, perhaps replacing the score only if it is higher than on the previous attempt.

Any of these outcomes may be appropriate under certain circumstances.

The first option occurs automatically if the LO proceeds without considering existing status. Some LMSs handle the second option by providing a special review mode that does not record new results. You can also create internal LO logic to handle the second and third options. Have the LO check for *lesson_status* = "passed" immediately. For the second option, have the LO send the original status and score values it received from the LMS, rather than setting new ones. For the third option, have the LO send either the old or new score, whichever is higher.

The one thing not to do in this situation is fail to send back any values for score and status. The specifications are unclear as to how the LMS should respond under these circumstances, so the result is unpredictable. It is much better to control the situation yourself.

How Do I Calculate and Report the LO Score?

The first thing to understand about scoring LOs is that a scored LO must produce and report a single overall score. This doesn't mean that you can't have quizzes or other scored interactions scattered throughout the LO and that such interactions can't be weighted differently. If you do this, however, you must provide the programming logic that allows the LO to calculate a final summary score.

The process of reporting the score calculated for an LO seems straightforward enough, but the specifications have a few quirks. The acceptable values

TABLE 9.7

Acceptable Score Values by Specification and Version

Specifications	Data Element Names	Acceptable Values
AICC version 2.x (HACP only)	*score*	Any integer number from -32,768 to +32,767[a]
AICC version 3.x, SCORM version 1.1 (HACP and API)	*score, cmi.core.score.raw*	Any decimal number[b]
SCORM version 1.2	*cmi.core.score.raw*	A normalized decimal number between 0 and 100[c]

[a]*Source:* From AICC CMI Subcommittee (Hyde, J., chair), *CMI Guidelines for Interoperability*, revision 2.2. AICC, 1998, p. 73. Available at: http://www.aicc.org.

[b]*Source:* From AICC CMI Subcommittee (Hyde, J., chair), *CMI Guidelines for Interoperability*, revision 3.5. AICC, 2001, p. 75. Available at: http://www.aicc.org.

[c]*Source:* Dodds, P., Ed., *Sharable Content Object Reference Model (SCORM): The SCORM Content Aggregation Model*, version 1.2. Advanced Distributed Learning, 2001, pp. 3-27–3-28. Available at: http://www.adlnet.org.

for the *score/cmi.core.score.raw* data element differ between specifications and versions. Table 9.7 summarizes the requirements.

Notice in particular the change between versions of the SCORM. The SCORM committee seems to be walking a fine line between allowing freedom for LO designers and tracking in a format that is readily understood without intimate knowledge of the LO. Requiring the score to be a normalized number in the 0–100 range (essentially a percentage) significantly restricts the former but ensures the latter. The requirement may create confusion, however, because the name of the data element includes *raw,* which implies a non-normalized score.

AICC version 3.x and both versions of the SCORM offer an alternative method of clarifying the scoring scale by allowing the maximum and minimum scores to be defined. In the HACP model, these scores are added to the score data element in the format *score=raw,max,min.* You can provide one or both of these extended values, as appropriate for your LO's scoring system. Conforming LMSs are required to support these values. All versions of the API model include two optional data elements, *cmi.core.score.max* and *cmi.core.score.min.* If your LMS supports them, you can use them in the same way as the HACP extended values. In the SCORM 1.2, these optional values seem redundant and may not even be usable. They are also defined as normalized numbers between 0 and 100, so they cannot be used to specify a true maximum or minimum score that falls outside this range.

What If My LO Generates Multiple Scores?

The data models contain only one required score element, so you cannot count on the ability to track scores for subsections of your LO. However, some LMSs support optional data elements for tracking scores by objective. If you plan to use objectives-based tracking, see the specification documents for details. Keep in mind, though, that only the summary score for the LO is used in determining the value of *lesson_status / cmi.core.lesson_status.*

How Do I Parse and Compose HACP Messages?

Some authoring tools, including Macromedia Authorware, Macromedia Dreamweaver with the CourseBuilder extension, and Click2Learn ToolBook, will handle all or part of this task for you. Check the documentation for your authoring product to see what it has available and how to use it.

If you are not using such an authoring tool, or you are having problems and need to troubleshoot the messages, you will need good programming skills to create the necessary routines. The Web site for this book, http://www.elearning-standards.com, provides programming suggestions and sample routines that you can adapt to your specific circumstances.

Standards-Friendly Authoring Tools for Interoperability

Several commercial authoring packages and course generation systems provide tools that simplify the creation of lessons that use standards-based data tracking. The following are among the best:

- Macromedia Authorware — Authorware is the most comprehensive and flexible standards-based authoring tool. It provides built-in communication functions that can be used with all required and optional data elements. It also offers automated data tracking that can be used with a standards-based LMS. At the same time it allows tremendous flexibility for building customized routines. Version 6.0 is certified as an authoring tool by the AICC. Authorware's only major disadvantage is that it requires learners to download and install a browser plug-in. See http://www.macromedia.com for product information on Authorware, Dreamweaver, and Flash.
- Click2Learn Toolbook Instructor — Toolbook Instructor has a Web-packaging option that automatically produces lesson files with HACP–based tracking. All the author needs to do is assign values to a specified set of variables that are used by the packaging program. No plug-in is required to run these lessons. However, some of Toolbook's advanced authoring features cannot be used in Web-packaged lessons, and not all optional data elements are available

for use. Version 7.2 is certified as a course generation tool by the AICC. See http://www.click2learn.com for product information.

- Macromedia Dreamweaver with the CourseBuilder extension — Dreamweaver is a Web-page development tool. CourseBuilder is a free download file from the Macromedia Exchange that adds courseware development features, including quiz questions and basic AICC tracking capabilities. The quiz samples that come with CourseBuilder are somewhat challenging to adapt, but far easier than building the tracking code from scratch. Because it produces native HTML plus JavaScript files, the lessons it produces cannot receive incoming data from a HACP LMS.
- SCORM Runtime Wrapper extensions for Macromedia Dreamweaver and Flash — Like CourseBuilder, these are available as free downloads from Macromedia. They provide templates that include basic Sharable Content Object Reference Model functionality for Dreamweaver and Flash, respectively. The Flash version is quite minimal and is designed primarily as a model for the developer to expand on.

Conclusion

In this chapter, we have covered standards-based data tracking in considerable detail. You should now be prepared to use such tracking in the LOs that you create. Ultimately, you will still need to tackle the standards documents themselves, but you should be much better prepared to search them and to understand the material they present.

The standardization of data tracking is the foundation of interoperability. In the next chapter, we will look in detail at developing meta-data for all types of LOs so that they can be readily shared.

References

1. AICC CMI Subcommittee (Hyde, J., chair), *CMI Guidelines for Interoperability*, Appendix B, revision 3.5. AICC, 2001, section B.3. Available at: http://www.aicc.org.
2. AICC CMI Subcommittee (Hyde, J., chair), *CMI Guidelines for Interoperability*, Appendix B, revision 3.5. AICC, 2001, section B.2.2. Available at: http://www.aicc.org.
3. AICC CMI Subcommittee (Hyde, J., chair), *CMI Guidelines for Interoperability*, Appendix A, revision 3.5. AICC, 2001, section A.4.0. Available at: http://www.aicc.org.

4. AICC CMI Subcommittee (Hyde, J., chair), *CMI Guidelines for Interoperability*, Appendix A, revision 3.5. AICC, 2001, sections A.5.0 and A.6.0. Available at: http://www.aicc.org.

10

A Guide to Creating Meta-Data Files

Introduction

This chapter helps prepare you to create your own meta-data files for LOs and structures. It builds on the concepts introduced in Chapter 5. As in that chapter, the first several pages are devoted to a more detailed look at XML. The XML concepts explained here will be needed to fully understand the meta-data–specific portion of the chapter, as well as the material in the remaining chapters.

The later part of this chapter covers the ADL SCORM specification for meta-data in considerable detail. It is not a substitute for the actual SCORM and IMS specifications, but it should prepare you to interpret and edit many of the elements in existing meta-data examples and to supply appropriate data when using an automated meta-data–generating tool.

XML Concepts and Terminology

In this section, we take a closer look at XML. This is not an exhaustive lesson on how to write XML. There are plenty of good books and resources on the Internet that can teach you to write it by hand if you should need to do so. More importantly, there are so many XML editing and checking tools available that you should not have to resort to hand coding. However, you should have a fair understanding of how XML works in order to read and implement the specifications and troubleshoot your documents.

Elements and Attributes

The two main components of XML are the *element* and the *attribute,* as illustrated in Figure 10.1.

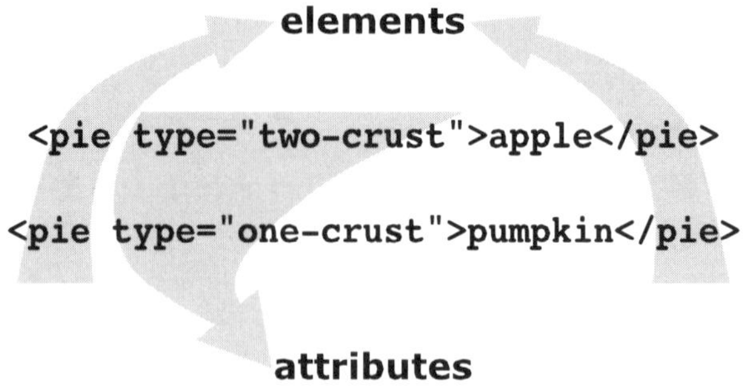

elements

```
<pie type="two-crust">apple</pie>

<pie type="one-crust">pumpkin</pie>
```

attributes

FIGURE 10.1
XML elements and attributes.

- An element is a holder for data. It can contain either the data itself or one or more nested elements. Some elements may contain both data and nested elements. As we have seen previously, elements are set off in the XML documents by pairs of named tags.
- An attribute provides additional information that qualifies or modifies the data in an element. The relationship between elements and attributes is similar to that between nouns and adjectives.

Consider the following example taken from a SCORM meta-data document.

```
<location type="URI">http://www.courses.com/Course01/
SCO_01.htm</location>
```

This example contains one element set off by the *<location>* and *</location>* tags. Typical element names give some idea of what kind of information they contain, in this case some kind of location. *Location* is a very broad term, however, so you would need to see the example in context to really know what it signifies. This particular element contains the location at which you can access the actual SCO content file described by the meta-data.

The SCORM specification allows for two different ways of expressing the location of a content file. The *<location>* element can contain either an address on the Internet or a simple text description of where the file can be found. The attribute *type* is used to indicate which kind of location data is being provided. In this example, *type="URI"* indicates that the location element contains an Internet address. If the location type were a text description, the element might look like the following:

```
<location type="text">4th floor CD storage, Volume 8</
location>
```

The following rules govern the use of elements and attributes in XML:

- Element and attribute names may not include any embedded spaces. An element or attribute could be named *size* or *file_size,* but not *file size.*
- Tags are element names surrounded by pointed brackets. They are used in pairs that enclose the data or other elements contained in an element. The closing tag of a pair includes a "/" character before the element name.
- Attributes are expressed as name–value pairs (i.e., *attribute_name="attribute_value"* or *type="text"*). They are placed directly after the element name inside an opening tag. The value part of an attribute is always surrounded by quotation marks.
- More than one attribute may be included in a given tag.

The Well-Formed Document

XML offers almost unlimited latitude in terms of naming elements and defining what they mean and how they work together. The price of this freedom, however, is a very rigid set of rules for how a document must be structured. An XML document that conforms to the rules is called a *well-formed document*. A document that is not well formed will be rejected by almost any software that reads or parses XML (see Figure 10.2).

FIGURE 10.2
Is your document well formed?

Although the rules for well formedness are strictly enforced, most of them are simple to understand. The following are some of the restrictions to which a well-formed document must conform:

- The document must have exactly one top-level element that contains all other elements.
- Every opening tag must have a corresponding closing tag. If an element is empty, the opening and closing tags may be combined using the special format *<empty_tag_name />*.
- All elements must be correctly nested, with no overlapping of their closing tags.
- Element names may contain only letters, numbers, hyphens, periods, and underscores.
- The first character in an element name must be either a letter or an underscore.
- Characters that are used for markup (such as "<" and ">") cannot be used in content. Special replacements are available for them. For example, the element *<equation> x < 3 </equation>* would not be legal in a well-formed document because an XML parser would confuse the "less-than" character in the equation with the beginning of a new tag. The "<" can be replaced with the special combination "<" — *<equation> x < 3 </equation>*. This allows the equation to be understood correctly without confusing the parser.

Data Types and Vocabularies

It is often necessary for specifications to limit what kind of data can be included in an element or used as an attribute value. For example, an element named *starting_time* should probably contain data that a computer application can interpret as a time. If, instead, it contained a person's name or a color, the application would not be able to perform operations such as calculating an elapsed time.

The World Wide Web Consortium (W3C) has defined a considerable number of general-purpose data types. These include *string, integer, ID, language, time,* and *date.* Individual groups are free to define additional data types to meet their own needs, and the IMS and ADL have defined many of them for use in their specifications.

Some data types, such as *string, integer,* or *time,* can be defined by general rules for the values that can be assigned to them. However, other data types are defined by a set of discrete values. The values for the W3C-defined *language* data type, for example, must be drawn from a list of two- and three-letter language codes specified by the ISO.

A vocabulary is a set of values that a data element or attribute can take on (see Figure 10.3). The ISO list of language codes is one such vocabulary.

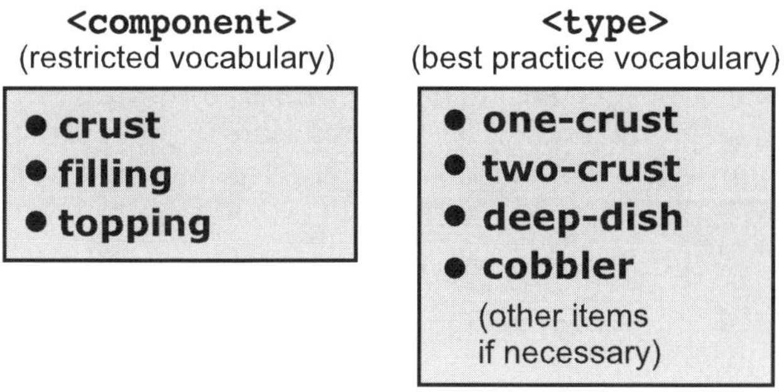

<component>
(restricted vocabulary)

- **crust**
- **filling**
- **topping**

<type>
(best practice vocabulary)

- **one-crust**
- **two-crust**
- **deep-dish**
- **cobbler**

(other items
if necessary)

FIGURE 10.3
Vocabularies in XML.

Meta-data specifications make particularly extensive use of vocabularies. A vocabulary may be restricted to the listed values, or it may be what is called a best-practice vocabulary that can accommodate additional values when necessary.

Namespaces

One issue that can arise in using XML is that the same element name can be used in different documents to mean entirely different things. Consider how an element named *<bulb>* would likely be used to describe the inventory of a nursery versus that of a lighting supply store. If the two stores merged as parts of a new home-improvement store, attempting to integrate their XML inventory documents would result in a naming conflict, as illustrated in Figure 10.4. To prevent such conflicts, XML uses the concept of *namespaces.* A namespace is a way of indicating the context from which an element is drawn.

A namespace is typically declared as an attribute of the top-level element in an XML document using the following format: *xmlns:prefix="location."* The prefix can be any desired string of characters. The location is presented

FIGURE 10.4
A naming conflict: <bulb>.

in the form of an Internet address. However, it is used only as an identifier; it does not have to be a valid URI that could be accessed on the Internet. Once a namespace is declared, elements or attributes from the namespace are used in the form *prefix:elementname.* Here is an example of using namespaces in the inventory document for our hypothetical home improvement store.

```
<inventory xmlns:nur="www.sunshinenursery.com/
inventory" xmlns:lgt="lightupyourlife.com/inventory">
    . . . . .
    <nur:bulb>daffodil</nur:bulb>
    . . . . .
    <lgt:bulb>75 watt incandescent</lgt:bulb>
    . . . . .
</inventory>
```

Meta-data and other e-learning XML documents typically declare two or three namespaces. See the examples available on the ADL and IMS Web sites.

Document Type Definitions and Schema — Reference Models for XML Documents

As you can imagine, XML documents can be very complicated. To ensure that a document meets all the necessary requirements for elements, attributes, data types, vocabularies, and so on, a reference model document can be used.

The document type definition (DTD) defines the elements, attributes, and certain other characteristics for XML documents. DTD documents have their own language and are saved with the extension *.dtd.* Early versions of the e-learning specifications were based on DTDs. However, the current versions have abandoned DTDs in favor of XML Schema.

XML Schema define and control the structure of XML documents. XML Schema documents use the extension *.xsd.* However, they are actually written in XML. A document that is based on an XML Schema must declare the schema in a manner similar to a namespace declaration. The format for the declaration is *xsi:schemaLocation=" [location(s)]".* Locations are Internet addresses or file paths. Unlike the locations for namespaces, those for schemas must be valid locations at which the schema documents can be found. More than one location can be specified, separated by spaces. An XML Schema document is available for each of the current specifications that uses an XML binding. See the examples available on the ADL and IMS Web sites.

The SCORM Meta-Data Information Model

The remainder of this chapter deals with the SCORM Meta-Data Information Model. We begin with an extended example of meta-data, followed by a discussion of the individual parts that make up the meta-data specification.

An Annotated Example — Meta-Data for a SCO

The following meta-data document is an expansion of the simplified example from Chapter 5. It includes all the required elements for a SCO as well as some of the more interesting optional elements.

Annotations have been inserted throughout the XML document. Appendix A, Listing 10.1 shows the uninterrupted meta-data as it would appear in a real-world application. As mentioned previously, the line numbers are included for clarity only and are not part of the actual XML.

```
001 <?xml version="1.0" encoding="UTF-8"?>
002 <lom xmlns="http://www.imsglobal.org/xsd
    imsmd_v1p2" xmlns:xsi="http://www.w3.org/2001/
    XMLSchema-instance"
003 xsi:schemaLocation="http://www.imsglobal.org/xsd/
    imsmd_v1p2 imsmd_v1p2p2.xsd">
```

Line 001 is an XML version declaration required at the beginning of all complete XML documents. The *<lom>* element that follows in line 002 is almost lost among the namespace and schema declarations that accompany it. It is the root element of the XML and contains everything else.

There are two namespace declarations, one to the IMS Learning Object Meta-Data (LOM) specification and the other to the W3C's XML Schema specification. The *xsi:* prefix is used immediately to declare *schemaLocation,* the Web location of the meta-data schema on the IMS site.

```
004     <general>
005         <title>
006             <langstring>Pie Crust Techniques
    </langstring>
007         </title>
```

The *<general>* section begins with the *<title>* element. The *<langstring>* tag in line 006 indicates a special data type defined in the specification. It is used to provide the option of presenting textual information in more than one language. See the "Special Data Types" section later in this chapter for more details.

```
008          <catalogentry>
009               <catalog>Catalog of Culinary Art
     Courses</catalog>
010               <entry>
011                    <langstring>p-006</langstring>
012               </entry>
013          </catalogentry>
014          <language>en-US</language>
```

The *<catalogentry>* (lines 008–013) and *<language>* (line 014) elements are part of the *<general>* category. *<language>* is an optional element that indicates the main human language used in the SCO. It must be expressed using the standard two- and three-letter language codes with optional country modifiers specified by the ISO (in *ISO 639* and *ISO 3166*).

```
015          <description>
016               <langstring>How to make a pie crust
     </langstring>
017          </description>
018          <keyword>
019               <langstring>pie</langstring>
020          </keyword>
021          <keyword>
022               <langstring>baking</langstring>
023          </keyword>
```

The <general> category continues with *<description>* and *<keyword>* elements. Keywords (lines 018–023) are used by catalog searches. It is a good idea to include several of them to maximize the chances of your SCO being found.

```
024          <aggregationlevel>
025               <source>
026                    <langstring xml:lang=
     "x-none">LOMv1.0</langstring>
027               </source>
028               <value>
029                    <langstring xml:lang=
     "x-none">2</langstring>
030               </value>
031          </aggregationlevel>
032     </general>
```

<aggregationlevel> completes the *<general>* category in this example. It is an optional element that indicates the level of granularity of the learning component. There is a defined vocabulary for *<aggregationlevel>* that contains the values "1," "2," "3," and "4." The value "2" used in line 029 of the example is defined in the specification as representing "a collection of atoms, e.g., an HTML document with some embedded pictures or a lesson."

<aggregationlevel> is an example of a special data type required for elements that draw their content from defined vocabularies. This data type contains two subelements. *<source>* (lines 025–027) contains a reference to the source document for the vocabulary list. *<value>* (lines 028–030) contains the actual term selected from the referenced list. For more details, see "Vocabulary Type" in the "Special Data Types" section later in this chapter.

```
033        <lifecycle>
034            <version>
035                <langstring>2.0</langstring>
036            </version>
037            <status>
038                <source>
039                    <langstring xml:lang="x-none">
    LOMv1.0</langstring>
040                </source>
041                <value>
042                    <langstring xml:lang="x-none">
    Final</langstring>
043                </value>
044            </status>
```

As we saw in Chapter 5, the <lifecycle> category provides information about the SCO's history and current state of development. *<status>* (lines 037–044) is another vocabulary element. The vocabulary is defined as "Draft," "Final," "Revised," and "Unused." It indicates the development status of the SCO. Notice the implication here: meta-data should be updated every time that a learning component is revised.

```
045            <contribute>
046                <role>
047                    <source>
048                        <langstring xml:lang=
    "x-none">LOMv1.0</langstring>
049                    </source>
050                    <value>
051                        <langstring xml:lang=
    "x-none">Author</langstring>
052                    </value>
053                </role>
```

<contribute> is an optional *<lifecycle>* element that identifies the people or organizations involved in creating and maintaining the SCO. Each person or organization who played a significant role in the current state of the learning component may be represented by a separate *<contribute>* element.

The *<role>* element (lines 46–53) describes the type of contribution made by this particular contributor. Its vocabulary includes such items as "Author," "Publisher," "Graphical Designer," and "Instructional Designer."

It is a best-practice vocabulary, meaning that if you cannot find an appropriate term on the list, you can use one of your own choosing.

```
054              <centity>
055                   <vcard>
056                        begin:vcard
057                        fn:Frank Baker
058                        end:vcard
059                   </vcard>
060              </centity>
```

The *<centity>* element provides identifying information about the contributor. It takes the form of a vCard, which is an electronic analogue to a business card. The vCard format is not yet rigorously defined by the specifications. Our example includes only the full name (*fn*) of the person (line 057), but a vCard can contain a variety of identification and contact information.

```
061              <date>
062                   <datetime>2002-01-27</datetime>
063              </date>
064         </contribute>
065    </lifecycle>
```

The *<date>* element represents the date of the contribution. The *<datetime>* tag in line 062 indicates that the date is expressed using the ISO 8601 standard. Date elements are expressed using a special data type that is defined in the specification. See the "Special Data Types" section below for more information.

```
066    <metametadata>
067         <metadatascheme>ADL SCORM 1.2
   </metadatascheme>
068    </metametadata>
```

The *<metametadata>* category contains meta-data about the meta-data document itself. It can include *<catalogentry>*, *<contribute>*, and *<language>* elements that are treated in the same manner as those for the learning component. This example includes only the required *<metadatascheme>* element, which indicates the specification on which the meta-data document is based.

```
069    <technical>
070         <format>text/HTML</format>
071         <size>130671</size>
072         <location type="URI">pie101.htm</location>
```

The *<technical>* category contains the technical requirements and characteristics of the learning component. In line 070, *<format>* describes the technical data type or types used in the learning component, and in doing so implies the software needed to access it. The *<size>* of the resource in line 071 is given in bytes. The *<location>* element in line 072 is typically the local or Web address at which the primary physical file of the learning component is located. However, a text description of the location can be used instead by changing the *type* attribute's value to "TEXT."

```
073            <requirement>
074                <type>
075                    <source>
076                        <langstring xml:lang="x-none">
    LOMv1.0</langstring>
077                    </source>
078                    <value>
079                        <langstring xml:lang="x-none">
    Operating System</langstring>
080                    </value>
081                </type>
082                <name>
083                    <source>
084                        <langstring xml:lang="x-none">
    LOMv1.0</langstring>
085                    </source>
086                    <value>
087                        <langstring xml:lang="x-none">
    MS-Windows</langstring>
088                    </value>
089                </name>
090                <minimumversion>95</minimumversion>
091            </requirement>
092        </technical>
```

The *<requirement>* element can be used to specify the software, hardware, or other technologies required to use the learning component. The current specification focuses on operating system and browser requirements and provides best-practice vocabularies for specifying them. However, other requirements such as browser plug-ins could be included here as well.

```
093        <educational>
094            <learningresourcetype>
095                <source>
096                    <langstring xml:lang="x-none">
    LOMv1.0</langstring>
097                </source>
098                <value>
099                    <langstring xml:lang="x-none">
    Narrative Text</langstring>
100                </value>
101            </learningresourcetype>
```

<educational> is an optional category that contains elements describing various pedagogical characteristics of the learning component. There are a number of available subelements besides the two used in this example.

The *<learningresourcetype>* element (lines 094–101) describes the general nature of the resource. Its best-practice vocabulary includes such types as "Exercise," "Simulation," "Figure," "Exam," and "Experiment." More than one type can be listed, with the most dominant first. For example, if the bulk of the learning component is just reading material, but it also includes a small simulation activity, a *<learningresourcetype>* element containing "Narrative Text" might be followed by one containing "Simulation."

```
102            <interactivitylevel>
103                <source>
104                        <langstring xml:lang="x-none">
    LOMv1.0</langstring>
105                </source>
106                <value>
107                    <langstring xml:lang="x-none">
    medium</langstring>
108                </value>
109            </interactivitylevel>
110        </educational>
```

The *<interactivitylevel>* element describes the degree of interaction between the learner and the learning component. The vocabulary for this element contains five levels ranging from "very low" to "very high." A so-called "page turner" would be at the "very low" end of the scale, whereas a self-directed simulation activity would probably have a "very high" interactivity level.

```
111        <rights>
112            <cost>
113                <source>
114                    <langstring xml:lang="x-none">
    LOMv1.0</langstring>
115                </source>
116                <value>
117                    <langstring xml:lang="x-none">
    yes</langstring>
118                </value>
119            </cost>
120            <copyrightandotherrestrictions>
121                <source>
122                    <langstring xml:lang="x-none">
    LOMv1.0</langstring>
123                </source>
124                <value>
```

```
125                         <langstring xml:lang="x-none">
    yes</langstring>
126                     </value>
127                 </copyrightandotherrestrictions>
128                 <description>
129                     <langstring>Requires payment of a fee
    to be negotiated with the vendor and use of the
    vendor's logo.</langstring>
130                 </description>
131             </rights>
```

The *<rights>* category defines the copyright and usage restrictions on the learning component. Both the *<cost>* (lines 112–119) and *<copyrightandother-restrictions>* (lines 120–127) elements are required and have restricted vocabularies consisting of "yes" and "no." If either of them is listed as "yes," the *<description>* element (lines 130–131) can be used to provide further information about the terms of .use.

```
132             <classification>
133                 <purpose>
134                     <source>
135                         <langstring xml:lang="x-none">
    LOMv1.0</langstring>
136                     </source>
137                     <value>
138                         <langstring xml:lang="x-none">
    Educational Objective</langstring>
139                     </value>
140                 </purpose>
```

The *<classification>* category describes a learning component in terms of one or more classification schemes. The element can be repeated several times in reference to difference learning taxonomies and other classification schemes. This example represents the bare minimum required by the specification.

<purpose> (lines 133–140) describes the purpose for making a particular classification. If there is more than one *<classification>* element, each will most likely have a different *<purpose>*. The best-practice vocabulary for the *<purpose>* element includes such terms as "Discipline," "Prerequisite," "Educational Objective," and "Skill Level."

```
141                 <description>
142                     <langstring>This SCO addresses the
    following objective: The student will be able to
    describe the basic steps in the pie crust-making
    process.</langstring>
143                 </description>
```

```
144          <keyword>
145               <langstring>cooking basics
     </langstring>
146          </keyword>
147       </classification>
148  </lom>
```

The *<description>* (lines 141–143) contains a text description of how the learning component fulfills the particular purpose of the given classification. The *<keyword>* element in lines 144–146 differs from the general keywords in that it describes the learning component in relation to the stated purpose for the classification.

The *</lom>* tag in line 148 marks the end of the meta-data.[1]

The Meta-Data Information Model

There are two parts to the SCORM meta-data specification, the Meta-Data Information Model and the Meta-Data XML Binding. Although we have used this chapter to look extensively at XML, the information model stands alone. Ultimately, non-XML formats may be specified as alternate representations of the information model.

The Meta-Data Information Model describes the individual data elements used to build SCORM-conformant meta-data. Chapter 5 listed the elements required for a SCO or Asset. The annotated example earlier in this chapter introduced some additional elements. For a complete list of the elements that make up the Information Model, see the specification document itself.

Special Data Types

A given meta-data element may contain other elements, or it may contain one of four types of data:

- String
- LangString
- Date
- Vocabulary

String data is defined conventionally as any sequence of characters. The other three are special complex types that are themselves defined within the SCORM specification. We have already seen these special data types in action in our annotated example. Now we will discuss them in more detail.

LangString Type

The LangString data type allows text to be represented in one or more languages. LangStrings are typically used for text elements that are intended to be displayed to humans. In XML, the *<langstring>* tag is used. An optional *xml:lang* attribute is used to identify the language. Although the specification allows this attribute to contain any string value, it is common practice to use the standard language codes specified by the ISO (*ISO 639-1* and *639-2*).

If no language attribute is specified, the default language for the meta-data document is assumed. The default language can be specified in the *<metametadata>* section of the document. If it is not, it must be inferred from the other data in the document.

The following is an example of a SCO *<title>* element presented in English, Spanish, and French.

```
<title>
    <langstring xml:lang="en">Dogs</langstring>
    <langstring xml:lang="es">Los Perros
</langstring>
    <langstring xml:lang="fr">Les Chiens
</langstring>
</title>
```

There is no limit to the number of *<langstring>* tags that can be used as long as each represents a different language.

Date Type

The Date type is defined to be flexible. It allows the date to be expressed in an *ISO 8601* standard *datetime* format or to be described in a LangString, or both. Most likely the description element would be used in cases in which an exact date is not available. Here is an XML example that includes both formats:

```
<date>
    <datetime>2002-01-27</datetime>
    <description>
        <langstring xml:lang="en">Near the
end of January 2002</langstring>
    </description>
</date>
```

The ISO standard includes a number of different formats. It is considered a best practice to use the format *yyyy-mm-dd* for dates and *hh:mm:ss* for times.

Vocabulary Type

The Vocabulary type is used for element values that are drawn from predefined lists. It is designed for flexibility by indicating the source of the vocabulary list used as well as the specific value. The source of the vocabularies used in the SCORM 1.2 specification is the IEEE LOM Specification, which is represented in vocabulary elements as "LOMv1.0." Vocabulary items identified as "Restricted" must be based on this source. Best-practice vocabulary items can be based on a different source if necessary. The value portion of the data type may contain any one of the terms in the relevant vocabulary list.

As an example of using an alternate vocabulary, the LOM best-practice vocabulary provided for the *<learningresourcetype>* element does not include "Reference Material," which you may consider the only appropriate term to describe your resource. You could create an alternate vocabulary list that includes your term. Because it is not a well-known list, you might publish it on the Internet and use the source element to provide a URI to its location. In XML, your *<learningresourcetype>* element would look something like this:

```
<learningresourcetype>
    <source>
        <langstring xml:lang="x-none">http://www.mysite.org/myvocab.htm</langstring>
    </source>
    <value>
        <langstring xml:lang="x-none">Reference Material</langstring>
    </value>
</learningresourcetype>
```

The values for the source and value components of a vocabulary type are LangStrings, but they use the special language value "x-none" to indicate that they are "tokens" rather than ordinary data. A token is intended to be recognized and used for a special purpose by computers. Vocabulary tokens are used as the names of search categories. A catalog user may want to see a list of all available reference material resources. A computer can easily locate all items with a *<learningresourcetype>* value of "Reference Material" but would miss items in which the value is misspelled or translated into a different human language. For this reason, a token must always use the exact language and spelling provided in the specification.

This Vocabulary data type is peculiar to the LOM specification. Other specifications handle vocabularies differently.[2]

Meta-Data Application Profiles

Meta-data can be applied to assets, SCOs, and content aggregations. Each of these learning components has slightly different requirements. For example, *<catalogentry>* information is crucial for SCOs and content aggregations but may be irrelevant for assets that are not intended to stand alone. The specification provides application profiles that define how the information model applies to each type of learning component. The requirements are presented in a table that lists each element and indicates whether it is mandatory or optional for a given application.

Oddities of the Specification

Some aspects of the specification may seem strange at first glance. One seeming oddity is the concept of *smallest permitted maximum.* This is a requirement placed on software that processes meta-data. Smallest permitted maximums are used in two different contexts. When applied to a string or LangString element, the value requires the software to make the associated data field long enough to accommodate at least the given number of characters. This prevents characters from being chopped off the end of long text strings. When a smallest permitted maximum is specified for an element that can appear several times (such as *<keyword>*), it requires the software to accommodate at least that many instances of the element. If you stay within the smallest permitted maximums, when creating meta-data, you can be confident that no conforming software will drop any of your data.

Another seeming peculiarity in the specification is the definition of elements that cannot legally be used. These elements, which are labeled in the specification as "RESERVED," are all identifiers that are intended to be globally unique. As you can imagine, developing a scheme for creating IDs that are guaranteed to be unique (and remain so indefinitely) is a daunting task. Several such schemes exist, but the IMS and ADL have not yet settled on one. Until the standards bodies officially adopt a method for creating and distributing identifiers, these elements will not be used.

The XML Binding — Turning the Data Elements into XML

A sizeable portion of the LOM specification is devoted to describing how the elements in the information model are to be represented in ("bound to") XML. The XML-binding section is probably easier to understand initially than the information model itself because it includes an actual example of each data element.

Common Development Problems and Solutions

If I can't use the restricted identifier elements, how can I uniquely identify my learning content?

The current recommendation for a workaround is to use a catalog_entry element. The combination of a known catalog name and a unique entry within that catalog is generally sufficient to uniquely identify learning content. If necessary, you can create your own catalog for this purpose.

When I looked at the actual specification, I found that some of the elements that this book lists as required have a multiplicity (number of times they are allowed to be used) of "0 or more." How can a required element be used zero times?

The answer to this question lies in the application profiles. As mentioned earlier, some elements are necessary for SCOs and content aggregations, but not for assets. The basic definition in the specification applies to all three applications, but our examples were specifically for SCOs. So, for example, *<catalogentry>* is required and must be used at least once for an SCO. However, it is optional for an asset.

Tools for Creating Meta-Data

The good news about meta-data is that you do not have to write the XML all by yourself. Several tools, some of them free, are available to help you create meta-data files. Most provide you with a simple form to fill out, then generate the appropriate XML code for your data. Here are a couple:

- The *SCORM Meta-Data Generator Version 1.1* is available for free download at http://www.adlnet.org. It requires the latest Java plug-in from Sun Microsystems, which it prompts you to download if you do not already have it. It includes built-in explanations of the meta-data elements.
- Macromedia Authorware *SCORM Metadata Editor* ships with the Authorware application. It is launched from within Authorware. Like the previous tool, it supports only version 1.1 of the specification. It includes brief explanations of the elements and indicates which are mandatory.

There are also a number of general-purpose programs available for creating and validating XML documents. These typically help you to create freeform XML or XML that is based on template documents (DTDs and XML Schemas) such as those provided for the SCORM/IMS meta-data. Some may also be used to validate a given XML document against the appropriate template. Commercial packages for Windows platforms include the following:

- XML Extensibility (http://www.extensibility.com)
- XML Spy (http://www.xmlspy.com)
- Corel® XMetaL® (http://www.xmetal.com)
- Epic Editor® (http://www.arbortext.com)
- XML Pro from Vervet Logic (http://www.vervet.com)

In addition to these, Microsoft offers a free package called XML Notepad. It is available for download at http://www.msdn.com.

Conclusion

At this point, you should have good understanding of the basics of LO meta-data. However, meta-data is only one part of the overall Content Aggregation Model portion of the SCORM. We have somewhat arbitrarily separated it from the packaging portion of the model so that we could include a grounding in XML without creating an overwhelmingly long and complicated chapter. In the next chapter, we will present the details of content packaging and will explain how meta-data fits into the overall content aggregation scheme.

References

1. Dodds, P., Ed., *Sharable Content Object Reference Model (SCORM): The SCORM Content Aggregation Model,* version 1.2. Advanced Distributed Learning, 2001, section 2.3.5. Available at: http://www.adlnet.org.
2. Dodds, P., Ed., *Sharable Content Object Reference Model (SCORM): The SCORM Content Aggregation Model,* version 1.2. Advanced Distributed Learning, 2001, section 2.2.3.2. Available at: http://www.adlnet.org.

11

A Guide to Creating Course Structure Manifests and Interchange Files

Introduction

This chapter provides a more detailed look at the special files used to communicate the structure of a course from one LMS to another. It provides a detailed annotated example of the structure and the required data elements for a SCORM content aggregation manifest. It also includes annotated examples of the AICC course interchange files (CIFs).

Although this chapter is not a substitute for the actual specification documents, it should prepare you to interpret and edit existing manifests and CIFs.

Example Course Structure

The example files in this lesson are based on a small sample course titled "Pies 101." Here is an outline of the course:

- Course: *Pies 101* — This course shows the learner how to make a pie.
  - LO: *Pies, Pies, and More Pies* — An introductory discussion of the various types of pies
  - Block: *Making Pies* — Pie-making methodology
    - Block: *Pie Crust Techniques* — How to make a pie crust
      - LO : *Pie Crust Pretest* — Tests prior knowledge of making pie crusts
      - LO: *Pastry Crusts* — How to mix, roll out, and bake pastry pie crusts

    - LO: *Crumb Crusts* — How to create crusts from cookie and graham cracker crumbs
- Block: *Pie Filling Techniques* — How to make a pie filling
    - LO: *Pie Filling Pretest* — Tests prior knowledge of making pie fillings
    - LO: *Fruit Fillings* — How to prepare fillings from fresh, dried, or canned fruit
    - LO: *Other Fillings* — How to make cream, custard, cheese, and other nonfruit fillings
- LO: *Specialty Pies* — Applying ordinary techniques to achieve extraordinary pies

The following behaviors are expected from the course if they are supported by *both* the specification in question and the given LMS:

- Each LO has a minimum passing score of 80%.
- "Pies, Pies, and More Pies" is a prerequisite to the "Making Pies" block.
- Both the "Pie Crust Techniques" and "Pie Filling Techniques" blocks are prerequisite to the "Specialty Pies" LO.
- The learner can complete either of the techniques blocks by passing only its pretest LO, in essence testing out of the content LOs in the block.

Figure 11.1 shows how the "Pies 101" menu might appear in a student's browser.

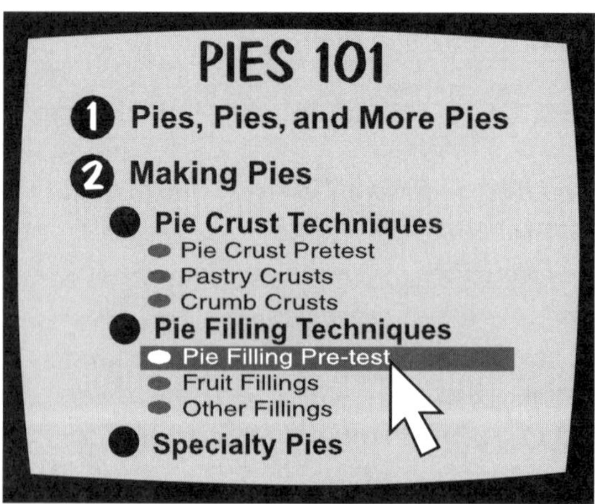

FIGURE 11.1
Pies 101 course menu.

SCORM Content Aggregation Packaging

In Chapter 6 we briefly discussed the two types of packages defined by the SCORM Content Packaging Information Model: the content package for transporting unstructured bundles of learning content and the content aggregation package for interchanging learning content that is organized into a block or course. In this chapter we will confine our discussion to content aggregation packages.

An Annotated Example — A Manifest for Pies 101

The following is a manifest document for a "Pies 101" content aggregation package. It includes all the required elements for describing the course, along with some key optional elements.

Annotations have been inserted as needed within the XML document. Listing 11.1 in Appendix A shows the uninterrupted manifest as it would appear in a real-world application. As with previous examples, the line numbers are not part of the actual XML.

```
001 <manifest identifier="Pies101"
    xmlns="http://www.imsproject.org/xsd/imscp_rootv1p1p2"
    xmlns:adlcp="http://www.adlnet.org/xsd/adlcp_rootv1p2"
    xmlns:imsmd="http://www.imsglobal.org/xsd/
    imsmd_rootv1p2p1"
    xmlns:xsi="http://www.w3.org/2001/XMLSchema-instance"
    xsi:schemaLocation="http://www.imsproject.org/xsd/
    imscp_rootv1p1p2
    imscp_rootv1p1p2.xsd http://www.imsglobal.org/xsd/
    imsmd_rootv1p2p1 imsmd_rootv1p2p1.xsd http://
    www.adlnet.org/xsd/adlcp_rootv1p2 adlcp_rootv1p2.xsd">
```

<manifest> (line 001) is the root element for the XML document and contains everything else. The *identifier* attribute is required and must be unique within the manifest.

All the necessary namespace and schema location declarations also get dumped into this tag. Note in particular the *adlcp:* and *imsmd:* namespaces. *adlcp:* is used for elements that are special ADL extensions to the basic IMS packaging model. Many of these elements are adapted from the AICC specification. *imsmd:* references the IMS Learning Object Meta-Data specification and is used for meta-data that is included within the manifest.

```
002     <metadata>
003         <schema>ADL SCORM</schema>
004         <schemaversion>1.2</schemaversion>
```

```
005          <imsmd:lom>
006              <imsmd:general>
007                  <imsmd:title>
008                      <imsmd:langstring xml:lang=
        "en-US">Manifest Example</imsmd:langstring >
009                  </imsmd:title>
010              </imsmd:general>
011          </imsmd:lom>
012      </metadata>
```

The optional *<metadata>* element can appear in several different contexts within the manifest. Here it provides meta-data about the manifest document itself. This example includes in-line meta-data inside the tags with the *imsmd:* namespace prefix (lines 005–011). Later we will see some examples of *<metadata>* elements that reference external meta-data documents.

```
013      <organizations default="root">
014          <organization identifier="root">
015              <title>Pies 101</title>
016              <adlcp:description>This course shows the
        learner how to make a pie></adlcp:description>
```

The *<organizations>* element is required in a content aggregation manifest. It contains one or more *<organization>* elements (line 014) that provide a complete description of the structure of the overall course or block represented by the manifest. If there are multiple *<organization>* elements, each represents a different way of structuring the learning content. Each organization element must have an *identifier* attribute that is unique within the manifest. The *default* attribute in the *<organizations>* tag references the *identifier* of the organization that is to be used by default. It is required even if there is only one possibility, as in this example.

```
017              <item identifier="A0" identifierref=
        "R_A0">
018                  <title>Pies, Pies, and More Pies
        </title>
019                  <adlcp:description>An introductory
        discussion of the various types of pies
        </adlcp:description>
020                  <adlcp:masteryscore>80
        </adlcp:masteryscore>
021              </item>
```

The *<item>* element defines a SCO or a block within the course. These elements are sequenced and nested to duplicate the course's hierarchical structure. The item above represents the first lesson or SCO in the course — "Pies, Pies, and More Pies." The *identifier* attribute is required and must be unique within the manifest. The *identifierref* attribute points to a *<resource>* element defined later in the manifest. The *<resource>* element, in turn, points to the actual content files for the SCO. SCO-level items require an *identifierref*; block-level items seldom include one.

The *<title>* (line 018) is the only required element for an item. LMSs will display the title on course menus. Most will also display the descriptive text in the *<adlcp:description>* element (line 019). The *<adlcp:masteryscore>* value (line 020) is used by LMSs that support the optional *cmi.student_data.mastery_score* data element. It represents the minimum passing score and can be used by the LMS to override any status set by the SCO itself.

```
022                 <item identifier="B0">
023                     <title>Making Pies</title>
024                     <adlcp:description>Pie-making
    methodology</adlcp:description>
025                     <adlcp:prerequisites type="aicc_
    script">A0</adlcp:prerequisites>
```

The *<item>* above represents the "Making Pies" block. Notice that it does not have an *identifierref* attribute. This is typical of block-level items, which ordinarily serve only as grouping devices that are not associated with actual content. The *<adlcp:prerequisites>* element (line 025) indicates that the item having the specified identifier must be completed before a learner can enter this block. In our example, item A0 is the "Pies, Pies, and More Pies" SCO.

```
026                     <item identifier="B1">
027                         <title>Pie Crust Techniques
    </title>
028                         <adlcp:description>How to make
    a pie crust</adlcp:description>
030                         <item identifier="A1"
    identifierref="R_A1">
031                             <title>Pie Crust Pretest
    </title>
032                             <adlcp:description>Tests
    prior knowledge of making pie crusts
    </adlcp:description>
033                             <adlcp:masteryscore>80
    </adlcp:masteryscore>
034                         </item>
035                         <item identifier="A2"
    identifierref="R_A2">
036                             <title>Pastry Crusts</title>
037                             <adlcp:description>How to
    mix, roll out, and bake pastry pie crusts
    </adlcp:description>
038                             <adlcp:masteryscore>80
    </adlcp:masteryscore>
039                         </item>
```

```
040                       <item identifier="A3"
    identifierref="R_A3">
041                           <title>Crumb Crusts</title>
042                           <adlcp:description>How to
    create crusts from cookie and graham cracker crumbs
    </adlcp:description>
043                           <adlcp:masteryscore>80
    </adlcp: masteryscore>
044                       </item>
045                   </item>
```

Lines 026–045 contain the nested block item "Pie Crust Techniques," which includes three LO items, "Pie Crust Pretest" (lines 031–034), "Pastry Crusts" (lines 035–039), and "Crumb Crusts" (lines 040–044).

Each *<item>* element, no matter how deeply nested, has the same basic structure. This arrangement can be likened to the traditional sets of Russian folk dolls in which each doll opens to reveal a slightly smaller copy of itself, as illustrated in Figure 11.2.

```
046                   <item identifier="B2">
047                       <title>Pie Filling Techniques
    </title>
048                       <adlcp:description>How to make
    a pie filling</adlcp:description>
050                       <item identifier="A4"
    identifierref="R_A4">
051                           <title>Pie Filling Pretest
    </title>
052                           <adlcp:description>Tests
    prior knowledge of making pie fillings
    </adlcp:description>
053                           <adlcp:masteryscore>80
    </adlcp:masteryscore>
054                       </item>
055                       <item identifier="A5"
    identifierref="R_A5">
056                           <title>Fruit Fillings
    </title>
057                           <adlcp:description>How to
    prepare fillings from fresh, dried, or canned fruit
    </adlcp:description>
058                           <adlcp:masteryscore>80
    </adlcp:masteryscore>
059                       </item>
060                       <item identifier="A6"
    identifierref="R_A6">
061                           <title>Other Fillings
    </title>
```

```
062                            <adlcp:description>How to
    make cream, custard, cheese, and other non-fruit
    fillings</adlcp:description>
063                            <adlcp:masteryscore>80
    </adlcp:masteryscore>
064                        </item>
065                    </item>
```

FIGURE 11.2
Nested <item> elements.

Lines 046–065 contain the "Pie Filling Techniques" nested block, the structure of which closely resembles that of the previous block.

```
066                    <item identifier="A7" identifierref=
    "R_A7">
067                        <title>Specialty Pies</title>
068                        <adlcp:description>Applying
    ordinary techniques to achieve extraordinary pies
    </adlcp: description>
069                        <adlcp:prerequisites type=
    "aicc_script">B1&B2</adlcp:prerequisites>
070                        <adlcp:masteryscore>80</adlcp:
    masteryscore>
071                    </item>
072                </item>
073            </organization>
074        </organizations>
```

Lines 066–071 represent the *<item>* element for the final LO in the course. This LO has a complex prerequisite, requiring completion of two different blocks before allowing entry to the LO. To define complex prerequisites, the SCORM uses a scripting language developed by the AICC for describing prerequisites using logical expressions. For example, the prerequisite expression "(A0&B1) | (3*{C0, C1, C2, C3})" means that the learner must complete either items A0 and B1 or else any three of the four C items. In XML, this prerequisite would be represented as follows:

```
    <adlcp:prerequisites type="aicc_script">(A0&B1)|
    (3*{C0, C1, C2, C3})</adlcp:prerequisites>
```

At present, the required *type* attribute in the *<adlcp:prerequisites>* tag must contain the value "aicc_script" to indicate the use of AICC-based prerequisite descriptions. Other schemes for describing prerequisites may be added in the future. See the "Complex Prerequisite and Completion Logic" section near the end of this chapter for more details.

Lines 072–074 complete the *organizations* portion of the manifest.

```
075     <resources>
076         <resource identifier="R_A0" type="webcontent"
    adlcp:scormtype="sco" href="../courses/pies/pies_
    L1.htm">
077             <metadata>
078                 <adlcp:location>pies_L1.xml</adlcp:
    location>
079             </metadata>
080             <file href="../courses/pies/pies_L1.htm"/>
081             <dependency identifierref="R_G1" />
082         </resource>
```

The *<resources>* element provides the link between the course structure described in the *<organization>* element and the actual learning-content files. It contains a list of individual *<resource>* elements that serves as a virtual packing list for all the content files included in a content package. It also provides the LMS with the URLs that it needs to launch the SCOs in the course.

The *<resource>* shown above (lines 075–082) is the "Pies, Pies, and More Pies" SCO. All four of the attributes included in the *<resource>* tag are required for a SCO. The *identifier* was previously referenced by the corresponding *<item>* element in the *<organization>* section. Currently, the only defined value for *type* is "webcontent." The *adl:scormtype* may be either "sco" or "asset." The *href* attribute is the file location used by the LMS for launching the SCO. Resources that are not directly launched by the LMS (i.e., most assets) do not use this attribute.

The *<metadata>* element shown in lines 077–079 contains a reference to an external meta-data file for the SCO. Rather than referencing an external file, one could include in-line meta-data at this location in the manifest. However, using in-line meta-data for resources can result in a very long and unwieldy manifest.

The *<file>* element's *href* attribute (line 080) gives the location of the SCO or asset file. For SCOs it typically matches the *href* attribute in the *<resource>* element, but it may be different. A *<file>* element may contain a *<metadata>* element, or it may be empty as shown here. Notice the "/" at the end of the tag. This indicates an empty element for which the opening and closing tags have been merged into one.

The *<dependency>* element (line 081) points to a secondary resource used by the current resource, such as a graphic used by an HTML file. In this example, the resource "R_G1" is defined later in the file as a graphic named "applepie.jpg." A resource can include an unlimited number of *<dependency>* elements.

```
083         <resource identifier="R_A1" type="webcontent" adlcp:scormtype="sco" href="../courses/pies/pies_L2.htm">
084             <metadata>
085                 <adlcp:location>pies_L2.xml</adlcp:location>
086             </metadata>
087             <file href="../courses/pies/pies_L2.htm" />
088             <dependency identifierref="R_G2" />
089             <dependency identifierref="R_G3" />
090         </resource>
091         <resource identifier="R_A3" type="webcontent" adlcp:scormtype="sco" href="../courses/pies/pies_L3.htm">
092             <metadata>
093                 <adlcp:location>pies_L3.xml</adlcp:location>
094             </metadata>
095             <file href="../courses/pies/pies_L3.htm" />
096             <dependency identifierref="R_G4" />
097         </resource>
098         <resource identifier="R_A4" type="webcontent" adlcp:scormtype="sco" href="../courses/pies/pies_L4.htm">
099             <metadata>
100                 <adlcp:location>pies_L4.xml</adlcp:location>
101             </metadata>
102             <file href="../courses/pies/pies_L4.htm" />
103         </resource>
(remaining SCO resources would go here)
```

The section above lists the next three SCO resources in the course. These correspond to "Pie Crust Pretest" (lines 083–090), "Pastry Crusts" (lines 091–097), and "Crumb Crusts" (lines 098–103). The remaining SCO resources have been omitted here because they are all very similar. The complete listing in Appendix A includes all the resources.

```
104            <resource identifier="R_G1" type="webcontent"
    adlcp:scormtype="asset">
105                <file href="../courses/pies/graphics/
    applepie.jpg" />
106            </resource>
```

The resource identified as "R_G1" (lines 104–106) is an example of an asset resource. Notice that the *<resource>* element does not include an *href* attribute because the LMS does not need to launch the file. Additional asset resources are included in the portion of the manifest shown below. A typical course would contain many more assets than are listed here.

```
107            <resource identifier="R_G2" type="webcontent"
    adlcp:scormtype="asset">
108                <file href="../courses/pies/graphics/
    rollingpin.jpg" />
109            </resource>
110            <resource identifier="R_G3" type="webcontent"
    adlcp:scormtype="asset">
111                <file href="../courses/pies/graphics/
    crust.jpg" />
112            </resource>
113            <resource identifier="R_G4" type="webcontent"
    adlcp:scormtype="asset">
114                <file href="../courses/pies/graphics/
    apples.jpg" />
115            </resource>
116        </resources>
117</manifest>
```

The closing *</manifest>* tag in line 117 completes the manifest file.[1]

The Content-Packaging Information Model

The complete SCORM Content Packaging Information Model includes a number of additional elements and attributes that did not appear in our example. Consult the specification document and the examples provided by ADL for details.

The AICC CIFs

As discussed in Chapter 6, the AICC specification defines seven CIFs, of which four are required at the lowest level of course structure complexity.

Each of these files can be recognized by a specific filename extension. In this section we will look at the details of these files.

Example: An Annotated Set of CIFs for Pies 101

The following annotated set of CIFs defines the "Pies 101" course. It includes the four required files, plus the optional *Prerequisites* (.pre) and *Completion* requirements (.cmp) files. Because we did not define objectives for "Pies 101," the file set does not include the *Objectives Reference* file (.ort). As with the XML files, the line numbers in these files are for our convenience only. Including line numbers in the actual files would cause an error.

The Course (.crs) File

The *Course* file includes information about the course as a whole. Definitions of the *Course* file keywords are provided after the sample listing.

```
[Course]
Course_Creator = Sharon Brown
Course_ID = pies_C1
Course_System = Dreamweaver
Course_Title = Pies 101
Level = 3
Max_Fields_CST = 4
Total_AUs = 8
Total_Blocks = 3
Version=3.5

[Course_Behavior]
Max_Normal=3

[Course_Description]
This course shows the learner how to make a pie.
```

Keyword definitions are as follows:

- [Course] group
  - Course_Creator — The person or group who authored the course
  - Course_ID — A unique identifier assigned to the course as a whole
  - Course_System — Name of the primary authoring tool or system used to create the course
  - Course_Title — Title of the course displayed by the LMS on student menus

- Level — Complexity level of course interchange described by these files. Level 1 requires the *Course, Descriptor, Assignable Unit,* and *Course Structure Table* files. Level 2 adds the *Prerequisites* and *Completion Requirements* files. Level 3 adds the *Objectives Relationships* file and allows complex prerequisites and completion requirements. Because our example uses a complex prerequisite it is considered level 3.
- Max_Fields_CST — Maximum width in columns of the *Course Structure Table.* This value is equal to the number of top-level members in the largest block (or in the course itself) plus one. In our example, each of the three blocks contains three members. The "Pie Crust Techniques" and "Pie Filling Techniques" blocks each contain three assignable units (AUs). The "Making Pies" block contains two blocks and a "loose" AU. Adding one to this maximum yields a value of 4 for Max_Fields_CST.
- Total_AUs — Total number of AUs in the course
- Total_Blocks — Total number of blocks in the course
- Version — Version of the AICC specification to which the course is written

- [Course_Behavior] group
  - Max_Normal — Maximum number of lessons that a learner may have in progress at the same time
- [Course_Description] "Group"
  - (no element name) — Text description of the course that the LMS may display to learners

The Descriptor (.des) File

This file contains a comma-delimited table. Each line represents a row in the table, and the text in quotation marks between the commas is what goes in the individual table cells for the row. See Table 11.1 for an example of how the data in the descriptor file would appear in conventional table format. The first line contains the headings for the table columns, which may appear in any order. The remaining lines each describe one of the AUs or blocks that make up the course. Definitions for the table columns are provided after the sample listing.

```
"System_ID","Title"," Description","Developer_ID"
"A0","Pies, Pies, and More Pies","An introductory discussion of the various types of pies","pies_L1"
"A1","Pie Crust Pretest","Tests prior knowledge of making pie crusts","pies_L2"
"A2","Pastry Crusts","How to mix, roll out, and bake pastry pie crusts","pies_L3"
```

```
"A3","Crumb Crusts","How to create crusts from cookie and graham cracker crumbs","pies_L4"
"A4","Pie Filling Pretest","Tests prior knowledge of making pie crusts","pies_L5"
"A5","Fruit Fillings","How to prepare fillings from fresh, dried, or canned fruit","pies_L6"
"A6","Other Fillings","How to make cream, custard, cheese, and other nonfruit fillings","pies_L7"
"A7","Specialty Pies","Applying ordinary techniques to achieve extraordinary pies","pies_L8"
"B0","Making Pies","Pie-making methodology","pies_B1"
"B1","Pie Crust Techniques","How to make a pie crust","pies_B2"
"B2","Pie Filling Techniques","How to make pie fillings","pies_B3"
```

TABLE 11.1

The Descriptor (.des) File Displayed as a Conventional Table

System_ ID	Title	Description	Developer_ID
A0	Pies, Pies, and More Pies	Introductory discussion of the various types of pies	pies_L1
A1	Pie Crust Pretest	Test of prior knowledge of making pie crusts	pies_L2
A2	Pastry Crusts	Lesson on mixing, rolling out, and baking pastry pie crusts	pies_L3
A3	Crumb Crusts	Lesson on creating crusts from cookie and graham cracker crumbs	pies_L4
A4	Pie Filling Pretest	Test of prior knowledge of making pie fillings	pies_L5
A5	Fruit Fillings	Lesson on preparing fillings from fresh, dried, or canned fruit	pies_L6
A6	Other Fillings	Lesson on making cream, custard, cheese, and other nonfruit fillings	pies_L7
A7	Specialty Pies	Lesson on applying ordinary techniques to achieve extraordinary pies	pies_L8
B0	Making Pies	Lesson on pie-making methodology	pies_B1
B1	Pie Crust Techniques	Lesson on making a pie crust	pies_B2
B2	Pie Filling Techniques	Lesson on making pie fillings	pies_B3

Column definitions are as follows:

- System_ID — ID assigned to every course element, typically by a course exporting system. IDs beginning with "A" represent AUs and those beginning with "B" represent blocks. This ID is used in the other files to reference this particular element. If you must create this file by hand, it is recommended that you use the same naming convention. Each System_ID must be unique within the course.
- Title — Title of the course element displayed by the LMS on learner menus
- Description — Text description of the course element, typically made available to learners by the LMS
- Developer_ID — Identifier assigned to the element by its developer; ideally, this identifier should be universally unique, but the specification does not identify a method for producing unique identifiers.

The AU (.au) File

Like the *Descriptor* file, this is a comma-delimited table, with the column order defined by the first line's list of column headings. It includes a line for each AU in the course. Notice that some of the fields in the example contain no data between their quotation marks. This is typical. The *.au* file is designed to include all possible information about the AUs, some of which is not used very often. Definitions for the table columns are provided after the sample listing.

```
"System_ID","Type","/Command_Line","Max_Time_Allowed",
"Time_Limit_Action","Max_Score","Core_Vendor","System_
Vendor","File_name","Mastery_Score","Web_Launch","AU_
Password"
"A0","","../courses/pies/pies_L1.htm","","","","","
Dreamweaver", "../courses/pies/pies_L1.htm","80","",""
"A1","","../courses/pies/pies_L2.htm","","","","","
Dreamweaver", "../courses/pies/pies_L2.htm","80","",""
"A2","","../courses/pies/pies_L3.htm","","","","","
Dreamweaver", "../courses/pies/pies_L3.htm","80","",""
"A3","","../courses/pies/pies_L4.htm","","","","","
Dreamweaver", "../courses/pies/pies_L4.htm","80","",""
"A4","","../courses/pies/pies_L5.htm","","","","","
Dreamweaver", "../courses/pies/pies_L5.htm","80","",""
"A5","","../courses/pies/pies_L6.htm","","","","","
Dreamweaver", "../courses/pies/pies_L6.htm","80","",""
```

```
"A6","","../courses/pies/pies_L7.htm","","","","","
Dreamweaver", "../courses/pies/pies_L7.htm","80","",""
"A7","","../courses/pies/pies_L8.htm","","","","","
Dreamweaver", "../courses/pies/pies_L8.htm","80","",""
```

Column definitions are as follows:

- System_ID — Same as in the *Descriptor* file.
- Type — Developer-defined category for the AU, such as "lesson" or "posttest."
- Command_Line — Launch address for the AU.
- Max_Time_Allowed — Time limit for completion of the AU. This value is assigned to the optional *max_time_allowed* data element if the LMS supports it. Otherwise it is ignored.
- Time_Limit_Action — Action that the LMS should take when Max_Time_Allowed is exceeded. The value is assigned to the optional *time_limit_action* data element if the LMS supports it. Otherwise it is ignored.
- Max_Score — Maximum score that the learner could have achieved in the AU. It allows the LMS to compute a percentage score from the raw score returned by the AU.
- Core_Vendor — Special information required by a given lesson. The value is assigned to the *[Core_Vendor]* data element in the LMS.
- System_Vendor — Name of the primary authoring tool used to develop the AU.
- File_Name — Full name of the primary file for the AU. Some LMSs use this value to launch the AU.
- Mastery_Score — Minimum passing score for the lesson. This value is assigned to the *mastery_score* data element in the LMS.
- Web_Launch — Any special data that needs to be added to the launch URL for the lesson to start up successfully
- AU_Password — Password that can be sent by the AU to authenticate request messages. This value is assigned to the *AU_password* data element in the LMS.

The Course Structure Table (.cst) File

This file is a comma-delimited listing of course components that indicates the order in which they will occur and how they are grouped into blocks. The *System_ID* values assigned to the specific AUs and blocks are used in the representation. The identifier used for the course as a whole is "Root." In our example, the entire course comprises the "Pies, Pies, and More Pies" AU (A0) and the "Making Pies" block (B0). The block in turn comprises the

"Pie Crust Techniques" (B1) and "Pie Filling Techniques" (B2) blocks plus the "Specialty Pies" (A7) AU. The remaining AUs are nested inside blocks B1 and B2.

```
"Block","Member","Member"
"Root","A0","B0"
"B0","B1","B2","A7"
"B1","A1","A2","A3"
"B2","A4","A5","A6"
```

The Prerequisites (.pre) File

The *Prerequisites* file lists the individual elements that have prerequisites and what those prerequisites are. It uses a comma-delimited table with a heading row and a row for each element that has a prerequisite. The data in our example indicates that the AU A0 is a prerequisite for block B0 and that both blocks B1 and B2 are prerequisites for AU A7. Even more complex prerequisite logic is possible, as described later in this chapter.

```
"structure_element", "prerequisite"
"B0","A0"
"A7","B1&B2"
```

The Completion Requirements (.cmp) File

The *Completion Requirements* file is a vehicle for specifying alternative conditions for completion of a given course element and, optionally, defining the sequence in which course elements should be presented based on these requirements.

The default conditions for completion of course elements are straightforward:

- A simple objective is completed when the AU reports its completion to LMS.
- An AU is completed when the AU reports a "Passed" or "Completed" status or a score that meets or exceeds the mastery score.
- A complex objective or a block is completed when all its component elements are completed.

Completion requirements allow nondefault conditions to determine whether a course element is completed.

The *Completion Requirements* file for "Pies 101" is shown here. It indicates that blocks B1 and B2 are considered completed if their corresponding pretest AUs (A1 and A4, respectively) report a status of "Passed." Notice that there was no way to provide this information in the SCORM manifest. Under the current version of SCORM, the learner cannot receive completion credit for any course components as a result of completing different components.

```
"Structure_Element","Requirement","Result"
"B1","A1=Passed","Completed"
"B2","A4=Passed","Completed"
```

Column definitions are as follows:

- Structure_Element — System ID of a block, AU, or complex objective for which a special completion requirement is being set
- Requirement — Logic statement involving the status of one or more course structure elements that can be evaluated as "true" or "false"
- Result — Status to which the element is set if the requirement evaluates to "true"; if the requirement evaluates to "false," the element's status remains unchanged

There is more to completion requirements than our "Pies 101" example is able to show. We will revisit this topic with another example in the next section.

More about Optional CIF Files

Our "Pies 101" example did not make use of the optional *Objectives Relationships* file, and it did not completely explain the use of *Completion Requirements.* These files deal with tracking and sequencing options that have no analogue in the current version of the SCORM. This section discusses *Objectives Relationships* briefly and provides a more complete example of the capabilities of *Completion Requirements.*

The Objectives Relationships (.ort) File

The relationship between instructional objectives and the structural elements of a course can be quite complex. Sometimes an AU may cover several objectives, whereas other times, more than one AU is required to meet a single objective. Some objectives are themselves complex, requiring mastery of several subobjectives. The *Objectives Relationship* file spells out all of the dependencies between AUs, blocks, and objectives.

Like AUs and blocks, objectives are assigned *System_IDs.* Objective IDs begin with the letter J. The *Objectives Relationships* file has the same structure as the *Course Structure Table* file. Each row lists an element of the course structure (a block, an AU, or a complex objective) by its ID, followed by the IDs of all the objectives that are included in that element. A portion of an *.ort* file might look like the following:

```
"course_element","member","member","member"
"B0","J0","J3","J4"
"A0","J1","J2"
"J5","J6","J7"
```

Once objectives are brought into play, several of the other files are affected. The *Course* file requires three additional keywords to accommodate the use of the *Objectives Relationships* file: *Max_Fields_ORT, Total_Complex_Obj,* and *Total_Objectives.* The *Prerequisites* and *Completion Requirements* files can define their rules in terms of objectives instead of or in combination with AUs and blocks.

The Completion Requirements (.cmp) File

As mentioned previously, there is more to be said about completion requirements. The following example illustrates several new points.

```
01  "Structure_Element","Requirement","Result","Next",
    "Return"
02  "A3","A1=Passed","Passed"
03  "A3","A2","Passed"
04  "A4","A4=Failed","Failed","A15","A4"
```

A line-by-line explanation follows:

- Line 01 includes two additional column headers, "Next" and "Return." The use of these headers is explained in the discussion of line 04 below.
- Notice that lines 02 and 03 each set a different completion requirement for lesson "A3." If either of the two conditions is met, "A3" will be set to a status of "Passed."
- If no explicit status is included in the requirement value, as in line 03, the requirement is considered "true" for a status of "Passed" or "Completed," and "false" for any other status.
- Line 04 illustrates the use of the optional "Next" and "Return" values. When used with an LMS that is capable of automatically launching AUs, using these values provides adaptive control over the launch sequence.
  - The "Next" value contains the System ID of the next AU that should be launched if the completion requirement is met. In the example, if "A4" is failed, "A15" is launched automatically (provided the LMS is capable of auto-launch). "A15" might be a remediation lesson.

- The "Return" value, which is used only in conjunction with "Next," contains the System ID of the AU to which the learner should be returned after completion of the "Next" AU. In our example, the Return value tells the LMS to launch "A4" again once "A15" is completed.[3]

Complex Prerequisite and Completion Logic

As noted earlier, the AICC has defined a scripting language for expressing complex prerequisites and completion requirements. This language, which consists of a set of logical operators and a few general rules, has also been adopted by the SCORM for describing prerequisites.

Statuses and Status Categories

Prerequisites and completion requirements are based on the status values assigned to blocks, lessons, and objectives. Blocks and complex objectives are considered either "incomplete" or "complete," based on the statuses of their member elements or special completion requirements. AUs and simple objectives may be assigned any of six official statuses, which in turn may be grouped into "incomplete" and "complete" categories, as follows:

- Incomplete category
  - Not Attempted (N)
  - Browsed (B)
  - Incomplete (I)
  - Failed (F)
- Complete category
  - Completed (C)
  - Passed (P)

If a prerequisite or completion requirement expression does not specify a required status for a course element, it is treated as complete or incomplete based on the category in which its actual status falls. For example, a prerequisite specified as "A0=P" is satisfied only if AU A0 has a status of "Passed." However, if the prerequisite is listed as "A0," it is satisfied if A0 is either "Passed" or "Completed."

Logic Statements

A logic statement is an expression that can take on one of two values, such as "true"/"false" or "complete"/"incomplete." As we saw in the last section, the status of any course element can be treated as either "complete" or "incomplete." By adding some symbols borrowed from mathematics, we can build combinations of course elements that produce an overall "true"/ "false" result. Here are some examples.

- "A0 & A1" is true if both A0 and A1 have statuses of "Completed" or "Passed."
- "A0=P | A1=C" is true if either A0 has a status of "Passed" or A1 has a status of "Completed."
- "3*{J0,J1,J2,J3,J4}" is true if any three of the listed objectives have statuses of "Completed" or "Passed."

The special symbols used in logic statements, such as "&," "|," and "*," are called *logic operators*. Table 11.2 lists and explains the logic operators used, as defined by the AICC specification.[4]

Common Development Problem and Solution

In the AICC Course Interchange Files, which items must be enclosed in quotation marks?

The short answer is, "We're not sure." The examples in the specification are inconsistent, and there are no real guidelines given. It appears that quotation marks are not used in the Course file. For the other files, most of the examples in the specification document place each separate item in quotation marks. However, a few examples do not use them. For simplicity we recommend placing all items in quotation marks except in the Course file.

There is one other point that should be noted by those whose background is in writing rather than programming. Contrary to standard English punctuation rules, the commas between items in a file must go *outside* the quotation marks. The following line would make no sense to a computer that is expecting to find the items separated by commas:

```
"name," "address," "telephone number"
```

Tools for Content Packaging

A number of tools are available to help you create manifest files for Sharable Content Object Reference Model (SCORM) content packages and content aggregation packages. These include general-purpose Extensible Markup Language (XML) editors such as those listed in Chapter 10, as well as the following:

TABLE 11.2

AICC Logic Operators

Symbol	Meaning	Examples
=	*Equals* — The combination is true if the values on both sides are the same. This symbol is used to specify the required status for a lesson or simple objective.	J5=C — True if objective J5 has a status of "Completed" A4=F — True if lesson A4 has a status of "Failed"
&	*And* — The combination is complete or true only if the items on both sides of the symbol are complete or true.	B1 & A10 — True if both B1 and A10 have statuses of "Passed" or "Completed" A3=P & A4=P — True if both A3 and A4 have statuses of "Passed"
|	*Or* — The combination is complete or true if either of the items surrounding the symbol is complete or true.	B1 | A10 — True if either B1 or A10 has a status of "Passed" or "Completed" A3=P | A4=P — True if either A3 or A4 has a status of "Passed"
~	*Not* — The value of the item immediately after the symbol is reversed.	~A6 — True if A6 does *not* have a status of "Passed" or "Completed" ~J11=F — True if J11 has any status except "Failed"
( )	*Evaluate first* — The expression inside the parentheses must be evaluated before combining its results with other parts of the statement; parentheses can be nested inside one another.	B3 & B4 | B5 — True if both B3 and B4 are complete or else if B5 is complete. Note that is possible to meet the requirement by completing only one block — B5. B3 & (B4 | B5) — True if B3 and either B4 or B5 are complete. Note that two blocks must be complete to meet this requirement.
{ , }	*Set* and *separator* — Groups a list of course elements together; the elements inside the braces (curly brackets) are separated by commas. Sets are used in conjunction with the X* operator described in the next row.	{J1,J2,J3} — A set by itself is not evaluated
X*	*X out of* — Used in front of a set to specify a number of set members that must be completed; X represents an integer no larger than the number of members in the set.	2*{J1,J2,J3} — True if any two of the three listed objectives has a status of "Completed" or "Passed"

Source: All data from AICC CMI Subcommittee (Hyde, J., chair), *CMI Guidelines for Interoperability,* revision 3.5. AICC, 2001, section 6.6.2. Available at: http://www.aicc.org.

- An LMS — SCORM-conforming LMSs can export content aggregation manifest files. Whether or not this export capability is particularly useful depends on whether the LMS allows you to define learning objects and build the content structure from scratch. If the LMS requires the content structure to be imported in the first place, you will need an external tool.

- Microsoft LRN Toolkit — This toolkit is available for free download from Microsoft. It includes an editor that allows the user to build a course structure from existing components, preview the course in a viewer, and create a directory that includes the manifest and content files. There are several good course samples available for download as well. It includes some added utilities for quickly converting PowerPoint presentations and Front Page webs to courses. It can also be used to convert SCORM 1.1 Content Structure Files to SCORM 1.2 manifests. You can download it at http://www.microsoft.com/downloads.
- Macromedia Dreamweaver Manifest Maker extension — This extension to Dreamweaver creates a manifest from a site defined in Dreamweaver. The manifest is for an unstructured content package, not a content aggregation package. However, adding an *<organization>* section to the manifest is significantly simplified by the fact that all the resources are defined for you. Manifest Maker is available from Macromedia's Web site: http://www.macromedia.com.

Unfortunately, we know of no tools except LMSs that will write AICC Course Interchange Files.

Conclusion

This completes our detailed tour through the AICC and SCORM specifications involving LOs and courses. In earlier chapters we saw how interoperability allows LOs to be used with any standards-conformant LMS and how meta-data can be provided to make learning components easier to locate and use. This chapter has detailed how the structure of courses and blocks can be communicated by the content developer in a manner that allows an LMS to replicate that structure. In our next and final chapter, we will turn once again to assessment and delve into the details of the IMS Question and Test Interoperability specifications.

References

1. Dodds, P., Ed., *Sharable Content Object Reference Model (SCORM): The SCORM Content Aggregation Model,* version 1.2. Advanced Distributed Learning, 2001, sections 2.3.5 and 2.3.6. Available at: http://www.adlnet.org.

2. AICC CMI Subcommittee (Hyde, J., chair), *CMI Guidelines for Interoperability,* revision 3.5. AICC, 2001, section 6.0. Available at: http://www.aicc.org.
3. AICC CMI Subcommittee (Hyde, J., chair), *CMI Guidelines for Interoperability,* revision 3.5. AICC, 2001, sections 6.5–6.7. Available at: http://www.aicc.org.
4. AICC CMI Subcommittee (Hyde, J., chair), *CMI Guidelines for Interoperability,* revision 3.5. AICC, 2001, section 6.6.2. Available at: http://www.aicc.org.

12

A Guide to Creating Standards-Based Test Items and Assessments

Introduction

This chapter provides a detailed look at the *IMS Question and Test Interoperability* (QTI) *Specification.* It builds on the concepts and examples introduced in Chapter 7. It includes a high-level description of assessment delivery software and explains how the specification categorizes questions by their response types. It completes the example item from Chapter 7 by adding a response-processing component. It then goes on to discuss the construction and functionality of complete assessments and concludes with an annotated example of a detail results report.

The material in this chapter should provide a good working introduction to the QTI specification documents. However, its focus is necessarily limited; in particular, it explicates only a single common item type. If you expect to author items and assessments, you must ultimately refer to the actual specification documents.

The Assessment–Section–Item Information Model

As discussed in Chapter 7, there are two information models contained in the QTI specification, the Assessment–Section–Item (ASI) model and the Results-Reporting Information model. The ASI model describes the structure of assessments, the structure and content of items, mechanisms for selecting and ordering the items to be included in an assessment, and mechanisms for processing item responses and overall assessment outcomes. In this section we will take a closer look at the components of the ASI model.

The Assessment Engine

To understand the ASI model, we need to know a little bit about the software that is used to present assessments to learners. Generically, such software is called an assessment engine. An assessment engine has two main components, a rendering engine to display the items and a response-processing component to evaluate the learners' responses and provide feedback.

Rendering engines are similar in concept to Web browsers. They use an internal set of display rules to decide how to display the various item elements. Some rendering engines take more formatting guidance from the item description than others. In particular, QTI v.1.2 has introduced a set of *<flow_>* tags that provide a way to set off portions of the item content into blocks or paragraphs. Some rendering engines will use these tags to adjust formatting, whereas others will ignore them.

The response-processing component of an assessment engine determines the correctness of the user's responses and tracks scoring information. It also controls the display of feedback to the user. Feedback can include hints, right and wrong indicators, and display of the correct answer.

Response Types and Rendering Formats

The types of questions supported by QTI are categorized into five major groups. These groups are based on the response type of the question. The QTI working group decided that the nature of the required response, rather than the presentation (rendering) format, best reflects the underlying structure and logic of a question. For example, it is relatively easy to see that true–false, multiple-choice, and multiple-response (i.e., multiple choice with more than one possible correct answer) questions all have pretty much the same underlying logic. The learner makes a selection from a predefined set of responses. A slider that can be set to any member of a series of discrete numeric values looks quite different from a typical set of answer choices. However, it serves the same function of providing a group of predefined choices. On the other hand, a fill-in-the-blank question uses quite different logic.

Table 12.1, adapted from the QTI specification, describes the basic response types defined in the QTI specification.

The Response Type column lists the defined response types. The abbreviations in this column (e.g., "LID") form part of the names of the data element containers that hold item response information. For example, a set of multiple-choice responses is placed in a *<response_lid>* element. A *<response_str>* element would contain information for a fill-in-the-blank or short-answer item.

The Data Structure column contains some rather arcane information that we will not discuss in detail.

The final three Rendering Formats columns break down the possible rendering formats based on how many responses are expected of the learner

TABLE 12.1

Basic Response Types

Response Type	Data Structure	Rendering Formats		
		Single	**Multiple**	**Ordered**
Logical identifier (LID)	The response-type identity or list of identities. The order of the list is first choice, second choice, etc.	Multiple choice True/false Slider	Multiple response	Order objects Connect-the-points Match object Order object Drag object Drag target
X-Y coordinates (XY)	The "x-y" co-ordinates of the centre of the object for each response identity or a list of "x-y" co-ords. The order of the list is first choice, second choice, etc.	Image hot spot	Order objects	Connect-the-points
String (STR)	The typed string for each response identity.	Fill-in-blank Select text Short answer Essay		
Numerical (NUM)	The entered number for each response identity.	Fill-in-blank Slider		
Logical groups (GRP)	The response identity and group identity tuples for each matched set of objects.	Match objects Drag object Drag target	Match objects Drag objects Drag targets	Match objects Order objects

Source: From Smythe, C., Shepherd, E., Brewer, L., and Lay, S., *IMS Question & Test Interoperability: ASI Best Practice & Implementation Guide,* final specification, version 1.2, Table 3.2. IMS Global Consortium, February 2002, copyright © IMS Global Learning Consortium, Inc. Available at http://www.imsproject.org.

and on whether or not the order of responses is important. These formats are listed by what the specification calls "colloquial question types." Some of these types require further explanation:

- Image hot spot — The learner must click on a specific area of an image.
- Select text — The learner must select a specific excerpt from a paragraph or list.

- Slider — The learner must choose a number by moving a slider to the required value. The available slider values are defined by a maximum, minimum, and increment.
- Drag objects, drag targets — The learner must drag one or more objects to predefined locations or target objects. It is not clear why the specification separates these two types; their official descriptions appear virtually identical.
- Match objects — The learner must match pairs or groups of objects, typically by drag-and-drop operations.
- Ordered objects — The learner must place text or objects in a defined order, either by drag-and-drop operations or by clicking in the required order.
- Connect-the-points — The learner must connect a set of points in a specific order, typically by clicking on them in the required order.[1]

Notice that a number of the colloquial question types can be represented by more than one response type and that some of them seem misplaced. For instance, why is "Order objects" placed under the Multiple heading instead of the Ordered heading in the X-Y Coordinates row? A few errors appear to have crept into the specification, and this may be one of them. However, the overall mapping of the items is sound and provides a good insight into the logic behind the specification.

Response Processing

In Chapter 7 we looked at the presentation portion of a simple multiple-choice question. The XML description and a typical rendering for that question are shown in Figures 12.1 and 12.2, respectively. In this section, we will discuss the remaining sections of a complete QTI item.

The high-level structure of a complete item is as follows:

```
<item>
    <qticomment></qticomment>
    <presentation>
        . . .
    </presentation>
    <resprocessing>
        . . .
    </resprocessing>
    <itemfeedback>
        . . .
    </itemfeedback>
</item>
```

```
<item title = "Multiple Choice Example" ident = "Unique_EX001">
  <qticomment>This is a simple multiple choice example. The rendering is a standard
  radio button style. No response processing is incorporated.</qticomment>
   <presentation label = "Example001">
    <flow>
        <material>
         <mattext>Which of the following is a synonym for "sleep"?</mattext>
         </material>
         <response_lid ident = "MCa_01" rcardinality = "Single" rtiming = "Yes">
            <render_choice shuffle = "Yes">
               <flow_label>
                  <response_label ident = "A">
                      <material>
                         <mattext>slumber</mattext>
                      </material>
                  </response_label>
                </flow_label>
               <flow_label>
                  <response_label ident = "B">
                     <material>
                          <mattext>wakefulness</mattext>
                        </material>
                    </response_label>
               </flow_label>
                 <flow_label>
                    <response_label ident = "C"> r chuffle = "No">
                       <material>
                           <mattext>none of the above</mattext>
                        </material>
                    </response_label>
               </flow_label>
            </render_choice>
        </response_lid>
     </flow>
   </presentation>
 </item>
```

FIGURE 12.1
QTI test question description, presentation portion.

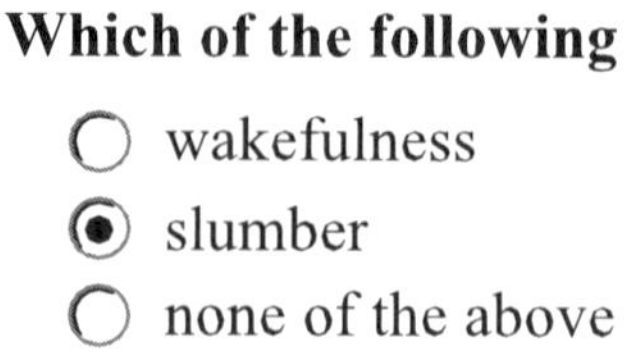

Which of the following is a synonym for "sleep"?

○ wakefulness

◉ slumber

○ none of the above

FIGURE 12.2
QTI test question — typical rendering.

The *<resprocessing>* section contains directions for checking the correctness of the learner's response, recording the result, and displaying appropriate feedback. The *<itemfeedback>* section is a repository for feedback messages (see Figure 12.2).

The following example presents the *<resprocessing>* and *<itemfeedback>* sections for our ongoing sample item. Appendix A, Listing 12.1 shows how these sections fit into the complete item definition. Remember that the line numbers are not part of the XML.

```
01    <resprocessing>
02        <outcomes>
03            <decvar varname="SCORE" vartype="Integer"
      defaultval="0"/>
04        </outcomes>
```

The *<outcomes>* element in line 02 sets up one or more variables that can be used to hold scoring data. The *<decvar>* element (line 03) can appear as many times as necessary to define different variables. The varname attribute sets the name of the variable. The *vartype* attribute indicates the type of data the variable can contain, in this case an integer. The value for *vartype* must be selected from a mandatory vocabulary. The *defaultval* is the starting value for the variable. The values of *varname* and *defaultval* are shown here for clarity. Both default to the values given and may be omitted. *vartype* has no default value and is always required.

```
05        <respcondition title="Correct Response Test">
06            <conditionvar>
07                <varequal respident="MCa_01">A
      </varequal>
08            </conditionvar>
09            <setvar varname="SCORE" action="Set">
      1</setvar>
10            <displayfeedback linkrefid="Correct"/>
11        </respcondition>
12        <respcondition title="Incorrect Response
      Test">
13            <conditionvar>
14                <not><varequal respident="MCa_01">
      A</varequal></not>
```

```
15                </conditionvar>
16                <displayfeedback linkrefid="Incorrect"/>
17            </respcondition>
18        </resprocessing>
```

The *<respcondition>* element is where the actual correctness testing and processing takes place. The *title* attribute is optional, but it is useful if a number of *<respcondition>* elements are used.

The *<conditionvar>* elements (lines 06–08 and lines 13–15) set up the actual test conditions. This example contains two conditions, one for the correct answer (lines 05–11) and one that will recognize any incorrect answer (lines 12–17). First it uses the *<varequal>* element to test whether the learner's response equals the correct answer, A. Next it uses the combination of the *<not>* and *<varequal>* elements to test whether the response is *not* equal to A (i.e., it is either B or C).

A number of different elements can be used to build a test condition. For example, rather than testing equality, one can test for less-than or greater-than conditions using *<varlt>* or *<vargt>*. As we saw in line 14, these conditions can be modified using the *<not>* tag. They can also be combined using *<and>* or *<or>* tags. The logical expressions that can be built with these elements can be as complex as needed to describe the required response conditions.

The *<setvar>* and *<displayfeedback>* elements (lines 9–10 and 16, respectively) indicate how the test delivery software should respond if the given test condition is true. When the correct answer condition is true, *<setvar>* sets the value of the SCORE variable to 1. The incorrect answer condition does not include a *<setvar>* element. The value of SCORE remains 0.

<displayfeedback> tells the software to present feedback to the learner. The *linkrefid* attribute contains the identifier of the feedback information to be used, as we will see in the final section of the item file.

```
19        <itemfeedback ident="Correct">
20            <material>
21            <mattext>That's right.</mattext>
22        </material>
23    </itemfeedback>
24        <itemfeedback ident="Incorrect">
25            <material>
26                <mattext>Sorry, that's incorrect.
    </mattext>
27            </material>
28        </itemfeedback>
29    </item>
```

An *<itemfeedback>* element (lines 19–23 and 24–28) is used for each different feedback message that is to be displayed to the learner. The value of the *ident* attribute is the *linkrefid* referenced in the *<displayfeedback>* tag. The closing *</resprocessing>* and *</item>* tags complete the item.[2]

Building an Assessment

So far we have been concerned primarily with individual item definitions. This is appropriate, because few of the current assessment engine products go beyond this point. However, the data model is named *Assessment–Section–Item* for a reason. In this section we will consider how sections and assessments are built from individual items.

Figure 12.3 illustrates the structure of a simple assessment. Notice the following:

- An assessment is built up of one or more sections. It may not include "loose" items.
- A section may include individual items, other sections, or both. Sections may be nested as deeply as necessary.

The structure of an assessment or section document mirrors the structure of the assessment itself. For example, the high-level structure of the assessment shown in Figure 12.3 would be as follows:

```
<questestinterop>
    <assessment>
        <section>
            <item></item>
            <section>
                <item></item>
                <item></item>
            </section>
            <section>
                <item></item>
                <item></item>
                <item><item>
            </section>
            <item></item>
        </section>
    </assessment>
</questestinterop>
```

The complete section and item definitions can be included directly in the assessment document or referenced externally.

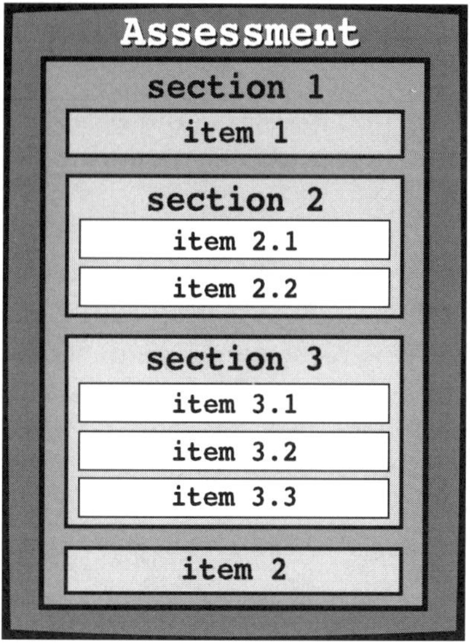

FIGURE 12.3
Structure of a simple assessment.

In addition to representing its structure, the definition of a section or an assessment can include any or all of the following:

- A time limit
- A list of objectives
- Presentation text or other content relevant to the entire assessment or section, such as directions or section headings
- Rules for selecting sections and items from a pool and displaying them in a particular order
- Rules for scoring the overall section or assessment
- Rules for presenting feedback

Selection and Ordering

As noted in the previous section, assessments and sections can include rules for selecting and ordering items for presentation. Version 1.2 supports such cases as the following:

- Random selection, with or without repetition
- Random selection by topic (e.g., three items from topic 1 and seven from topic 2), either mixed together or presented in topic groups
- Random selection with certain "golden questions" that are always to be selected

- "Testlets" in which several items are based on the same stimulus (such as a reading passage)

Within the ASI specification, selection and ordering are accomplished by dividing the process into three parts — sequencing, selection, and ordering.

- *Sequencing* determines whether or not the same objects can be presented more than once in a given assessment. The default sequence does not allow repetition.
- *Selection* determines which objects are to be presented, based on a specified rule or condition. These may include simple numeric rules such as "pick 20 of these 50 items" or criteria based on section or item meta-data, or both. For example, each section might include meta-data that defines a "difficulty" parameter. A selection rule could be defined to present any two sections that have a difficulty of "moderate."
- *Ordering* determines the order in which the selected objects are presented. Objects may be presented in an order that is fixed by the structure of the assessment, in the order they were selected, or in a random order.

Within any given assessment or section, selection and ordering information applies only to the objects at the top level within it. These objects constitute the "scope" of the selection and ordering rules. In Figure 12.3, for example, suppose Section 1's selection and ordering rules call for all objects to be presented in random order with no repeats. This would allow presentation sequences such as the following:

- Section 3 — Item 1 — Item 2 — Section 2
- Item 2 — Section 2 — Item 1 — Section 3

However, the items in Section 2 and Section 3 are not part of Section 1's scope. Unless each of these inner sections has its own randomizing rule, the items within them will always be presented in their default order.

The selection and ordering rule that we have described for Section 1 would look like this in XML:

```
01  <selection_ordering sequence_type="Normal">
02      <selection />
03      <order order_type="Random" />
04  </selection_ordering>
```

The value of the *sequence_type* attribute in line 01 is restricted to "Normal" (no repeats) or "RandomRepeat." "Normal" is the default value and could have been omitted. The selection rule we have described for this example is to use all objects. This is the default, so the *<selection />* element on line 02 is empty. A number of different elements could have been placed within the *<selection />* container to specify more complex rules. The value of the *order_type* attribute in line 03 is restricted to "Sequential" (the default) or "Random."[3]

Outcomes Processing

We have seen how to set a score for a single item. Other item–result information can also be captured by using additional variables. Ordinarily, however, we are more interested in the results of a complete assessment. Outcomes processing addresses the way scores are "rolled up" from item to section to assessment.

Outcomes processing is not as straightforward as it might appear at first glance. Most of us have encountered assessments in which different items have different weights. For example, a series of multiple-choice questions may be worth one point each, whereas a short essay on the same test is worth 50 points. Most of us have also seen assessments in which there is a penalty for guessing. In the United States, college entrance exams are well-known examples of this scoring method, in which a percentage of the number of incorrect answers is subtracted from the number of correct answers. Weighted items and guessing penalties are among the different types of scoring that the QTI specification takes into account.

Outcomes processing applies to the same scope rule as selection and ordering. Only the top-level objects within a section (or assessment) are affected by that section's outcomes-processing rules. In the example section in Figure 12.3, a sum-of-scores outcome rule in Section 1 will calculate a score based on the individual scores of Items 1 and 2 plus the composite scores of Sections 2 and 3. Each of these sections must have its own outcomes-processing rule to produce a score for use by Section 1.

The actual scoring computation is a function of the assessment engine. The outcomes-processing data identify the scoring algorithm to be used and pass the necessary data to the assessment engine in variables such as SCORE.

Scoring Algorithms

The QTI specification defines several scoring mechanisms that assessment engines can be expected to support. It calls these *in-built algorithms*. Some of the more familiar algorithms are as follows:

- Number correct — The total number of right answers, based on a variable that simply identifies the correctness of each item's response as true or false
- Sum of scores — The total of all item and section scores, based on the SCORE variable that we have seen in our examples

- Best K out of N — Total score of the K items with the best scores among the N items presented to the learner (e.g., throwing out the lowest 2 scores of 10 and using the rest)
- Negative scores (guessing penalty) — The number of correct answers minus a specified fraction of the number of incorrect answers

Each scoring algorithm has several variations that handle weighted scores, scores based on only the items the learner actually attempts, and so forth.

How Outcomes Are Specified

To show how outcomes processing is specified, let us once again consider the section illustrated in Figure 12.3. Assume that we want to obtain a score for Section 1 using a basic sum of scores algorithm. Assume further that each item assigns a value to the variable SCORE in the manner that we saw in the section on response processing and that Sections 2 and 3 have used their own sum-of-scores algorithms to produce a composite value for their SCORE variables. Then the outcomes processing portion of Section 1 would look like the following:

```
01   <outcomes_processing scoremodel="SumOfScores">
02       <outcomes>
03           <decvar varname="SCORE" defaultval="0"
     vartype="Integer" minvalue="0" maxvalue="7"
     cutvalue="5" />
04       </outcomes>
05   </outcomes_processing>
```

Notice how concisely the processing is described. The scoring algorithm is identified in the *scoremodel* attribute of the *<outcomes_processing>* element in line 01. The attributes of the *<decvar>* element in line 03 provide all the remaining information.

The value of 7 assigned to *maxvalue* is based on the assumption that the score for each correct item is 1 and that the identical scoring mechanism is used in Sections 2 and 3. This would result in maximum composite scores of 2 for Section 2 and of 3 for Section 3. Adding in the single points for Items 1 and 2, the overall maximum score would be 1 + 2 + 3 + 1 = 7.

The *cutvalue* attribute represents the minimum passing score for the section. Its value is arbitrary.[4]

The Results Reporting Information Model

In Chapter 7 we looked briefly at results reporting in QTI and saw an example of the summary results for an assessment using the QTI Results-Reporting model. Although summary information may be sufficient for some applications, there is also a need to capture detailed results down to the individual item level, including such data as the following:

- The type of question
- The correct answer
- The learner's answer
- The number of times the learner attempted the item
- The amount of time the learner took to answer
- The score assigned to the learner's answer
- The minimum and maximum possible scores
- The minimum passing score

Data specific to sections and assessments, such as total number of items, and number of items presented and attempted, can also be captured.

A complete detail report for an assessment would include data for every section and item it contains. Obviously, such a report could be immense. Additionally, a separate report would be generated for each learner who participates in the assessment. Fortunately, recording of results should be an automated process performed by the system that delivers the assessment.

The following annotated example contains Tom Sawyer's result for our ongoing example item. Appendix A, Listing 12.2 shows the uninterrupted XML for the result.

```
01  <qti_result_report>
02      <result>
03          <context>
04              <name>Tom Sawyer</name>
05          </context>
06          <item_result ident_ref="Unique_EX001">
07              <response ident_ref="Mca_01">
08                  <response_form cardinality="single"
    render_type="choice" response_type="lid">
09                      <correct_response>A</correct_
    response>
10                  </response_form>
```

The *<context>* element (lines 03–05) contains information about the learner. Typically this section would contain considerably more information about the learner than just a name. The *<item_result>* element identifies the item by referencing its unique identifier. The first part of the *<response>* section (lines 07–09) contains data about the item itself. This information matches corresponding information in the item document. Compare this listing with Listing 12.1 in Appendix A to see how the data match up.

```
11                      <num_attempts>1</num_attempts>
12                      <response_value>A</response_value>
13                  </response>
```

Lines 11 and 12 describe the actual response made by the learner. Tom got the correct answer (A) in a single attempt. Keep in mind that the correct answer identifier is independent of the order in which the responses are displayed to the learner. Because the first two responses can be shuffled, Tom may well have seen the question presented as in Figure 12.1, in which the correct answer occupies what might be considered the B position.

```
14                  <outcomes>
15                      <score varname="SCORE" vartype=
        "Integer">
16                          <score_value>1</score_value>
17                          <score_min>0</score_min>
18                          <score_max>1</score_max>
19                          <score_cut>1</score_cut>
20                      </score>
21                  </outcomes>
22              </item_result>
23          </result>
24      </qti_result_report>
```

The *<outcomes>* section contains scoring information. The variable that will hold the score is identified as SCORE by the *varname* attribute in line 15. This matches the variable name used in the results-processing section of the item. *<score_value>* (line 16) contains the learner's actual score. The *<score_min>*, *<score_max>*, and *<score_cut>* elements (lines 17–19) contain fixed values that were defined in the item.[5]

Authoring and Presentation Tools for Items and Assessments

As of this writing, there are relatively few products that provide significant support for development or presentation of QTI–based assessments and items. The following list includes the most noteworthy:

- *Macromedia Authorware* v. 6.0 allows import and export of a few of the simpler QTI item types via knowledge objects (KOs). It does not support sections or assessments. See http://www.macromedia.com for product details.
- *IMS Assesst Designer* is a very inexpensive QTI assessment creation tool. Its interface is primitive, and at the time of this writing it supports only version 1.01 of the QTI specification. However, it supports the development of complete assessments, and the free trial version is a good way to quickly experiment with the specification. See http://www.xdlsoft.com/ad/ for product details and download.
- *Questionmark Perception* is a mature, full-featured assessment authoring and delivery platform that can be integrated with a standards-based LMS. Its native item format is proprietary, but the current version can also import and export QTI version 1.1 items. Sections and assessments are not yet supported, although they are planned for future versions. See http://www.questionmark.com for product details.
- *Riva e•test* is a wholly Web-based enterprise-level system for managing, deploying, and reporting assessments. It supports development and deployment of QTI items, assessments, and item banks. It can be integrated with standards-based LMSs. See http://www.riva.com for product details.
- *Can Studios Ltd. Canvas Learning,* in beta testing at the time of this writing, will include two components, an authoring, design, and preview environment and a delivery engine (player). It will support QTI version 1.2 and can be integrated with a standards-based learning management system. An online preview is available that gives a good idea of what is possible using QTI. See http://www.the-can.com for product details.

Conclusion

This completes our look at the IMS QTI specification. As we have seen, this is a large and complex specification. We have attempted to cover the most important concepts in reasonable detail and to provide useful examples. Ideally, you should not have to write your own XML code, although you may sometimes need to edit or troubleshoot existing code. As authoring and development tools mature, creating QTI-conformant items, sections, and assessments should become relatively simple.

References

1. Smythe, C., Shepherd, E., Brewer, L., and Lay, S., *IMS Question & Test Interoperability: ASI Information Model Specification*, final specification, version 1.2. IMS Global Consortium, 2002, section 3.2. Available at: http://www.imsproject.org.
2. Smythe, C., Shepherd, E., Brewer, L., and Lay, S., *IMS Question & Test Interoperability: Results Reporting XML Binding*, final specification, version 1.2. IMS Global Consortium, 2002, section 3.5. Available at: http://www.imsproject.org.
3. Smythe, C., Shepherd, E., Brewer, L., and Lay, S., *IMS Question & Test Interoperability: ASI Selection and Ordering*, final specification, version 1.2. IMS Global Consortium, 2002, sections 2.3–2.5. Available at: http://www.imsproject.org.
4. Smythe, C., Shepherd, E., Brewer, L., and Lay, S., *IMS Question & Test Interoperability: ASI Outcomes Processing*, final specification, version 1.2. IMS Global Consortium, 2002, sections 2.3–2.4. Available at: http://www.imsproject.org.
5. Smythe, C., Shepherd, E., Brewer, L., and Lay, S., *IMS Question & Test Interoperability: Results Reporting Information Model*, final specification, version 1.2. IMS Global Consortium, 2002, section 3.7. Available at: http://www.imsproject.org.

Appendix A

Code Listings

This appendix contains the code for several of the longer annotated examples as it would appear in actual use, uninterrupted and without line numbers.

Listing 7.1 – QTI Assessment Summary Report

```
<qti_result_report>
  <result>
       <context>
            <name>Tom Sawyer</name>
            <generic_identifier>
                 <type_label>SSN</type_label>
                 <identifier_string>DoL:222334444A
</identifier_string>
            </generic_identifier>
            <date>
                 <type_label>Exam</type_label>
                 <datetime>2003-02-06T00:00:00</datetime>
            </date>
       </context>
       <summary_result>
            <type_label>Assessment</type_label>
            <generic_identifier>
                 <type_label>Assessment Id</type_label>
                 <identifier_string>WeTest:33-184
</identifier_string>
            </generic_identifier>
            <date>
                 <type_label>Exam</type_label>
                 <datetime>2003-02-06T00:00:00</datetime>
            </date>
```

```
            <status>
                <status_value>Complete</status_value>
            </status>
            <duration>P0Y0M0DT1H23M0S</duration>
            <score varname = "SCORE" vartype = "Integer">
                <score_value>82</score_value>
                <score_min>0</score_min>
                <score_max>100</score_max>
                <score_cut>60</score_cut>
            </score>
            <grade members = "A,B,C,D,F" varname = "GRADE">
                <grade_value>B</grade_value>
                <grade_cut>D</grade_cut>
            </grade>
        </summary_result>
    </result>
</qti_result_report>
```

Listing 10.1 – Metadata for a SCO

```
<?xml version="1.0" encoding="UTF-8"?>
<lom xmlns="http://www.imsglobal.org/xsd/imsmd_v1p2"
xmlns:xsi="http://www.w3.org/2001/XMLSchema-instance"
xsi:schemaLocation="http://www.imsglobal.org/xsd/imsmd_v1p2
imsmd_v1p2p2.xsd">
    <general>
        <title>
            <langstring>Pie Crust Techniques</langstring>
        </title>
        <catalogentry>
            <catalog>Catalog of Culinary Art Courses</catalog>
            <entry>
                <langstring>p-006</langstring>
            </entry>
        </catalogentry>
        <language>en-US</language>
        <description>
            <langstring>How to make a pie crust</langstring>
        </description>
        <keyword>
            <langstring>pie</langstring>
        </keyword>
        <keyword>
```

```
            <langstring>baking</langstring>
        </keyword>
        <aggregationlevel>
            <source>
                <langstring xml:lang="x-none">LOMv1.0
</langstring>
            </source>
            <value>
                <langstring xml:lang="x-none">2</langstring>
            </value>
        </aggregationlevel>
    </general>
    <lifecycle>
        <version>
            <langstring>2.0</langstring>
        </version>
        <status>
            <source>
                <langstring xml:lang="x-none">LOMv1.0
</langstring>
            </source>
            <value>
                langstring xml:lang="x-none">Final
</langstring>
            </value>
        </status>
        <contribute>
            <role>
                <source>
                    <langstring xml:lang="x-none">LOMv1.0
</langstring>
                </source>
                <value>
                    <langstring xml:lang="x-none">Author
</langstring>
                </value>
            </role>
            <centity>
                <vcard>
                    begin:vcard
                    fn:Frank Baker
                    end:vcard
                </vcard>
            </centity>
            <date>
                <datetime>2002-01-27</datetime>
            </date>
```

```
        </contribute>
    </lifecycle>
    <metametadata>
        <metadatascheme>ADL SCORM 1.2</metadatascheme>
    </metametadata>
    <technical>
        <format>text/HTML</format>
        <size>130671</size>
        <location type="URI">pie101.htm</location>
        <requirement>
            <type>
                <source>
                    <langstring xml:lang="x-none">LOMv1.0
</langstring>
                </source>
                <value>
                    <langstring xml:lang="x-none">Operating
System</langstring>
                </value>
            </type>
            <name>
                <source>
                    <langstring xml:lang="x-none">LOMv1.0
</langstring>
                </source>
                <value>
                    <langstring xml:lang="x-none">MS-Windows
</langstring>
                </value>
            </name>
            <minimumversion>95</minimumversion>
        </requirement>
    </technical>
    <educational>
        <learningresourcetype>
            <source>
                <langstring xml:lang="x-none">LOMv1.0
</langstring>
            </source>
            <value>
                <langstring xml:lang="x-none">Narrative Text
</langstring>
            </value>
        </learningresourcetype>
        <interactivitylevel>
            <source>
```

```
                <langstring xml:lang="x-none">Narrative Text
</langstring>
            </source>
            <value>
                <langstring xml:lang="x-none">medium
</langstring>
            </value>
        </interactivitylevel>
    </educational>
    <rights>
        <cost>
            <source>
                <langstring xml:lang="x-none">LOMv1.0
</langstring>
            </source>
            <value>
                <langstring xml:lang="x-none">yes</langstring>
            </value>
        </cost>
        <copyrightandotherrestrictions>
            <source>
                <langstring xml:lang="x-none">LOMv1.0
</langstring>
            </source>
            <value>
                <langstring xml:lang="x-none">yes</langstring>
            </value>
        </copyrightandotherrestrictions>
        <description>
            <langstring>Requires payment of a fee to be
negotiated with the vendor and use of the vendor's logo.
</langstring>
        </description>
    </rights>
    <classification>
        <purpose>
            <source>
                <langstring xml:lang="x-none">LOMv1.0
</langstring>
            </source>
            <value>
                <langstring xml:lang="x-none">Educational
Objective</langstring>
            </value>
        </purpose>
        <description>
```

```
          <langstring>This SCO addresses the following
objective: The student will be able to describe the basic steps
in the pie crust-making process.</langstring>
      </description>
      <keyword>
          <langstring>cooking basics</langstring>
      </keyword>
  </classification>
</lom>
```

Listing 11.1 – Content Aggregation Manifest

```
<manifest identifier="Pies101" xmlns="http://
www.imsproject.org/xsd/imscp_rootv1p1p2" xmlns:adlcp="http://
www.adlnet.org/xsd/adlcp_rootv1p2"
xmlns:imsmd="http://www.imsglobal.org/xsd/imsmd_rootv1p2p1"
xmlns:xsi="http://www.w3.org/2001/XMLSchema-instance"
xsi:schemaLocation="http://www.imsproject.org/xsd/
imscp_rootv1p1p2 imscp_rootv1p1p2.xsd http://
www.imsglobal.org/xsd/imsmd_rootv1p2p1
imsmd_rootv1p2p1.xsd http://www.adlnet.org/xsd/
adlcp_rootv1p2 adlcp_rootv1p2.xsd">
  <metadata>
      <schema>ADL SCORM</schema>
      <schemaversion>1.2</schemaversion>
      <imsmd: lom>
          <imsmd: general>
              <imsmd: title>
                  <imsmd: langstring xml:lang=
"en-US">Manifest Example</imsmd:langstring >
              </imsmd: title>
          </imsmd: general>
      </imsmd: lom>
  </metadata>
  <organizations default="root">
      <organization identifier="root">
          <title>Pies 101</title>
          <adlcp:description>This course shows the learner how
to make a pie></adlcp:description>
          <item identifier="A0" identifierref="R_A0">
              <title>Pies, Pies, and More Pies</title>
              <adlcp:description>An introductory discussion
of the various types of pies</adlcp:description>
              <adlcp:masteryscore>80</adlcp:masteryscore>
          </item>
```

```
                <item identifier="B0">
                    <title>Making Pies</title>
                    <adlcp:description>Pie-making methodology
</adlcp:description>
                    <adlcp:prerequisites type="aicc_script">A0
</adlcp:prerequisites>
                <item identifier="B1">
                    <title>Pie Crust Techniques</title>
                    <adlcp:description>How to make a pie crust
</adlcp:description>
                    <item identifier="A1" identifierref=
"R_A1">
                        <title>Pie Crust Pre-test</title>
                        <adlcp:description>Tests prior
knowledge of making pie crusts</adlcp:description>
                        <adlcp:masteryscore>80
</adlcp:masteryscore>
                    </item>
                    <item identifier="A2" identifierref=
"R_A2">
                        <title>Pastry Crusts</title>
                        <adlcp:description>How to mix, roll
out, and bake pastry pie crusts</adlcp:description>
                        <adlcp:masteryscore>80
</adlcp:masteryscore>
                    </item>
                    <item identifier="A3"
identifierref="R_A3">
                        <title>Crumb Crusts</title>
                        <adlcp:description>How to create
crusts from cookie and graham cracker crumbs</
adlcp:description>
                        <adlcp:masteryscore>80
</adlcp:masteryscore>
                    </item>
                </item>
                <item identifier="B2">
                    <title>Pie Filling Techniques</title>
                    <adlcp:description>How to make a pie
filling</adlcp:description>
                    <item identifier="A4"
identifierref="R_A4">
                        <title>Pie Filling Pre-test</title>
                        <adlcp:description>Tests prior
knowledge of making pie fillings</adlcp:description>
                        <adlcp:masteryscore>80
</adlcp:masteryscore>
                    </item>
```

```
                    <item identifier="A5" identifierref=
"R_A5">
                        <title>Fruit Fillings</title>
                        <adlcp:description>How to prepare
fillings from fresh, dried, or canned fruit</adlcp:description>
                        <adlcp:masteryscore>80
</adlcp:masteryscore>
                    </item>
                    <item identifier="A6" identifierref=
"R_A6">
                        <title>Other Fillings</title>
                        <adlcp:description>How to make cream,
custard, cheese, and other non-fruit fillings
</adlcp:description>
                        <adlcp:masteryscore>80
</adlcp:masteryscore>
                    </item>
                </item>
                <item identifier="A7" identifierref="R_A7">
                    <title>Specialty Pies</title>
                    <adlcp:description>Applying ordinary
techniques to achieve extraordinary pies</adlcp:description>
                    <adlcp:prerequisites
type="aicc_script">B1&B2</adlcp:prerequisites>
                    <adlcp:masteryscore>80
</adlcp:masteryscore>
                </item>
            </item>
        </organization>
    </organizations>
    <resources>
        <resource identifier="R_A0" type="webcontent"
adlcp:scormtype="sco" href="../courses/pies/pies_L1.htm">
            <metadata>
                <adlcp:location>pies_L1.xml</adlcp:location>
            </metadata>
            <file href="../courses/pies/pies_L1.htm" />
            <dependency identifierref="R_G1" />
        </resource>
        <resource identifier="R_A1" type="webcontent"
adlcp:scormtype="sco" href="../courses/pies/pies_L2.htm">
            <metadata>
                <adlcp:location>pies_L2.xml</adlcp:location>
            </metadata>
            <file href="../courses/pies/pies_L2.htm" />
            <dependency identifierref="R_G2" />
            <dependency identifierref="R_G3" />
        </resource>
```

```
      <resource identifier="R_A2" type="webcontent"
adlcp:scormtype="sco" href="../courses/pies/pies_L3.htm">
           <metadata>
                <adlcp:location>pies_L3.xml</adlcp:location>
           </metadata>
           <file href="../courses/pies/pies_L1.htm" />
           <dependency identifierref="R_G4" />
      </resource>
      <resource identifier="R_A3" type="webcontent"
adlcp:scormtype="sco" href="../courses/pies/pies_L4.htm">
           <metadata>
                <adlcp:location>pies_L4.xml</adlcp:location>
           </metadata>
           <file href="../courses/pies/pies_L4.htm" />
      </resource>
      <resource identifier="R_A4" type="webcontent"
adlcp:scormtype="sco" href="../courses/pies/pies_L5.htm">
           <metadata>
                <adlcp:location>pies_L5.xml</adlcp:location>
           </metadata>
           <file href="../courses/pies/pies_L5.htm" />
      </resource>
      <resource identifier="R_A5" type="webcontent"
adlcp:scormtype="sco" href="../courses/pies/pies_L6.htm">
           <metadata>
                <adlcp:location>pies_L6.xml</adlcp:location>
           </metadata>
           <file href="../courses/pies/pies_L6.htm" />
      </resource>
      <resource identifier="R_A6" type="webcontent"
adlcp:scormtype="sco" href="../courses/pies/pies_L7.htm">
           <metadata>
                <adlcp:location>pies_L7.xml</adlcp:location>
           </metadata>
           <file href="../courses/pies/pies_L7.htm" />
      </resource>
      <resource identifier="R_A7" type="webcontent"
adlcp:scormtype="sco" href="../courses/pies/pies_L8.htm">
           <metadata>
                <adlcp:location>pies_L8.xml</adlcp:location>
           </metadata>
           <file href="../courses/pies/pies_L8.htm" />
      </resource>
      <resource identifier="R_G1" type="webcontent"
adlcp:scormtype="asset">
           <file href="../courses/pies/graphics/applepie.jpg" />
      </resource>
```

```
        <resource identifier="R_G2" type="webcontent"
adlcp:scormtype="asset">
            <file href="../courses/pies/graphics/
rollingpin.jpg" />
        </resource>
        <resource identifier="R_G3" type="webcontent"
adlcp:scormtype="asset">
            <file href="../courses/pies/graphics/crust.jpg" />
        </resource>
        <resource identifier="R_G4" type="webcontent"
adlcp:scormtype="asset">
            <file href="../courses/pies/graphics/apples.jpg" />
        </resource>
    </resources>
</manifest>
```

Listing 12.1 – Complete QTI Multiple Choice Item with Response Processing

```
<item title = "Multiple Choice Example" ident = "Unique EX001">
  <qticomment>This is a simple multiple choice example. The
rendering is a standard radio button style. Response processing
is incorporated.</qticomment>
  <presentation label = "Example001">
        <flow>
            <material>
                <mattext>Which of the following is a synonym for
"sleep"?</mattext>
            </material>
            <response_lid ident = "MCa_01" rcardinality =
"Single" rtiming = "Yes">
                <render_choice shuffle = "Yes">
                    <flow_label>
                        <response_label ident = "A">
                            <material>
                                <mattext>slumber</mattext>
                            </material>
                        </response_label>
                    </flow_label>
                    <flow_label>
                        <response_label ident = "B">
                            <material>
                                <mattext>wakefulness
</mattext>
```

```
                        </material>
                    </response_label>
                </flow_label>
                <flow_label>
                    <response_label ident = "C" rshuffle =
"No">
                        <material>
                            <mattext>none of the above
</mattext>
                        </material>
                    </response_label>
                </flow_label>
            </render_choice>
        </response_lid>
    </flow>
  </presentation>
  <resprocessing>
    <outcomes>
        <decvar varname="SCORE" vartype="Integer"
defaultval="0"/>
    </outcomes>
    <respcondition title="Correct Response Test">
        <conditionvar>
            <varequal respident="MCa_01">A</varequal>
        </conditionvar>
        <setvar varname="SCORE" action="Set">1</setvar>
        <displayfeedback linkrefid="Correct"/>
    </respcondition>
    <respcondition title="Incorrect Response Test">
        <conditionvar>
            <not><varequal respident="MCa_01">A
</varequal></not>
        </conditionvar>
        <displayfeedback linkrefid="Incorrect"/>
    </respcondition>
    </resprocessing>
  <itemfeedback ident="Correct">
    <material>
        <mattext>That's right.</mattext>
    </material>
  </itemfeedback>
  <itemfeedback ident="Incorrect">
    <material>
        <mattext>Sorry, that's incorrect.</mattext>
    </material>
    </itemfeedback>
</item>
```

Listing 12.2 – Single-Item QTI Detail Report

```
<qti_result_report>
  <result>
      <context>
          <name>Tom Sawyer</name>
      </context>
      <item_result ident_ref="Unique_EX001">
          <response ident_ref="Mca_01">
              <response_form cardinality="single"
render_type="choice" response_type="lid">
                  <correct_response>A</correct_response>
              </response_form>
              <num_attempts>1</num_attempts>
              <response_value>B</response_value>
          </response>
          <outcomes>
              <score varname="SCORE" vartype="Integer">
                  <score_value>1</score_value>
                  <score_min>0</score_min>
                  <score_max>1</score_max>
                  <score_cut>1</score_cut>
              </score>
          </outcomes>
      </item_result>
  </result>
</qti_result_report>
```

Appendix B

Some Useful Resources

This appendix includes detailed information on the specifications, Web addresses of the various standards bodies, and an assortment of other resources that we found useful during the development of this book and wanted to share with you. The Web site for this book, http://www.elearning-standards.com, maintains an updated list of links to recommended resources on the Web and other related materials.

Specification Information

The specification documents that we have referenced can be found at the following locations. Because of the changeable nature of Web sites, we have given only the URL to each organization's home page.

AICC Specification

- Web site: http://www.aicc.org
- Primary document file: CMI001 — *CMI Guidelines for Interoperability*
- Versions: 2.0 or higher for HACP, 3.0 or higher for API; latest is 3.5
- Other relevant document(s):
  - AGR010 — *Web-based Computer-Managed Instruction (CMI)*
  - CMI003 — *AICC/CMI Certification Testing Procedures*

SCORM Specification

- Web site: http://www.adlnet.org
- Primary document files, which can be downloaded in a single zip file:

    - *The SCORM Overview*
    - *The SCORM Content Aggregation Model*
    - *The SCORM Runtime Environment*
- Versions: 1.1 or higher, latest is 1.2
- Other relevant documents:
    - *The SCORM Addendums* (clarifications and error corrections to the main specifications)

QTI Specification

- Web site: http://www.imsproject.org
- Primary document files, which can be downloaded in a single zip file:
    - *IMS Question & Test Interoperability Overview*
    - *IMS Question & Test ASI Best Practice Guide*
    - *IMS Question & Test ASI XML Binding Specification*
    - *IMS Question & Test ASI Information Model*
    - *IMS Question & Test ASI Outcomes Processing Specification*
    - *IMS Question & Test ASI Selection and Ordering Specification*
    - *IMS Question & Test Results Reporting Best Practice and Implementation Guide*
    - *IMS Question & Test Results Reporting XML Binding Guide*
    - *IMS Question & Test Results Reporting Information Model*
- Versions: 1.1 and above; 1.2 is the latest
- Other relevant document(s):
    - *IMS Question & Test Interoperability Lite* — a simplified version of QTI that includes only the display of multiple-choice questions.

Other IMS Specifications Mentioned in This Book

- Web site: http://www.imsproject.org
- Specifications:
    - *IMS Content Packaging Specification*
    - *IMS Meta-Data Specification*
    - *IMS Simple Sequencing Specification*

Web Sites for Standards Bodies

The following are the home pages for the Web sites maintained by the standards bodies that we have discussed in our book:

- ADL/SCORM: http://www.adlnet.org
- AICC: http://www.aicc.org
- ARIADNE: http://www.ariadne-eu.org/
- IEEE/LTSC: http://ltsc.ieee.org/
- IMS: http://www.imsproject.org
- ISO: http://jtc1sc36.org/

Online Articles, Presentations, White Papers, and Forums

The following list includes some of our favorite resources on the Web. URLs are provided for sites other than those operated by the standards bodies.

- ADL Web site — There are numerous useful documents, presentations, videos, and a list of selected readings available at the Resources Center page of the ADL Web site. One of our favorites is *DeMystifying SCORM*, by Philip Dodds.
- IMS Web site — The Resources page of the IMS Web site includes links to a number of useful materials. In particular, the "Dr. Tom's Guides" series provides an excellent introduction to XML and meta-data.
- QTI User Forum on Topica (http://www.topica.com/lists/IMSQTI) — This is a useful discussion list for those involved in implementing the QTI specification.
- CETIS (http://www.cetis.ac.uk) — Another of our favorite sites is that of CETIS, the Center for Educational Technology Interoperability Standards. It offers the latest news, articles, discussion forums, and lots of other information about e-learning standards.
- Learnativity (http://www.learnativity.com) — This excellent site offers many articles and white papers about learning objects, standards, and many other related areas. It also contains a good list of links to other e-learning and standards-related sites.

Glossary

24/7 — twenty-four hours per day, seven days per week; usually refers to the availability of resources or services

accredited standard — a specification that has been through a standardization process and approved by an accredited standards body such as ISO or IEEE (see also the following terms: *ISO/IEC JTC1 SC36* and *IEEE/LTSC)*

ADL — acronym for *Advanced Distributed Learning Initiative* (the ADL was founded by the DoD); its goal is to develop a common technical framework for distributed learning environments (see also *DoD*)

AGR — acronym for *AICC Guidelines and Recommendations,* technical guidelines published by the AICC for specific areas of learning technology; they usually reference an AICC Specification document (see also *AICC*)

AICC — acronym for *Aviation Industry CBT Committee,* an international group of learning technology developers and vendors that develops guidelines for the development, delivery, and evaluation of technology-based learning

API — acronym for *Application Programming Interface,* a set of standard software calls, functions, and data formats that can be used by a computer program to access network services, devices, or operating systems

applet — a small application program embedded in a Web page

Application Programming Interface — see *API*

archive — a file that contains other files, usually in a compressed format; archive formats include .zip, .sit, .tar, .jar, and .cab

ARIADNE — acronym for *Alliance of Remote Instructional Authoring & Distribution Networks for Europe;* the ARIADNE Foundation was created to exploit and further develop the results of the ARIADNE and ARIADNE II European Projects, which created tools and methodologies for producing, managing, and sharing e-learning resources

ASP — acronym for *application service provider,* a service that provides remote access to an application program, typically using HTTP communication

assessment — in the QTI specification, a data structure that is equivalent to a test; contains all data necessary to present the test questions, process the learner's responses, and provide feedback (see also *QTI, section,* and *item*)

asset — in the SCORM specification, a piece of learning content that cannot stand by itself and does not include data tracking; typical assets include graphics, movies, or sections of text (see also *SCORM*)

assignable unit — see *AU*

attribute — a qualifier or modifier to the data in an XML element (see also *XML* and *element*)

AU — acronym for *assignable unit,* the term used in the AICC CMI Specification as equivalent to a learning object (see also *AICC, CMI,* and *LO*)

Aviation Industry CBT Committee — see *AICC*

block — an arbitrarily defined grouping of course components; a block may include assets, LOs, and other blocks (see also *LO*)

CBT — acronym for *computer-based training,* training normally delivered on a CD-ROM or via an organization's local area network

CE — acronym for *continuing education;* usually used in relation to credits awarded to students who complete further education courses

CIF — see *course interchange files*

CMI — acronym for *computer-managed instruction,* a predecessor and generally a functional subset of LMS; for the purposes of this book, the terms *CMI* and *LMS* should be considered interchangeable (see also *LMS*)

comma-delimited table — a representation of a table in a text file; commas are inserted between the values that would go in each table cell

completion requirement — stated criteria for completing an LO, block, or course, such as a requirement that a learner complete six of eight LOs for a course to be marked as complete (see also *block* and *LO*)

computer-managed instruction — see *CMI*

content aggregation — in the SCORM specification, a structured group of assets, SCOs, or content aggregations, typically equivalent to a course (see also *asset* and *SCO*)

content aggregation package — a group of physical files that makes up a content aggregation, collected for transfer between learning systems; it includes the content items and a manifest file that lists and describes the hierarchical structure of the components within the package (see also *content aggregation* and *manifest file*)

content package — one or more reusable assets, SCOs, or content aggregations collected for transfer between learning systems; differs from a content aggregation package by having no overall hierarchical structure (see also *asset, SCO,* and *content aggregation*)

content packaging — a standard way to transfer e-learning content between different administrative systems

content structure format (CSF) file — a file defined in SCORM version 1.1, used to transfer the structure of a course between administrative systems; replaced in SCORM 1.2 by the content aggregation manifest file (see also *SCORM, content aggregation,* and *manifest file*)

course interchange — the transfer of courses between administrative systems

course interchange files (CIF) — a set of files required by the AICC CMI specification for transfer of courses between administrative systems (see also *AICC*)

courseware — a term used to describe e-learning courses and their components: LOs, assessments, lessons, and so on

data element — an item of data in a data model; has a specific name and is assigned a value based on its definition in the data model (see also *data model*)

data model — a discrete set of data items defined for a particular use, such as data tracking or content sharing (see also *data element*)

***de facto* standard** — a specification or standard that has been widely implemented and is *generally accepted* as an industrywide standard

***de jure* standard** — a standard *in law;* another name for an *accredited standard*

DoD — acronym for U.S. Department of Defense

domain — a domain name, such as *elearning-standards.com,* that is an easily remembered, logical name used to reference a TCP/IP address, typically on a Web server

dot notation — a method for expressing a hierarchical relationship between a group of categories and items; for example, *animal.dog.collie* indicates that the category "animal" contains the subcategory "dog," which contains the individual item "collie"

DTD — acronym for *document type definition,* a reference document that defines the elements, attributes, and certain other characteristics for XML documents (see also *XML, element, attribute,* and *XML Schema*)

e-learning — electronically delivered learning; in particular, training or education that is facilitated by the use of well-known and proven computer technologies, specifically networks based on Internet technology

element — a holder for data or other elements in XML; an element is indicated by a pair of opening and closing tags (see also *XML* and *tag*)

frame — a subdivision of a browser window; using frames allows the browser to independently display two or more different Web pages and run any scripts that they may contain

granularity — the extent to which learning content is divided into individual pieces; an entire course presented in a single piece would have coarse granularity, whereas if the same content were broken into pieces that each cover a single concept, it would have fine granularity

HACP — acronym for *HTTP-based AICC CMI Protocol,* one of the communication methods specified in the AICC CMI specification (see also *AICC* and *HTTP*)

HTML — acronym for *Hypertext Markup Language,* a coding language used to instruct Web browsers how to display and format Web pages

HTTP — acronym for *Hypertext Transfer Protocol;* HTTP defines how messages are formatted and transmitted on the World Wide Web

Hypertext Markup Language — see *HTML*

Hypertext Transfer Protocol — see *HTTP.*

IEC — acronym for *International Electrotechnical Commission,* an international standards and conformity assessment body for all fields of electrotechnology; IEC partners with ISO (see also *ISO/IEC JTC1 SC36*)

IEEE/LTSC — acronym for *Institute of Electrical and Electronics Engineers Learning Technology Standards Committee,* a standards committee within the IEEE concerned with developing standards for e-learning

ILT — acronym for *instructor-led training,* training facilitated by a live instructor, such as in a classroom

IMS — abbreviation of *IMS Global Consortium,* an independent, subscription-based nonprofit organization of e-learning developers and vendors; produces specifications for exchanging information between learning components and systems

interoperability — the ability of different e-learning components, such as LMSs and LOs, to operate correctly with each other regardless of the source of the respective components (see also *LMS* and *LO*)

ISO/IEC JTC1 SC36 — acronym for *International Organization for Standardization/International Electrotechnical Commission Joint Technical Committee 1, Sub-Committee 36;* ISO/IEC JTC SC36 develops accredited standards for learning technology

item — in the QTI specification, a data structure that is equivalent to a test question; an item contains all the information required to display a single test question and process the learner's response (see also *QTI, assessment,* and *section*)

JavaScript — a cross-platform, object-based scripting language for client and server applications; JavaScript code can be run by most modern Web browsers and is typically used to enhance Web pages

keyword — name of an AICC data element; also, in meta-data, a term that can be searched for by a search engine (see also *AICC, data element,* and *meta-data*)

KO — knowledge object

LAN — local area network

launch — to locate and start up a piece of e-learning content

LCMS — acronym for *learning content management system,* an administrative system that provides management, organization, and search capabilities for e-learning content, such as assets, LOs, and content aggregations (see also *asset, LO,* and *content aggregation*)

learning content management system — see *LCMS*

learning management system — see *LMS*

learning object — see *LO*

LMS — acronym for *learning management system,* Web server–based software application that provides administrative and data-tracking functions for managing learners and provides learners with access to learning content

LO — acronym for *learning object,* the smallest chunk of e-learning content that can be tracked by an LMS (see also *LMS*)

logic operator — a symbol in an equation or a test condition that denotes a type of comparison between two values and returns a "true" or "false" value. Logic operators include "and," "or," and "not"

LOM — acronym for *Learning Object Meta-Data Model,* a set of meta-data developed by IMS and adapted by the SCORM, defined specifically for use in describing learning components, including assets, LOs, and content aggregations (see also *IMS, SCORM, asset, LO,* and *content aggregation*)

LUTC — an organization for insurance industry professionals formerly known as the Life Underwriter Training Council

manifest file — an XML file listing the contents and, when appropriate, describing the content structure of a SCORM content package or content aggregation package (see also *XML, SCORM, content package,* and *content aggregation package*)

meta-data — information about information; for example, the information in a library's card catalog can be described as meta-data. In the e-learning arena, meta-data is used to provide descriptive data about learning content

name–value pair — the name of a data item paired with its value; usually expressed in the following format: *name="Susan"*

nesting — placing a subsidiary item inside another larger item, such as an LO nested in a block; used in particular when an item can contain another item of the same type, such as a QTI section nested in a larger section (see also *QTI* and *section*)

object bank — in the QTI specification, a searchable, unstructured collection of items or sections gathered for transfer between assessment systems; a QTI assessment may present items selected directly from an object bank (see also *QTI, item, section,* and *assessment*)

outcome — in the QTI specification, the result of consolidating scores for items and sections to produce a final composite score for an entire test (see also *QTI, item,* and *section*)

package interchange file (PIF) — an archive file containing all components of a SCORM content package, including the physical content files, the manifest file, and any associated meta-data files (see also *archive, SCORM, content package, manifest file,* and *meta-data*)

parameter — a value that is passed to a programmed routine, typically in a function call; tracking data is passed between an LMS and an LO using parameters (see also *LMS* and *LO*)

parse — to scan a string of characters and pick out individual data items

prerequisite — a basic requirement that must be fulfilled before commencing a piece of learning; for example, completing an introductory lesson may be required before the learner is permitted to start an intermediate lesson

QTI — acronym for *Question & Test Interoperability,* a specification developed by IMS for sharing test questions and complete tests, and reporting their associated results (see also *IMS*)

Question & Test Interoperability — see *QTI*

render — to display based on instructions in a markup language such as XML or HTML (see also *XML* and *HTML*)

reusability — the ability of an LO to be reused in multiple different contexts or courses (see also *LO*)

SCO — acronym for *sharable content object,* the smallest chunk of content that can be launched and tracked by an LMS using the SCORM Runtime Environment; an SCO is the SCORM version of an LO (see also *LMS, SCORM,* and *LO*)

SCORM — acronym for *Sharable Content Object Reference Model*; SCORM is a reference model developed by the ADL that defines a Web-based learning content model, comprised of a set of interrelated technical specifications (see also *ADL*)

section — in the QTI specification, a structured group of items or other sections designed to be contained within an assessment (see also *QTI, item,* and *assessment*)

sequencing — determining the sequence in which LOs are to be launched, especially if they are launched automatically; also, in the QTI specification, determining the order in which test items and sections are presented in an assessment (see also *LO, QTI, item, section,* and *assessment*)

session — the period of time that a learner is connected to an LO. The LMS creates the session and assigns it an identifier when the LO is launched (see also *LO* and *LMS*)

standard — a document that specifies the solution to a known problem

tag — in XML and HTML, a marker that indicates the beginning or end of a section of text that has a particular meaning or is to be formatted in a particular way; a tag is expressed as an element name or a markup code inside pointed brackets, for instance, *<elementname>* (see also *XML, HTML,* and *element*)

TCP/IP — acronym for *Transmission Control Protocol/Internet Protocol,* communication protocol used to transmit data between servers and clients over the Internet

test suite — a set of computer programs or procedures designed to test and validate the functionality of other pieces of computer software; in the e-learning arena, test suites are used to test learning-management systems and content for conformance with specifications

URI — acronym for *uniform resource identifier,* a unique address for an object on the World Wide Web

URL — acronym for *uniform resource locator,* the most commonly used type of URI

URL encoding — coding of certain special characters, such as "=" and "&" in text messages for safe transmission via HTTP (see also *HTTP*)

WBT — acronym for *Web-based training,* training or education that depends on the Internet for its delivery, nowadays more commonly called e-learning

World Wide Web Consortium (W3C) — an organization that develops standards for the World Wide Web; its basic standards, which include HTML and XML, form the basis of virtually all e-learning standards (see also *HTML* and *XML*)

XML — acronym for *Extensible Markup Language,* a markup language for encoding structured data

XML binding — directions for expressing a data model using XML (see also *XML*)

XML namespace — a means of establishing the context from which XML elements are drawn; using namespaces allows the same element name to be used for different purposes without confusion (see also *XML* and *element*)

XML schema — a reference document that defines and controls the content and structure of XML documents; a schema serves a similar purpose to a DTD but provides more detail and control (see also *XML* and *DTD*)

XML vocabulary — a defined set of values that can be assigned to a specific XML element or attribute (see also *XML, element,* and *attribute*)

zip file — the most common type of archive file (see also *archive*)

Index

A

J

L

M

N

O

P

Q

R

S

T

U

W

X